Mark McCrum is the author of two other travel books: *Happy Sad Land*, about South Africa; and *The Craic*, about Ireland. In a varied career he has worked as an advertising executive, street artist, cinema manager, copywriter, video-games salesman and Father Christmas. As a journalist he has written for, amongst others, the *Evening Standard*, the *Independent*, the *Daily Mail*, the *Sunday Times*, *Vogue* and *Punch*. He also paints, and has had seven one-man shows of watercolours, in galleries from London to Botswana.

## By Mark McCrum

# NO WORRIES

## A Journey through Australia

## Mark McCrum

PHOENIX

A PHOENIX PAPERBACK

First published in Great Britain by Sinclair-Stevenson in 1997
This paperback edition published in 2000 by Phoenix,
an imprint of Orion Books Ltd,
Orion House, 5 Upper St Martin's Lane, London WC2H 9EA

Fourth impression 2003

A CIP catalogue record for this book is available from the
British Library.

ISBN 0 575 40246 6

Printed in Great Britain by
Clays Ltd, St Ives plc

*for Leonie*

# Contents

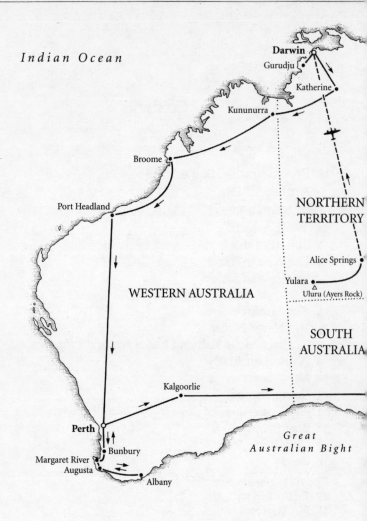

Indian Ocean

**Darwin**
Gurudju
Katherine
Kununurra

Broome

Port Headland

NORTHERN
TERRITORY

Alice Springs
Yulara
△ Uluru (Ayers Rock)

WESTERN AUSTRALIA

SOUTH
AUSTRALIA

Kalgoorlie

**Perth**
Bunbury
Margaret River
Augusta
Albany

Great
Australian Bight

Southern Ocean

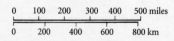

0    100   200   300   400   500 miles

0       200      400      600      800 km

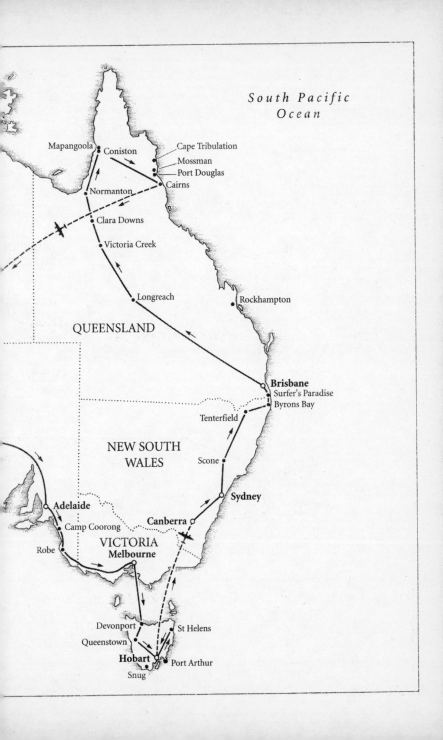

*South Pacific Ocean*

Mapangoola
Coniston
Cape Tribulation
Mossman
Port Douglas
Cairns
Normanton
Clara Downs
Victoria Creek
Longreach
Rockhampton

QUEENSLAND

Brisbane
Surfer's Paradise
Byrons Bay
Tenterfield

NEW SOUTH WALES

Scone

Adelaide
Camp Coorong
Sydney
Canberra
Robe
VICTORIA
Melbourne

Devonport
St Helens
Queenstown
Hobart
Port Arthur
Snug

# Preface to the 2000 Edition

When I arrived in Sydney on that sparkling, blue-skied September day in 1994, Rod McGee had just won the Olympic bid – now the Games are upon us. In the intervening five years much, on the surface, has changed. John Howard, glimpsed here as the newly appointed Leader of the Opposition, duly became Prime Minister. Emily Kame Kngwarreye, the celebrated Aboriginal artist, moved on to the giant studio in the sky. Queenslanders shocked liberal Australia and the world by electing to the Federal Parliament Pauline Hanson, fish and chip shop manager and enthusiastic opponent of multiculturalism. While, in a referendum on the Republic, Australians were true to the monarchist sentiments I'd heard in the most surprising places, and voted to keep the Queen.

Nor have the private characters I wrote about remained preserved in aspic. Martin and Christine are no longer in charge of their wild 'Coniston Plains' cattle-station; they're now running a roadside motel. While 'Miss Emma', the governess who brought me this news, has moved to London and married a Russian.

But much else remains the same. The backpackers are, from a friend's recent report, still having a wild time in Surfers' Paradise and Byron Bay; 'the Patriarch' still rules the roost at Clara Downs; the miners still ogle the skimpies in Kalgoorlie, while the Aboriginals drink in the dirt in Boulder park.

At the start of this book I am sent on my – somewhat nervous – way by a distinguished British publisher, who encourages me with talk of 'the very large book market in

Australia'. The firm he had founded had recently been taken over by another, larger company, and he was optimistic about my prospects. But, when I returned from Oz almost a year later, this publisher had been sacked – ironically by his new Australian boss. 'I'm rather off Australians at the moment,' he told me ruefully, when I phoned. Somewhat discouraged by this development, I sat down none the less and wrote my book. When it appeared, almost two years later, this larger publishing house was itself in the throes of being taken over by an even bigger American firm. The Australian boss was sent packing, the Australian offices of the old house closed down, and the newly published *No Worries* was only available in Australia to assiduous private investigators.

So it's a particular thrill for me that, as the result of yet another takeover, it's been picked up by a new publisher and is to be reissued in Australia too.

I only hope that Australians will enjoy this Pom's eye view of their country. As anyone who reads this book will soon discover, it didn't take me long to fall in love with 'the lucky country' – and by the end I nearly didn't make it home at all. On my first evening back I met up with my parents in their London club. It was a warm April evening and I marched up the stairs to the restaurant smartly dressed in suit and shirt, tan gleaming. No sooner had I sat down than a waiter came over. 'There's a gentleman over there complaining that you're not wearing a tie,' he told me. Peering through the panelled gloom, I saw a scowl above a fat, pinstriped belly and sincerely wished I had never got on that returning plane.

*Mark McCrum,*
*Primrose Hill,*
*2000*

## Author's Note

Some of the people mentioned in the Acknowledgements appear in the pages that follow, though I have changed many of the names of private figures. The worst part of a travel writer's job is having to be honest about people who have been kind to you, and I hope, as always, that I have not caused offence. If I have, I can only apologise. Wherever I went I made it clear that I was writing a book; and it would be a pointless exercise if I was untruthful to what I heard and saw.

## On Aborigine/Aboriginal

Although many English and Australian dictionaries still give 'Aborigine' as the correct noun to describe an Aboriginal Australian, this has now been replaced, in Aboriginal circles at least, by 'Aboriginal', as both noun and adjective. Except when quoting, therefore, I have followed this preferred newer usage.

# Introduction

I had no fascinating convict ancestor into whose history I was eager to delve. There was no nineteenth-century explorer whose mule train I'd suddenly conceived a yearning to follow. No compelling childhood fantasies; not even a lost, embroidered didgeridoo. My publisher sprang the project on me, over the liquid lunch I'd been looking forward to ever since I'd first met him, eighteen months and one book before.

'So you don't like the Greenland idea?' I heard myself mutter, fingering my carefully thought-out list of sure-fire bestsellers with exaggerated sobriety.

'People don't buy many books in Greenland,' he replied with a smile. 'Very large bookmarket in Australia.'

I looked out through the window at the stop-starting, whining, fuming traffic of Knightsbridge fouling the clear May sunshine. 'Okay,' I replied, with a sudden irresponsible lift in my heart.

My image of the Land Down Under was, I soon realised, a fantastically ill-considered cocktail of Castlemaine and Fosters ads, with stray bits of *Crocodile Dundee*, Dame Edna, *Strictly Ballroom* and *Neighbours* thrown in. It was a land of vast, dry, empty spaces where rough, suntanned rednecks drove down dirt roads in pick-up trucks piled high with tinnies of amber nectar, occasionally stopping to grunt appalling, chauvinistic remarks at their bedraggled womenfolk. If they weren't in 'the outback' they were down on the beach, chasing 'sheilas' with all the subtlety of the apocryphal Aussie surfer: 'G'day Sheila, wanna fuck?' – 'I do *now*, yer smoothtalkin' bastard.'

For the English, Australia and Australians were still – let's face it – a bit of a joke. Just the accent made us laugh. All the more so if it had any pretensions to anything. There'd been that famous Monty Python skit about Australian wine: 'Of the sparkling wines the most famous is Perth Pink. This is a bottle with a message in it and the message is – *bee-ware*. This is not a wine for drinking. This is a wine for laying down and *avoiding*.' Then there were the four philosophy lecturers at the University of Woolamaloo, all called Bruce: 'Now, Bruce teaches classical philosophy, Bruce teaches Hegelian philosophy, and Bruce here teaches logical positivism and is also in charge of the sheepdip. I'll just remind you of the faculty rules: Rule One – no pooftahs!'

Just to confirm our prejudices we had the Australians themselves. Barry Humphries' Bazza Mackenzie had marched through a cartoon-strip London fruitlessly seeking ice-cold tubes of amber nectar ('I'm that thirsty I could drink out of an Abo's loincloth'); chasing Pommie sheilas ('I could be up that like a rat up a drain'); 'splashing his boots' ('I'm flamin' urgently desirous to syphon the python'); and finally, always, 'chundering'.

Then there was Afferbeck Lauder's *Let's Stalk Strine*, with such key examples of Aussie-speak as EGG JELLY – '*there's nothing egg jelly the matter with her*'; GLORIA SOAME – *a suburban house containing fridge, telly, wall-to-wall carpets*; and ORPHEUS ROCKER – *psychopathic, neurotic, psychotic, slow, quick, eccentric, absent-minded, unstable, excitable, imaginative, introspective, creative, or in any way different*.

No, if we stopped to think about the place seriously the images were not encouraging. Sheep, flies, meat pies, cork hats, 'G'day mate', Kylie Minogue. Weren't these the things the average Pom would call out if a psychiatrist shouted 'Australia' at them?

Okay, so Sydney Harbour was supposed to be beautiful. The wines, we knew now, were not at all like Perth Pink. And films, yes, increasingly we loved those films. But that didn't mean we wanted to *go* there. Laughing at the crooked dance adjudicators of *Strictly Ballroom* or the dodgy local politician father in *Muriel's Wedding*; wincing at the homophobes of Cooper Pedy in *Priscilla* – the joke was a little more sophisticated than Monty Python, but only just. (That actor who played all those roles, what was his name, you know, the crimson-faced puffing one, I mean, surely, that's what most Aussies were *like*.)

Weren't all the interesting and talented ones over here anyway? Clive James, Barry Humphries, John Pilger, Germaine Greer, Michael Blakemore, Peter Conrad, Jill Kerr Conway, Robert Hughes, Kathy Lette . . . the list went on. If Australia was so bloody marvellous why didn't they all go back?

Clearly I had to get a more sophisticated picture. I went to the library and leafed through books with titles such as *The Australian Ugliness*, *The Great Australian Stupor* and *Australia Fair?* (all written by Australians). I discovered that Aussies believed in giving people 'a fair go'; they were wary of authority and loved the underdog; they had a laid-back, 'She'll be right' philosophy; they distrusted extreme politeness; above all, they loathed anybody who distinguished themselves, became 'a tall poppy' – even to the point of actively pretending to be stupid. 'To appear ordinary, just like everybody else, is sometimes a necessary condition for success in Australia.'

They were, despite their enviable classlessness, deeply racist. They treated the tiny remaining percentage (1.6 per cent, including mixed-bloods) of Aboriginals dreadfully. According to John Pilger (an Australian, naturally), the rate of black deaths in custody in Australia was, in the 1980s, *thirteen times* that of apartheid South Africa. As for immigrants, the White Australia policy, which had been officially supported by the Labour Party until 1965, had kept out 'coloureds' and 'Asians' almost entirely. Post-war Italian and Slav arrivals had been endlessly abused as 'wogs', 'dagoes' and 'bloody New Australians'.

'Australia,' Germaine Greer had written, 'is a huge rest home where no unwelcome news is ever wafted on to the pages of the worst newspapers in the world. The vast mass of the population snoozes away roused only for a football match or a free beer . . .'

The more I read, the more depressed I became. Quite apart from anything else, it was clear I was exactly the sort of Englishman the Aussies would like least. I was public-school educated and useless at sport. Not only useless but ignorant. I had no favourite football team, wasn't interested in rugby, had been put off cricket by forced participation as a child. (I'd been in the seventh eleven, which played with a tennis ball and was umpired by the headmaster's wife.) I was in fact the Ultimate Whingeing Pom.

I confided my doubts to friends, acquaintances, strangers. The general consensus was that I was making a mistake. 'I must say,' said one, 'that is one place I've never had a desire to go.' 'It's not top of my list,' said another. It was parochial, it was 'a cultural desert', everybody – 'I'm afraid' – had an inferiority complex. Others made jokes: 'Why do Australian birds fly upside down? Because there's nothing worth shitting on.' Or: 'You know that if an Englishman goes to Australia the IQ of both countries is increased.'

Only the people who'd actually been there recently struck a different note. 'You'll have a ball', 'It's beautiful', 'The food is fabulous', they enthused. But: 'I'll give you a tip,' said one, 'don't laugh at them until they do.' 'One thing my father did warn me,' said another, 'is: "Be careful not to be patronising."'

Hm. What an awful lot I had to learn.

# 'What Aspict?'

I'm on my third breakfast. Long, long ago (last night) it was late summer in LA; now it's early spring over the Tasman Sea. Sunday the 4th of September has vanished into a time warp. All around, the sky and sea are the same gorgeous aquamarine as the brochure.

Ah, at last, this must be Australia, looking at first like a group of grey, low-lying islands; then two of the islands become headlands and three blue inlets appear ... a harbour, *the* harbour, of course. Like a familiar photograph developing, the famous bridge becomes visible, then the white sails of the Opera House (much smaller than I imagined) beside it. To the left, a clutch of skyscrapers are pale cutouts against the gently shifting ochre clouds. It's all so *bright*.

At one end of the Arrivals hall there was a little café. The large blonde lady by the till looked even more exhausted than I felt. 'G'night,' she said, in an accent more Mediterranean than Australian. 'Sorry.' She gave me a weary smile. 'G'day.'

I'd told myself that taking a taxi was a good idea. It might be twenty dollars but this way I'd start my journey with a fair dinkum Aussie. From my American guidebook I knew to expect 'an enjoyable trip as well as pick up a little homespun philosophy with the latest slang and Strine along the way'. I also knew not to offend by getting into the back. No, in egalitarian Oz you got in the front. And called him 'mate'.

But opening the door I found my driver was a round-faced Fijian, who addressed me as 'sir' and nodded for me to get in the back. 'All these names are copy-cat names,' he told me, as we sped past the pretty wrought-iron balconies of Paddington and up Liverpool Street to Kings Cross. 'They can't even think up their own names.' 'Don't you like Australians?' I asked. 'They treat you like a-shit,' he told me. Then, 'Victoria Street, Victoria Street,' he muttered, pulling into the kerb to consult his map.

'The Cross' was clearly the place to start, being full of cheap hotels and backpacker hostels. It was also the red-light district, which might give me some useful colour. Didn't all the best travel books begin with the author checking unwittingly into a brothel? ('Oh ho ho, so you are not the chambermaid . . .') It was not to be. The hotel I'd selected had been turned into a refuge for battered women. A handwritten notice directed travellers to an address up the street.

Now the door would swing open and – 'G'day, mate!' – an enormous sunburnt ocker with a tattoo would knock me backwards with his greeting. 'It's smoko, cobber, I'm just brewing up the billy so grab a vegemite sarnie and we'll sort yer out with yer swag!' In the background would cower a thin, wan woman who agreed with everything she was told.

But Paul, of course, was slight and rather nervous, with glinting glasses and a straggly pepper and salt beard; and when Jacqui appeared through the hall, dark-haired and statuesque, it was clear she had at least a half-share in saying how the place was run.

Two hundred yards down the gently sloping, plane-tree-lined street I came to a long flight of stone steps. A panorama of central Sydney was spread before me. A steep drop to tattered grey and white warehouses in a narrow aquamarine bay; rising beyond, the green, tree-covered promontory of the Royal Botanic Gardens; beyond that the skyscrapers of the business district, squeaky-clean against the clear blue sky, looking more like an architect's drawing than a real city.

'It was impossible,' Trollope wrote, over a century ago, 'not to like the public gardens at Sydney – because one could sit under the trees and look upon the sea . . . grassy slopes on which you may lie and see the moon glimmer on the water as it only glimmers on land-locked curves of the ocean. You may lie there prostrate on the grass, with the ripple close at your feet within a quarter-of-an-hour of your club. Your after-dinner cigar will last you there and back if you will walk fairly and smoke slowly.'

Nothing had changed. The ripple was still at your feet, and through it you could see the rocky bottom as clearly as in a Cornish cove. It was spring, so the ornamental beds were awash with daffodils, tulips, swathes of pink and orange azaleas. Drifting across the sloping green lawns came the sound of someone practising the clarinet. Birds were singing, but what strange, curlewing cries they were. They sounded more like *The Clangers* than the gently spoken thrushes and sparrows of home.

I wandered on, jet-lagged and serendipitous. Sydney had won me over before I'd even got to the Opera House; before I'd even done the corny thing and taken the battered green and cream ferry to Manly, seen for myself the famous loveliness of the harbour: the myriad bays and inlets, the wooded headlands, the gardens that ran down to private jetties, the hidden boathouses, the jibs and mainsails of the criss-crossing dinghies bending in the breeze, the choppy blue-green sea, sparkling (truly) with a thousand dazzling diamonds of antipodean sunshine . . .

## Murder

As I lay in a deep sleep that evening – my guidebook tumbled onto the floor, the light still on beside me – thirty miles away, on the far side of the Western suburbs, an unknown gunman drove up to the front driveway of the State MP for Cabramatta, Mr John Paul Newman, and shot him dead in front of his young Chinese-born fiancée, Xiao Jing Wang (known affectionately to him as Lucy). STATE MP SHOT DEAD IN DRIVE-BY ATTACK yelled the headline in the *Sydney Morning Herald*. It was the 'first political assassination in Australian history'. Particularly controversial because Newman had been the white MP for a constituency with a thirty-five per cent Asian population. He'd been waging a high-profile political campaign against crime and street violence in Cabramatta and had received 'numerous death threats'. His car had been paint-bombed three times. A shot had been fired through the window of his electorate office after he'd taken out advertisments in Vietnamese and Chinese threatening to deport members of Asian gangs if they were found guilty of violent crimes.

So it was perhaps fortunate that the first of my contacts was what the Aussies call a journo. She was Helen, late-thirties, long strawberry-blonde hair, slash of crimson lipstick, just recruited onto the left-leaning *Herald* by new proprietor Conrad Black. As we sat in the trendy little Potts Point wine bar – all gleaming chrome and white-aproned waitresses – she seemed terribly distracted, kept staring off sideways at the wall.

'So, Sydney . . .' she was saying. 'Yuh . . . I interviewed Douglas Coupland, you know, the Generation X guy. He described Sydney as the alloy of all cities . . .' She tailed off again.

So what about the big news of the day, I asked, and she perked up. 'Yuh,' she said, 'that *is* amazing.' In the office they'd been trying to get someone to go down to Cabramatta, but they'd all been ducking and weaving because they knew they wouldn't get anything out of them. 'The Asian community, they just don't talk. They absolutely close ranks.'

But there was a twist to this thing. Bernie, this guy that dealt with the sex scandals and things – 'Like normally,' Helen laughed, 'you hear him shouting into the phone, "He was wearing *what*?"' – had found out that this Newman guy was a complete bastard to work for, he'd got through something like fifty secretaries since he'd been an MP, he'd had lots and lots of enemies, and the whole Asian-gang angle might well turn out to be a red herring.

Suddenly Helen had come alive and was ordering another bottle. We were talking about immigration and Australia's position on the Pacific Rim meaning that it was essentially an Asian country although it was, of course, having huge problems coming to terms with this; and then this definitely on-the-left, definitely liberal woman was saying, 'I'm not racist but what minimal violence there is in this society comes from Asians. People coming into houses and robbing people at knifepoint.'

When Helen had got up to go to the loo I'd noticed an unusual thing. In this bar with perhaps twelve occupied tables, there were no less than four men sitting alone with bottles of wine, reading books. Now we were joined by one of them, a plump forty-something in glasses. 'Come and meet Mark,' Helen shouted as he lumbered in his tweed jacket towards the front door.

'I'm sorry,' she said as he loomed over us, 'I've forgotten your name.'

'Noel,' he said, lips flickering with inebriated amuse-ment. 'It's French for Christmas. So you're writing a book about Australia. What aspict?'

'Oh, the whole thing,' I waved airily. 'Australia's the subject.'

He raised an eyebrow in Helen's direction. 'That's a big brief.'

When he'd gone Helen revealed the reason for her earlier distraction. She'd just split up with her boyfriend. Literally. On her way to meet me.

The next morning the *Herald*'s letters pages were full of suburban outrage. 'Stop pussyfooting around,' wrote Maureen A. Gillard of Ermington. 'Trash like this neither care about nor respect our laws and the solution is simple: deport them back to their own crime-ridden countries and let them live by their wits there.' As yet, nobody had a clue who'd murdered John Newman.

Tony Stephens was one of the *Herald*'s star feature writers. His photo-byline, with long, bearded face and sunken eyes, made him look like lugubriousness personified. But as we sped past the never-ending detached bungalows of the Western suburbs, a small, square smile made an appearance, and the eyes brightened up and were framed with laugh-lines.

'It'll be interesting to see how much security there is today. Even after this has happened it won't be like England. This is really new here, this sort of thing.' He laughed. 'A couple of years ago, in Darwin, there was this guy, he was drunk, went up to the Chief Minister of the Northern Territory while he was making a speech and cut his tie off.' Tony made a scissor-snip with his fingers. 'Like that. And I remember thinking at the time. This could only happen in Australia.'

At Our Lady of Mt Carmel Church, the queue of mourners stretched out through the gate and way off down the street. Here, visibly, were the 110 nationalities that lived in Cabramatta. Asians in brown suits, a pair of Mediterranean types in black bomber jackets, a group of white-haired chaps in sky-blue blazers. All around the huge beige-bricked church were colourful wreaths:

With our deep condolences, Serbian Orthodox, Saint Sava
  Assa.
The Australian Chinese Teo Chew Association.
We do not have adequate words. Rookwood Karate Club.

Inside, at the head of the aisle, the coffin was draped in the
Australian flag. Next to me in the journalists' pew was a
young Malay-featured woman in an elegant lime-silk
jacket; she was the reporter for the *Australian*. She pointed
out the bigwigs: Gough Whitlam, ex-Federal Prime Minister; Peter Sinclair, Governor of New South Wales; Mr
Fahey, State Prime Minister; Bob Carr, Leader of the State
Opposition. Then current PM Paul Keating and his wife
arrived in a flurry of deputies. Finally, the poor fiancée,
face contorted with grief, clutching a blank-eyed, grey-
haired old lady. 'There goes Luce and the Mum,' said the
plump journo on my other side.

Tall, white-haired Gough Whitlam read the first lesson;
John's brother, Peter Naumenko, the second. *Naumenko*. So
Newman had been an immigrant too.

Afterwards, while the coffin and cortège headed off on
its State Procession through the streets of Cabramatta, Tony,
the two long-haired photographers and I sped with Stuart
the driver straight to the cemetery.

'I saw you managed to get to Gough Whitlam,' I said to
Tony.

'Yes. He was dabbing at the old eyes there. Funny, I've
never seen him like that.' Newman's first wife and all his
children had been killed in a car crash in the late Seventies.
'After that he was in a very suicidal mood. Old Gough
came down and talked to him and persuaded him to carry
on.'

At the cemetery we walked through the gravestones.
'You see where they come from?' he said. SALWAROWSKY
HEINONEN lay next to HUSSAIN MOHAMMED. Tony
pointed at a row of ten-foot-high marble vaults, elaborately

decorated with columns, vases, carved flowers. 'This lot are the Italians. Pretty impressive eh?'

But John Paul Newman (né Naumenko) was not going to rest in such splendour. His grave was a three-foot by three-foot slot in a stack; four high, sixteen along, an in-death version of a Japanese love hotel.

'What a terrible place to be buried,' I said to Stuart the driver.

'There's a move to plant 'em upright now, pack more of 'em in.'

'It's a sad story, eh?'

'Bit of a dead story now, mate.' He chuckled heartily.

The hearses arrived, their shiny black roofs heavy with flowers. Two priests stood by the crimson velvet curtain that covered the mouth of the grave-slot. One sprinkled Holy Water. The crowd parted for the coffin.

But now came a cry from Lucy, a horrible, gut-wrenching, animal howl of grief. Her face was buried in the yellow roses and white chrysanthemums on the lid of the coffin. Her shoulders shook as she sobbed uncontrollably.

The crowd just stood and watched, shocked and stony-faced. Only the priest looked as if he knew how to handle such things. 'In the Name of the Father,' he began, mechanically. A lone photographer had pushed to the front of the crowd. His camera whirred and clicked intrusively.

Now the old mother had broken down. 'John, John,' she cried, clutching at the lid of the coffin, burying her head so you could only hear, ' . . . staying alive for hi-im, staying alive for me-e.'

Driving back east Tony was muted. 'I was talking to one of the Vietnamese women there,' he said eventually, 'she came over after the Fall of Saigon and Newman looked after her, welcomed her. Both the children of course speaking with broad Australian accents.' He laughed.

The two photographers were grumbling about the pictures they hadn't got. 'That bloke from AAP pitched up late and just barged straight to the front. We were all kept to one side. Then I'd just packed up my gear and she started freaking out. Christ that was annoying, mate.'

In the morning Tony's story was on the *Herald*'s front page. Inside, the heavyweight commentators delivered their verdicts. BIGOTRY SHAMES US ALL thundered Peter Smark:

> Whoever killed Dr Newman, and why (and we don't know either yet) there can be no justification for some of the letters reaching this newspaper and many of the calls to talk-back radio programmes these past two days. They show a redneck, fundamentalist racism which makes one wonder if this country really has come to terms with reality at all over the past few decades ...
>
> When will we all come to accept that we cannot sail this country away, and that while we can choose not to be part of Asia we do not have the choice not to be partly Asian? Nothing can alter the fact that we are already partly Asian, however hard some people try to pretend otherwise.

Michael was another of the *Herald* columnists. Helen had invited me along to his Saturday-night party in Clovelly, one suburb south-west of Bondi. It was to celebrate his fortieth birthday and also his 'renovation', which was attracting enthusiastic approval from the assembled gang of journos. 'This is the sort of renovation all the yuppies do,' Helen shouted, leading me through the yapping throng. 'They take one of these old houses and strip off the back, put in lots of big glass windows and a dick. Actually you should write about that. The dick is a big part of Australian culture.'

The deck in question was buzzing with new rumours about John Paul Newman. Bernie, the *Herald*'s sleaze and crime man, had the theory that the murderer was Lucy Chang's Chinese ex-husband. The police had been warning some journalists not to go too heavy on the Asian-gangs angle. 'Imagine how stupid some people are going to look if that's all it turns out to be – an overblown domestic.'

Stuart Hopkinson, tall, beaky-looking presenter of ABC's *Panorama*-style *Four Corners*, had a different angle. 'The fact is,' he said, leaning matily towards me over his frothing strawberry daiquiri, 'Newman was a criminal and he deserved to die. No really.' Stuart had a team of researchers down in Cabramatta as we spoke. And look, if I wanted to join him down there next week, it wouldn't be a problem. Basically it was coming through loud and clear from the interviews they'd already done that Newman had been far more complex than he'd been portrayed. He'd been in cahoots with local criminals. He was a shocking political opportunist who'd 'fearmongered' the level of crime and violence in the community to exploit the situation for his own political ends. 'And the people who are saying this,' Stuart shouted down at me, 'are, you know, level-headed, influential local people, even friends of his.'

'And you're going to say this in your programme?'

'Oh yes. The main point is that many of the leading politicians knew this. Australia's like that. There's this deep level of corruption.'

Stuart, Helen and Bernie all had two things in common, I discovered later; besides being journos, they were all Kiwis.

## Tyke the Piss!

' . . . So it's a wild garden, or a wild orchard, you could say, of thoughts and emotions and places that come and go . . .'

Oh dear. I'm at another party. This is all I seem to be doing now, tagging along with Helen to private views and openings and launches and standing with a glass in my hand while people say 'What aspict?' to me. This one's a literary launch, in the tartan-walled upstairs room of a pub in Paddo (as we call Paddington here). I'm squashed at the top of the stairs while everyone stands listening politely to the speech.

' . . . the other thing is its seamlessness, the way all the threads come together and I guess that's partly why Drusilla is so admired – '

CRASH! A large flushed man in a tweed jacket appears at the bottom of the stairs. 'Make sure I don't fall down,' he shouts, sideways, to an invisible companion. He climbs three steps and falls flat on his face. 'Ow-w,' he groans, then pulls himself up, pushes past me. 'Ignore the speeches,' he says loudly. 'Geddathebar!

'Shsh!' goes one of the gathered women.

' . . . for the price it really is an absolute pleasure and it is about women growing into their own lives and I think we can all be very grateful for that . . .'

'Oh *Christ*!' goes the drunk, staggering on a chorus of shushes towards the bright little Malaysian lady behind the bar.

But it's not a great outrage, we really don't expect anything better from our men and very soon the speeches are over and everyone's shrieking at each other. 'I did want to say, are you going to that belly-dance thing?'

'The Politics of Belly-Dancing?'

'Ye-es . . .'

'Can I have a glass for Drusilla?'

'I'm not usually like this,' says Helen, pushing up to me. 'What?'

'Going out every night. It's being single again.' Her ex has already found another woman, a complete airhead who's been hanging around him for years. His daughter goes to the same school as her daughter, 'that's the only thing they've got in common, that his daughter is her daughter's best friend.' She laughs, bitterly. 'And then I'm phoning up and he's saying, "I miss you, Helen." And then he tells me he just needs space and I said to him, "Well you should be able to find plenty of that between *her* ears." '

I laugh. 'Oh dear,' I say.

'I know I shouldn't be saying this stuff to him, she's not

even pretty and I'm phoning him up and saying, "Well, is the sex that good?" I know I shouldn't do it.'

Then Helen's gone home and I find myself downstairs having supper opposite Graham, a sales director from Melbourne with a thick walrus moustache and a huge spotted bow-tie. Having asked me 'What aspict?' he's now giving me his considered advice about how to pitch my book for maximum sales Down Under. 'Tyke the piss!' he bellows in my face.

Later we repair to the bar where he holds forth to me and two fellow salespeople – John, a Melburnian, and Nikki, a Sydneysider – about the superiority of Melbourne over Sydney. 'The truth of the matter,' he shouts, over Nikki's loud protestations, 'is that Melbourne is the place where people are serious but they can be frivolous at the same time. Okay, Sydney's the Emerald City, it's Sin City, it's there, the harbour, the sun glistens on the water, *okay*, but once you go underneath you don't see much at all, and nobody, *nobody*,' he waves a heavy finger to silence Nikki, 'will give you a relationship that goes much deeper than a quarter inch under the scum on the water at the top of Sydney Harbour. In Melbourne you find enduring friendships. My best mate and I have been friends, best friends for *thirty-two yee-ars*.' He smiles a slow and triumphant smile.

'My husband has been best friends with his best friend for twenty years and he's younger than you are!' Nikki shouts cogently.

'In Melbourne,' Graham bellows back, 'you can be driving down the street, and you think, I know who lives there, you just knock on the door and drop in . . .'

'It's the same in Sydney,' shouts Nikki.

'It's not.'

'It is.'

The next night I told a Sydneysider about this exchange and she laughed. 'But Melbourne people always end up coming to Sydney,' she said. 'I mean Sydney's attitude is: "Who *gives* a fuck?" '

Every morning I woke with a surprisingly unthick head (it must have been the air, I decided) and jogged out into the dazzling Australian sunshine, down the ninety-six steps, past the kiosk that sold meat pies to taxi drivers, past the tattered ex-docks of Woolloomooloo, up into the Botanic Gardens and round by the gently lapping waters of Farm Cove to the Opera House. However early I rose I would never be up before the Japanese, who would already be grinning and taking photos of each other at seven in the morning by the odd rock formation known as Mrs Macquarie's Chair. If I left the run till lunchtime the steep steps down to the water would be packed with muscly, fluorescent-clad jocks, mostly topless, using them as a kind of glorious open-air Stairmaster. Later still, I might catch a staged Japanese wedding, complete with bride and groom in wedding dress and suit, bogus 'priest', and supporting gaggle of photographer, stylist, make-up person and officious organiser. On and on they went, trying this pose and that, always making sure that in the background was that magic combination of Opera House and Harbour Bridge.

Back in Victoria Street I sat in the cafés drinking flat whites (as I had learnt to call the frothy Mediterranean-style coffee) and trying to get a handle on the accent of the young women passing by. 'The anly thing ee-ees she's laike a yee-ah aulder?' Every statement ended with the rising inflexion of a question; and 'no' was a word of two syllables – 'na-ow'. Very few of them said 'no worries', 'it's not a problem' being the preferred mantra.

Behind the shutters of my ground-floor hotel room I lay on my bed and shuffled the pack of visiting cards I'd picked up at the parties and wondered who I should interview to give me a real feel of Sydney. Should it be DAVID NET-THEIM, orotund-voiced actor, or his charming friend

ROBERT LLOYD, DESIGNER (bold black on a silver sheen). For all the supposed Australian scorn of 'tall poppies', Sydney seemed to be full of larger-than-life 'identities' that everyone knew about and looked up to. Some were obvious achievers, like Rod McGee, who'd just won the Olympic 2000 bid; or Rebel Penfold-Russell, heiress and producer of *Priscilla*. Others seemed purely social, part of the glitzily parochial harbourside scene I was getting a glimpse of night after night. 'Have you been to the North Shore yet?' a swishly suited gent had asked me, only yesterday. I'd told him about a Sunday brunch I'd enjoyed in Balmoral and he'd nodded approvingly, as if I were Leichhardt returning from the wildest outback. 'Good. You have to go,' he said. 'I can't *remember* the last time we went over the Harbour Bridge,' added his wife, who dripped with gold. 'You definitely need a map when you get there,' he agreed.

In between times I serial-phoned Stuart Hopkinson. Eventually he called back, genial as anything. Look, he was terribly sorry but the Newman story was getting more and more complex and he just hadn't had a spare minute and it was a shame because he'd been down there yesterday but it was someone who'd agreed to be interviewed at the last minute and they'd just choppered down there at four and been back by 5.30. But *basically*, the very interesting things that were emerging were: 1) that Newman had been very corrupt indeed, had had definite links with known criminals; 2) that the people most prejudiced against the new Asians were the first-generation post-war immigrants, the Italians, the Yugoslavs, of whom John Naumenko was one; 3) that Newman/Naumenko had deliberately painted a distorted picture of the community for his own political ends. The 'Asian gangs' were mostly just groups of dislocated teenagers rather than Triad-type hit-squads; and 4) paradoxically, charmingly, amusingly, many of the newest, Asian immigrants were the ones who were most passionate about being proper Australians. Stuart's team had filmed a cultural day at Cabramatta High School 'and it was extraordinary because the kids were all wearing these hats with corks in them and singing "Waltzing Matilda".' Stuart's laughter burbled out of the earpiece. 'Ultimately they're the Republicans. It's quite funny, the real Republicans are coming from these new communities.'

## Lord Waddy of Woolloomooloo

There was no way I could pretend I was neutral. I didn't need to talk to Malcolm Turnbull and Tom Keneally and be wowed by the force of their pro-Republican arguments. For a country to be nominally ruled by a leader resident 13,000 miles away, whether that leader was a Queen, a President or a teddy bear, struck me as utterly absurd. It seemed extraordinary that forty-six per cent of Australians still wanted it that way.

So I phoned Lloyd Waddy, National Convenor of Australians for a Constitutional Monarchy. He was immensely genial. By all means come and hear his arguments. Was I free for lunch? It would be his pleasure to take me to one of his clubs, the Sydney Club, or, since the weather was so pleasant at the moment, the Royal Yacht Club.

He wore dapper pinstripes and had a profile that Hogarth would have enjoyed. He was jovially proud of his convict ancestry. On his mother's side, the Hutchinsons had come over with the First Fleet. The original Waddy, on the other hand, had arrived as a soldier, in 1834. Either way, he was Old Stock. In England, I thought, he would have been Sir Lloyd, or even, perhaps, Lord Waddy of Woolloomooloo.

I got the usual little tour that you get from a proud clubman: the board with the engraved list of Commodores, the models of the hulls of celebrated yachts, the splendid harbour view. Upstairs, pink-faced chaps in suits and ties were tucking into a sumptuous buffet, everything from giant Sydney prawns to soft Tasmanian Brie.

It wasn't as simple, he told me, as just putting a line through Queen and writing President. Once you had a President you had to have a term and a term meant a politician. 'Beast' was the word he used. 'Once you create a President, how d'you restrain the beast you've created. A Republic means anyone can get control of the country. But no one has anything to fear from the House of Windsor, or from the Queen. And when you come down to it, who wants to give up a perfectly safe and secure system for something that might go wrong. Or for something you have to keep watching to make sure it doesn't go wrong.'

What Australia had was a perfectly good constitution that had worked longer than most democracies. 'There aren't so many others that have survived. If you add 'em up there's Britain, Canada, New Zealand, ourselves, the United States, which has had one bloody civil war, probably the worst civil war of all time, and where else?

'Four of those work on a constitutional monarchical system where the power and the glory are separated.' He pushed his soup bowl aside and waved a crust of French bread at me. 'The power of the Crown is not the power it exercises, it's the power it denies others. Those who run around saying, "Why can't I be the Head of Australia?" are the very people our system keeps out. Which I think is marvellous. You can have the power, or you can have the glory. People can all bow to you, and you get no power. Or you can follow along behind and you can have all the power.'

'So ideally you'd have the Queen for another hundred years?'

'And I think we will. People laugh at me when I say that. It's just not fashionable to say it. But it's the same problem we had in the 1890s, before federation. How else are you going to get a neutral pillar of society to hold this whole continent together. We're talking about a land-mass that stretches from London to Moscow. It's the world's biggest island, larger than the USA without Alaska. And it's very diverse, as you'll find out.'

## Asian Gangs

Not having the budget for a chopper I took the train, chuntering out through the Western suburbs, double-taking to see GUILDFORD, with arc-light sunshine and wind-whipped eucalyptus trees. On the platform were a pair of parchment-skinned grannies who might well have come from Guildford, England, side by side with two thickset Korean teenagers who, come to think of it, might well have come from Guildford, England too. What you didn't see much of were Afro-Carribeans. Well, the officially discriminatory White Australia policy had been in place until 1966; and since Governments had been letting in people whose skin-tone was darker than swarthy Mediterranean, the pressure had been essentially Asian. That at least was the story. 'There's been no reason for them to come here,' 'The tradewinds just haven't blown them here,' people told me.

When I finally arrived Cabramatta was more like Gerrard Street than Southall. HOT VON TOC NAM NU was squashed between HONG KONG WEDDING HOUSE and MY HUNG FABRICS. I stopped to ask a young Vietnamese selling T-shirts from a stall the way to the school. 'Ah, no worries, mate,' he replied, in broadest Aussie, 'it's just up the main drag there.'

Dennis Mackenzie, the handsome, forty-something headmaster of Cabramatta High, looked me up and down wearily. 'We're media'd out here,' he told me. Since the assassination they'd had just about everyone. *Four Corners*, *60 Minutes*, all the regular news programmes. But after last week's *60 Minutes* he was never going to watch or participate in it again. He was absolutely disgusted that a programme that was billed as a tribute to a local MP had been turned into a whole thing about racial hatred. They'd imported Nazi party racist-type people from Melbourne, he told me. 'It was whipped up.'

'They come in here, very sympathetic, just like you, and say they're going to put in all the positive stuff – but at the end of the day they've always got the edit button.'

What we were seeing in Cabramatta, obviously, was the impact of the immigration policies of the Seventies and Eighties. He'd seen it before, when he was a schoolboy, with the resettlement of the Italians from the Snowy Mountains irrigation scheme. 'The sort of reaction to them as new-comers – the name-calling and so on.' In the 1970s it was the people from the Middle East who'd been branded as the wogs; now it was the turn of the Indo-Chinese. 'It's like every dog has its day.'

As to how they were doing apart from the prejudice, there were of course some families who were well established, had businesses, were doing well, contributing to society. But there was no denying the difficulties that stemmed from an unemployment problem that was a result of the recession. Also there were youths who came out from Vietnam to join, say, a father whom they'd not seen for ten years, 'and then they find that in fact this father is remarried and the culture he's living in is an entirely different one from the one they've come from. That certainly causes problems.'

Then there were the assisted youth who'd been sponsored by uncles, aunties and so on; sometimes those relationships broke down. 'Because we not only face a generation gap, we have this significant cultural gap. We have families that hold traditional Vietnamese/Chinese/Khmer/Laotean/Thai values and maintain those sorts of values within an Australian context. But then their children are attending Australian schools and hanging around with Australian kids and there's no understanding at all. So that can lead to problems too. And in some cases lead to young people seeking an identity outside the home which is maybe the gang or the group culture. People talk about gangs but quite often it's just groups of young people who hang together because it provides them with an identity.'

Were there any kids in his school, I asked, whom he knew to be gang members. Dennis shrugged. 'Maybe there are ten, maybe fifteen, I don't know. I strongly suspect there are a couple. Now a lot of people will say, "How can you have people like that in your school?" Well the answer is that they don't impact in a negative way on the school. There's no evidence of any of their activities here. And as long as they are at school there's a chance that we can work and educate them so they'll be able to break that cycle themselves.'

In the main, though, his students were generally compliant and cooperative. There were forty-nine cultural groups represented at Cabramatta High, so with over sixty languages, it was hardly a hotbed of racial tension. 'Maybe that's because everybody's in the same boat of trying to establish themselves.'

When he'd filled me in on the academic successes they'd had, I asked him about his own reasons for being there. He sighed. 'I'm working here,' he said, 'and I see what people are trying to do with their lives and I don't think that sometimes they're given a fair go. And that gets my hackles up. So I'll defend them to the hilt.'

'Not given a fair go by other Australians?'

'Yeah. By other Australians who don't know much about the area in the main.'

'And if they did, they might understand?'

'They'd have more of an understanding certainly. But I don't think they'd *understand* . . .'

'What?'

'I don't think they *know* what some of . . .' He broke off; then began again in a different key. 'I can just talk about my students, what some of my students have been through, in terms of seeing members of their family killed, of spending a long time in camps, with all the attendant disease and violence and everything that goes on in those places, corruption that occurs, how some of them escaped, have seen their parents shot, sisters raped and everything else, on the way to Australia. And then come here and be treated like – like anything but human beings – by some people.'

Earlier in the century his own grandfather had been a £10-migrant from Glasgow. 'Glebe, where they lived, that was where all the gangs were, razor gangs in those days, and,' he laughed, 'my dad was regarded as being a bit of a lout because he wore twenty-two-inch cuffs. Nowadays people are louts because they wear a baseball cap back to front, or they wear baggy jeans, or because they don't want to do up the laces of their NIKE shoes.

'My grandfather was distinctly working class. And yet this country afforded his children the chance to break that mould. I don't say this with pride, but I was the first Mackenzie from our part of the Highlands to have the opportunity to go to university, which never would have happened at home.'

Dennis had mentioned that one of his school captains was a boat-person and I'd asked if I might meet him. If I'd hoped for a vivid tale of drama on the high seas I was to be disappointed. Evan had only been ten at the time of the trip from Vietnam to Thailand and barely remembered it. Only that his father had been aiming at Malaysia, lost the compass, and ended up in Thailand. After two years there they'd been sponsored by 'two old Australian couples' and now the whole family were citizens. Evan spoke better English now than he did Vietnamese and he 'definitely' considered himself more Australian than Vietnamese.

The only surprise was when I asked him about the Republic. He'd been on a school party to see Mr Sinclair, the Governor of New South Wales. 'And he gave me good insight on why we should keep Queen. He told me that when we change Queen and change our political system and everything it's going to require, how shall you say, a lot of time, and a lot of paperwork. I mean, if the system now is going fine why should we change it?'

If I'd been Lloyd Waddy I would have hugged him.

## Man O' Man

At first I'd thought James and Suzi were married. But when Suzi tripped off to the lavatory and I started talking about 'your wife' to James he shifted rather shyly from foot to foot and said, 'I'm not in the vagina business.'

'Oh,' I said. 'So she's just a friend?'

'Yes, we work together. She sings and I write music.' Another party was coming to an end and the waiters were taking down the huge canvas umbrella above the bar. 'I've never seen Australian men having trouble getting it down before,' James said, raising an eyebrow in my direction.

I wasn't looking for gay men; but they were everywhere. Not just in the cruisy bars of Oxford Street, or the restaurants in Darlinghurst (where dining as a mixed-sex couple, you might be the only hets in the place); wherever you turned, it seemed, you met them. They ranged from super-scene characters like the Italian waiter in the café on Victoria Street who'd taken my fifty-dollar note with a very frank look and told me he was used to big ones, through to Guy, a terribly straight-looking young man in a tweed jacket I'd met two nights before. 'I didn't realise he was gay for ages,' said the woman who'd introduced us. 'He's one of those guys you see who's really nice and turns out to be gay and you think – *what a waste!*'

Now it was Saturday night, and in Suzi's flat in Paddo James and his friends were drinking champagne and watching *Man O' Man*, a TV show where an audience of women voted for a line-up of gorgeous (and not so gorgeous) men. It was a knockout competition; all the women had little electric buzzers and at the end of each round the rejects were kissed by a glamour-puss blonde and pushed backwards, fully clothed, into a swimming pool.

'When they've got it down to just three,' Robert (who was wearing a dark beige skirt) explained, 'they take their clothes off and then the women pick the man of their dreams who's usually gay.'

'At least half of gay Sydney's been on that show,' said Greg, drily.

'Why do they go on?'

'You win this great trip for you and your boyfriend.'

'Oh *no*!' shrieked Robert. 'She's in the pool. Buggalugs is in the pool.'

There were only four contestants left.

'No,' said Robert, 'she's too tall. Australian girls don't pick tall guys.'

On the box the women were holding their breath as Sean was tested in the penultimate round: how would he react in a specific 'relationship situation'. Dave had already explained how he'd 'get to know' a woman at a bus-stop; now, 'Sean, what d'you do to get over a broken heart?'

'Keep busy,' Sean replied. 'Don't talk to whoever it was who broke your heart.' Screams and whoops from the women as our hostess moved on to Jeff the hunk. 'Jeff, how important is marriage to you in the Nineties?' A long pause, then, 'It depends on your individual self,' said Jeff. 'If I can go in that deep.'

'What d'you think, Elaine?' asked Robert. Elaine was a Junoesque older woman in her, what, late fifties, with a piled-up mass of blonde hair. Earlier James had described her as 'a real Grace Kelly in her day'. Now she sat with her finger in her mouth, captivated. 'Unfortunately I like them all, but I think number 2 will go.'

'He's going, number 7's going!' Splash! Number 7 was on his back in the pool.

'I told you so,' said Robert. 'Too tall.'

'Dinner's on!' called Suzi from the kitchen.

'We're watching *Man O' Man*,' said Elaine. 'Fuck the dinner.'

'One! One! One!' Robert was shouting. Number 1, the blond hunk, was going down very well. 'They're all pressing one,' said Elaine. Yes, the man who thought marriage depended on your individual self was easily the winner, and the other two were in the pool.

After supper I sat outside by the glowing barbie with James. 'It's kind of sweet that we've got a Queen,' he said. 'I'd much rather have her than Paul Keating. I mean could he handle a palace and ten corgis? No. Anyway, I love English culture. I loathe the way we're all being turned into Americans. I don't like to be snobbish but I hate anything that appeals to the masses.'

He came from a farming family in northern New South Wales. His father hated him being gay, but he'd never got on with his father, so what did it matter. It had a lot to do with the way he'd treated his mother. 'There were some things there that were unacceptable, if you like.' He looked down and gave me a half-smile. 'It may be the reason I'm gay, because I grew up to see women as objects. That was the way women were always portrayed to me.' In their family Mother was always making dinner, slaving away at the housework. 'I suppose the reason we all like *Absolutely Fabulous* so much is that it shows a couple of women who are controlling their own destinies.'

Helen was thinking of going abroad. She'd met her ex and his new woman at a party. 'I was sort of skulking behind this pot of plants and he looked over and I was laughing and he gave me this big glare – Darth Vader across the room – he knew *exactly* why I was so very amused. I thought she was going to be a big sex-kitten but boy she isn't, she was wearing this white sort of little blouse with a little frilly lace collar and black polyester trousers, I mean – *style bypass!*'

\*

Stuart's programme came out. Alleged that Newman had had criminal links. Revealed that he'd got through a phenomenal amount of secretaries. One very bitter ex-employee described him as the 'nearest thing to the devil' she'd ever met. Teenagers from the Asian gangs were interviewed by Stuart, backs to the camera, and told him that yes, they might carry knives but no, they'd never have done such a thing as this murder.

The journos had shot their investigative bolt; meanwhile, the news had moved on and the murderer roamed free.

# 2

# Country Life

At last, somehow, I had torn myself away from Sydney. Most Poms never managed it. For the rest of my trip I'd meet people who had come to Australia, spent six months in the Emerald City, then panicked and 'were doing the rest' in three.

I was riding north-west on a Country Train. That's how the two sections of Central Station were signed: CITY TRAINS and COUNTRY TRAINS. I'd been surprised by the old-fashioned quaintness of the expression and by the fact that you had to book at least a day in advance.

Most of the other passengers were schoolchildren going home for the September spring holidays. The air was filled with the rising inflection of questioning statements. The suburbs got hillier and leafier, then we were into a landscape of countless eucalypts on steep dry mountains. There were stretches of blue lake, moored boats, pretty little clapboard hideaways on the far shore.

Over the public address system, in an accent that veered erratically between Mediterranean and Orstrylian, came an endless string of completely pointless announcements. (Previously I'd thought the guard on the Gatwick Express was garrulous.) 'The buffets, situated in Cars A and D, are at present closed. An announcement will be made when they are open. Thank you for your attention ladies and gennlemen.' There were NO SMOKING signs *everywhere*. But no! 'This train has non-smoking policies. Smoking is not permitted in the carriages or toilets. Your cooperation with our non-smoking policies is appreciated. Thank you for your attention . . .'

We chuntered on. Here and there wistaria tumbled extravagantly down rocky embankments. Otherwise, eucalypts, eucalypts and more eucalypts. What were they all, these myriad varieties of the same species? I worried, I browsed in bookshops, eventually I realised that nobody else knew either. '*Eucalyptus Roadsideana* is a good one,' an academic I met in Canberra told me. 'If you have problems with that, *Eucalyptus Eucalyptofolia.*'

In the Hunter Valley, the drought that I'd read about every day in the papers was horribly evident. 'It's usually so green and pretty,' said Judy White, as we sped away from the little town of Scone through the biscuit-coloured hills, 'but this is as bad as you'll ever see it.' She was in her early sixties, I guessed; had once been a famous Sydney beauty; now, with children grown up and out of the way, she'd become an authoress, with one glossy book published about the famous White homestead, Belltrees, and another about the White family. They were, I'd been told, 'the nearest thing Australia has to aristocracy'. Their line stretched back unbroken to 1826, when James White, farmer of Crowcombe, Somerset, had arrived with £500, a wife and a flock of sheep.

In the middle of nowhere we came to a neat sign saying BELLTREES COUNTRY HOUSE. Down a long drive, past some estate cottages, a tiny school, a huge, abandoned sheep-shearing shed, round a corner, and there it was. Not as vast as I'd imagined from the way the socialites had gone on about it in Sydney, but still, impressive: red brick, green shutters, a long, white, wrought-iron balcony all the way along the first floor.

Once inside, you realised that the frontage was deceptively small. The bulk of the homestead stretched

backwards. Either side of the crimson carpet that dominated the panelled hall were a string of splendid reception
rooms. Here was a billiard room, with a full-sized table
and walls festooned with gymkhana victory ribbons; here
a library; here a sitting room, awash with framed photos
of the family . . .

Judy was waiting for me halfway up the splendid dark-
wood staircase. 'Of course,' she said, 'compared to your
English country houses this is so small. It'd just be the
lodge, wouldn't it?' She laughed. 'But I always say it's not
a historic house, it's a home. We keep all the rooms open
and the grandchildren run around everywhere.'

Now we were taking 'afternoon tea' out to 'the men',
who were pregnancy-testing cattle in the yard. There were
three, two strong young fellows with classic broad-
brimmed bush hats and one white-haired, red-faced old
boy. They were 'forcing the heifers', one by one, out of
a pen, down a narrow passage of iron bars and into a
contraption which held the head still while – huge
cow-eyes revolving with fear – the ear was tagged. The
pregnancy rate was below thirty per cent, they shouted, so
low they'd sent the vet home.

At the sight of beneficent Judy with tea and biscuits 'the
men' came over and just before I put my Pommie foot right
in it I realised that the white-haired old boy was Michael
White, Judy's husband and the owner of Belltrees, and the
two others were his sons, Anto and Peter. At home, I
thought, he would be a tweed-jacketed toff who, at best,
pottered around the farmyard giving orders; his sons
would be smooth-skinned Eurobond traders and come
down on odd weekends.

'So you're writing a book about Australia?' bellowed
Anto, at a decibel-level that would have put the most self-
confident hooray in England to shame. 'I could write a
book about Australia at the moment. One word, beginning
with F!' He laughed.

I went for a stroll in the slanting early evening sunshine.

Belltrees had been built right on the banks of the Hunter River (despite the drought there was still enough water to reflect the outlandishly green willows on either bank) at the centre of a horseshoe of hills, which rose, steeply triangular, from the all-but flat valley. Away to the left rose the mighty, forest-covered Mt Woolooma. It was the first rural Australian landscape I'd experienced. Beautiful, bizarre and, to me, rather eerie, it had more in common with Africa than England.

Dinner was an informal affair in the kitchen. 'We've just got a tray of quails there or some fillet if you'd prefer,' Judy said, pointing to an enormous roll of steak. After a few glasses of wine the conversation turned to Patrick, Michael's famous cousin, the writer and Australian Nobel Prizewinner. I was ashamed to admit that I hadn't read any of his books, *Voss* being one of those 'must get round to sometime' titles I'd been putting off for years. But it turned out that Michael hadn't read any of them either. 'I'm not intelligent enough for that sort of thing, I'm afraid,' he said, his round face pinkening as he laughed his affable laugh. 'I'm sure it's very good – he wouldn't have won the Nobel Prize if it wasn't – but it's not the sort of thing I like to read.' (He wasn't alone in this. One contemporary Australian review of *Voss* had read, 'In spite of England and America hailing this book as a masterpiece, in this country it is considered Australia's most unreadable book.')

Michael had been chatting to White's biographer, David Marr. 'Patrick read the manuscript before he died and you know what he said to David. "You've made me out to be a viper – I like it." ' Michael shook his head in amazement. ' "I like it"! He actually said that.'

In the morning Belltrees was hosting a wedding. The bride was the Japanese teacher from Scone High School, which amused Judy no end. In Queensland Japanese was already a compulsory second language; down here in New South Wales it was still something of a novelty.

'They all like a country wedding,' Judy told me, as I helped her hoist the big stereo speakers out through the 'French doors' onto the lawn. 'There are plenty of places in town they could have it, but they all like coming here.' Daughter Camilla was the organiser, running back and forth down the blossoming wistaria walk, her long blonde hair tied up in a black ribbon. The bridal party had spent a week making huge white tulle bows, 'but they just look terrible on those plastic chairs.'

In the dusty yard, meanwhile, Anto and Peter were waiting for the molasses man. Molasses was something the cattle desperately needed because of the drought. 'Things are so bad,' Judy told me, 'that he's got all the farmers in the palm of his hand. He can turn up when he likes – it's become a bit of a racket really.'

Suddenly Judy ran out of a side door. 'They're coming!' she shouted. Halfway across the lawn she stopped. 'Music!' she cried, and tripped back inside again. The notes of Chopin's 'Aeolian Harp' étude rippled out over the lovely garden.

Across the dried-up paddock from the tiny white clapboard church they trooped, the Japanese teacher up ahead in meringue cream, the groom and best man to one side; three blonde bridesmaids, in deep purple satin dresses split to the upper thigh, teetered over the tussocks in high heels behind.

Early afternoon: from the catering hut the freckled teenage waitresses, hair up, ran back and forth to the loud marquee. Lunch served, the cooks were gossiping. Some man had come out and wanted to use a phone to place a few bets on the races. 'Now he's gone off to his car to listen to the results,' said Camilla. 'It's hysterical. I said, "Don't you want to listen to the speeches." "No." He wasn't bothered. If that'd been my wedding I'd have clobbered him.'

Finally, at teatime, the molasses man arrived. Anto appeared in a black baseball cap and knee-high leather boots. 'Hello Brian, how're ya *goin'*?' More than a little wary of Anto – who was famed for his practical jokes – I was relieved that he was off to load sheep while I was to feed the cows with Peter, the quieter second son. (Along for the ride was his seven-year-old son Jasper and Jasper's grubby-faced chum Ethan.)

It was dry as a bone out there, the ivory grass nibbled back to nothing on the red-brown dirt. On a bare hillside we stopped by an empty trough. The molasses poured from the drum like thick dark treacle. 'You'd appreciate,' Peter shouted, over the rattle of the truck, 'that these animals have three stomachs. With the feed this dry you need something to help them get it down. Don't fall in boys,' he added to the two lads, who were craning over from the back of the lorry.

'Have you ever dropped anyone in?' I asked.

'If I had some smart-arsed Pommie jackaroo I might put him in there. The worst thing is, I'd have to leave him there for the cattle to lick him off – so as not to waste the molasses.' He met my eyes and laughed. I was glad I was the Visiting Writer of thirty-six, not the Jackaroo of eighteen on his first terrifying day. For certain I'd have ended up in the molasses.

'G'way! G'way!' Peter shouted as we rattled at speed across the fields, pursued by the famished cattle. 'Come on girls!' He turned to me. 'Look at them licking their lips.' At each trough the cows jostled, five feet away, tongues – literally – hanging out. 'Come on Marcus! Give 'em that Pommie accent. Come on girls, the Poms are here!'

As we came to the last trough, the setting sun now lighting up the empty hills so they were a magical ochre-orange, I saw my first ever kangaroo, indeed my first ever five kangaroos, absurdly touching animals, looking almost human as they bounded into the gloaming on two legs.

At dinner I enthused to Michael about this introduction to Australia's national animal. But it turned out they were pests. 'I can show you thousands,' he said. 'They eat as much as a sheep,' added Judy. 'They're pests,' Michael repeated. They knew where the feed was. And they had these forward-slanting teeth that meant they could get right down on the grass. In the old days you could shoot them and sell the skins. Not any more. It was another thing the Greenies had interfered with; they'd gone over to America, armed with photos of roos who'd met ugly deaths and convinced the Americans not to buy the skins. 'So now, when we shoot roos we just leave the carcasses out for the crows and foxes. It's such a waste.' Kangaroo leather was such beautiful leather, too; you could make ladies' handbags and belts and boots with it.

The Whites had once owned the whole of the Hunter valley, as well as the adjoining valleys of the Isis and the Page. 'It was, as Patrick used to remark, "their corner of the world". But it was not for him. Whenever he found himself in the bush he felt the old tug-o'-war between the landscape and the life: "I feel, this would be wonderful; then I realise I couldn't stand more than a fortnight. For me, the pavement and the crowd. You've got to have something to fight against; otherwise you'll die of bush ballads." '*

## Doug

Now it was ten to five in the morning and I was freezing to death in an all-night garage in Tenterfield. Up at the till was a pinch-faced blonde who clearly loathed Poms, particularly those of the backpacking variety.

'Is it all right to have a coffee here till it gets light?' I'd asked, as I'd humped my knapsack and ridiculous B.U.M. EQUIPMENT bag (such a great idea *that* had seemed in LA) in from the icy mist outside. 'Yeah,' she'd replied coldly. At the neon-lit canteen table it was so cold I got up and slid the door shut. After half a minute Blondie went over

* David Marr, *Patrick White: A Life* (Random Century, Sydney, 1991) – p. 594.

and reopened it. Why? Because she hated me. There was no possible other explanation.

All night on the Greyhound from Scone I'd been squashed up against a huge Aboriginal gentleman whose snores sounded like a motocross rally. In the seat behind, two Scandinavian females had kept up a constant stream of giggly, gurgly chatter. 'Nay, nay, spracken dracken hurdle gurdle nay nay,' they'd gone, falling deceptively silent before, like those most infuriating of car alarms, starting up again at full volume. 'Shh!' people had gone from time to time, but it was quite fruitless.

I waited, shivering and sipping coffee till it was just light, then trudged off up the hill into central Tenterfield. The only problem with having a cunningly selected article of luggage that turned in a jiffy from a canvas suitcase into a knapsack was that it wasn't a great case, and it was a worse knapsack. Anyway, I had a crap technique. Those other, proper, backpackers I'd seen every day in Sydney, their kettles and non-stick toasted-sandwich makers dangling proudly from upright aluminium frames, would have marched into Tenterfield as if carrying a feather pillow. Not me. I trudged along like the Hunchback of Notre Dame.

Eventually there was a crossroads and a cheery, up-early ocker in a bush hat to tell me that the first bus to Byron Bay left at two that afternoon. It now being 6.15 I decided, against all the advice I'd been given in Sydney, to hitch. The famous Backpacker Murderer had been recently caught. Not yet tried and found guilty, but arrested. Presumably they'd got the right man. Anyway, even if they hadn't, what were the chances of him being on the prowl in Tenterfield at 6.15 on a Monday morning? Live a little, die a little, you can hitch.

Beyond the garage on the edge of town I found the ideal spot. A nice stretch of straight road with a place to pull up just beyond. I sat on my suitcase/knapsack/roadside chair rubbing my hands against the cold. Rooks cawed, a cock crowed, other nameless Aussie birds made their weird, rasping, chuckling cries. Every ten minutes or so a car or 'ute' drove past, ignoring my upturned thumb.

I'm thirty-six, I was thinking. I have a university degree. I have friends who are directors of advertising agencies, partners in law firms, who edit magazines, who present the news, who have wives and children and spacious houses in Wandsworth full of toys and kitchen equipment. What am I doing; alone on this frozen green in the middle of nowhere? You have an adolescent desire To Be a Writer; and this, fifteen years later, after many trials and tribulations, is where you end up. Watching a man in a long purple T-shirt, white sneakers, and a black floppy hat, the Quentin Crisp of Tenterfield, teetering off to buy his morning newspaper.

After a while, I remembered my hitching technique, took a large piece of paper from my knapsack and wrote CASINO on it. I toyed with the idea of writing CASINO PLEASE but thought that might be altogether too Pommie and polite. CASINO PLEASE MATE (?) No, mightn't that be seen as a piss-take? By some murderous, Pom-hating Aussie, and I would end up, after all, six feet under in the Belanglo Forest.

Seven o'clock passed, then 7.20, then 8.04. The ruthless citizens of Tenterfield went on their merry way. Over the little triangular green the windows of the clapboard houses opened, people began their days. Quentin Crisp returned with a tetrapak of iced coffee, an old lady started poking around in her garden. I ran over. I was on the right road for Casino? 'Yes, yes, that's it. Best of luck, mate.' Warmed to the frozen cockles of my heart I ran back and smiled confidently at the next car. It didn't stop.

Half an hour later, just as I was about to abandon hope in favour of a simply enormous breakfast in central Tenterfield, a battered little van skittered to a halt in my brilliantly selected lay-by. Out stepped a man with a beergut and a wide-brimmed brown hat. He looked exactly like Dan in

*Roseanne*, give or take a few pounds on the stomach, the deep-red linen trousers and the billowing claret shirt.

All of a sudden I was transformed from tragic solipsistic thirty-something to gratefully eager teenager. As Dan started to lift his bags out of the offside seat, No, no, really, I said, I could squeeze in there, no worries. Dan said nothing, carrying on in his slow, deliberate way, moving his stuff to the back, where amid the junk and boxes and sawdust a grey, dingo-like dog stood chained up. 'I'll put my bags in there then?' Dan nodded and mumbled something incomprehensible.

We drove off. After a couple of minutes he leaned over and held out a big ham of a hand. 'Doug's me name,' he said. It could have been 'Doug's the name.' He spoke as if he had, not a plum, but a hot potato in his mouth.

I shouldn't be hitch-hiking. That much I did understand. There were a lot of something-something people out there. Things weren't what they used to be. In Orstrylia. Well versed in this sort of hitch-hikers' chat I nodded. 'It's a shame,' I said. 'Is,' he replied, shaking his head. 'Shame.'

We wound slowly down the tinderbox-dry slopes of the Great Dividing Range. The air was filled with a smoky haze: the green-grey eucalypts and crisp-brown olive trees fading to pale silhouettes in smudgy washes of blue and grey.

Doug had never been outside Orstrylia. Had no desire to. 'Even if I won the lotto. Wouldn't go.' No desire to see England, or the South Sea Isles, or America? 'Seen enough of 'em on TV.'

Two more hours brought us to Lismore, and suddenly the countryside was April green. 'This is like England,' I tried. 'Green.'

Doug nodded sadly. 'Spring,' he replied. 'Should be green everywhere.'

Then we were on the double track of the Pacific Highway and there was the sea below us. The lighthouse and double-curve of sand was Byron Bay, legendary home of Paul

Hogan, Mel Gibson, Olivia Newton-John and, so they'd said in Sydney, numerous hippies, New Agers and alternative-lifestylers. 'Take you in,' said Doug. 'Buy you beer.'

RETRAVISION, ROCK TOWERS REAL ESTATE, CRYSTAL TEMPLE — MASSAGE, REBIRTHING, PALMISTRY, TAROT AND PSYCHIC, palm trees, open-air cafés, glimpses of blue sea, pretty girls on bicycles, long-haired men in bare feet, expensive cars. It was a different world.

'There's a café,' I said. 'That'll be okay for a beer.' 'No,' Doug was firm. In his plump, sunbaked face his eyes flitted nervously. 'Need something-something dressed up,' he muttered.

Eventually we turned a corner and saw what we needed: an old-style Australian pub. Not a MOTEL but a HOTEL with the familiar strip along the veranda advertising TOOHEYS beer. Doug relaxed visibly. He pulled up in the yard at the back, gave his tame dingo a scratch under the chin and stumbled into the bar.

Where (it seemed to me then, so early in my journey, so naive) the two Australias collided. There was Doug, big and lumbering in his untucked shirt and ocker hat, ordering a schooner of Toohey's; and behind the bar was the crisp young blond of a barman with the singing Sydney accent. 'So what can I get you gentlemen?' he enquired with a flash of perfect white teeth.

'Schooner,' said Doug, nodding at the tap. Had he turned his head a fraction as that particularly lovely girl in the loose purple dress sashayed past? Or was he thinking: *This place isn't for me.* He pursed his lips and shook his head as I handed over five dollars for two schooners. 'Spensive,' he mumbled. He pulled out his wallet, showed me the crumpled blue tickets he used to buy beer in his club in Tweed Heads. You got ten for fifteen dollars fifty.

Outside he stood dumbly before me. 'Thanks Doug,' I said. 'Something-something-something hitch-hike,' he replied. I thanked him for this advice, shook his hand, and said goodbye for ever.

# 3

# The Lonely Planet

In Sydney I'd been tempted to abandon the solitary comfort of my hotel room for the cheese-on-toast friendliness of one of their numerous hostels. Surely they were the ones having all the fun? Walking up and down Victoria Street you'd catch snippets of their ever upbeat Eurochat as Sven from Sweden made lifelong friends with Randy from Akron, then fell out the next day over Susan from Stoke; as beaten-up Holdens or Round-Oz Greyhound tickets were bought, the grand route north to Cairns planned. Now, sweaty and exhausted in the bright, hot sunshine, a little woozy from my two schooners with Doug, I trudged across the railway track and entered the swinging world of the backpackers.

For half the price of my Sydney hotel I got a double room overlooking the garden. Straight over the railway and a thicket of dunes was the miraculous sweep of beach. Lying back – *twang* – on my mattress, I could hear the not-so-distant roar of the surf. Outside the wind tugged gently at the palm fronds against the endless blue sky. Yes, this'll do just fine, I thought.

Below in the garden the backpackers disported themselves. Here, in the shade, sat a swarthy Johnny Depp writing an airmail letter; there, on the sun-drenched lawn, a young Meg Ryan in a purple bikini gently basted. By the pool Sharon Stone sat naked astride Rufus Sewell, patiently oiling his shoulderblades.

I took a cold shower. On the back of every cubicle in the communal washroom was a printed notice saying,

IN THIS HOSTEL EVERYBODY HAS SEX ALL THE TIME
(USUALLY WITH TOTAL STRANGERS)
WHY NOT JOIN IN THE FUN?

No, it read, AIDS NEVER TAKES A HOLIDAY. And then, in jokey, desperate-not-to-be-patronising-to-yoof language advised you to wear a condom at all times. But it amounted to much the same thing.

In the evening I came back from a solitary walk round town to find a barbecue in progress. Merry groups of backpackers sat at the three or four long wooden tables in the yard munching steaks and sausages and salads, sharing packs of beer and bottles of wine, and generally having a whale of a time.

Suddenly, unaccountably, I felt as shy as if it were my first day at a new school. Obviously the thing to do was groove over and say, 'Hi, mind if I join you?' and obviously the answer would be, 'Fellow *traveller*, park your *ass* down here.' But I just couldn't do it.

In the middle of the longest table there were three older guys. Not older as in ten, fifteen years older, like me; but older as in twenty, thirty years older. There was a sulky-looking grey-bearded hippy, a grinning German with a shaved head and big red braces, and another grey-haired dude with hoary stubble and a black-suede jacket. It wasn't the young ones who were putting me off, it was these guys.

I took my book indoors to the communal area, sat down in a comfortable armchair and studied the same page for a good twenty minutes. Who needed all that laughter and fun out there?

All night a strong wind howled in the palms. I woke late; the sun, high in the sky, shone hot on my face through the gap in the curtains. But going downstairs I found it was not even 8 a.m. I headed off on my jog, miles and miles it seemed up the endless curve of beach. Way beyond the dog-walkers I paused by a couple doing yoga, hands together in an attitude of prayer.

'Is it okay to swim here?'

'No worries.'

'No sharks?'

The woman laughed, a throaty, hippy laugh. 'You'll be right,' she said. 'It's very safe.'

*You'll be right*, I thought, as I dodged nervously into the beautiful surf. It was the first time I'd heard the famous expression. But if there were sharks in Sydney harbour why not here? And those enormous jellyfish, washed up like slugs of blue phlegm all along the shore. Were they all dead? Maybe, with so many 'deadlies', in such an unpredictable climate, *She'll be right* was the only way to deal with it. 'It's bound to go wrong' was the reaction of someone from a tiny temperate island where only seven people had died of snakebite since the war.

## Single Mothers and Bitter Men

'So how d'you hook up with Judy White?' Phil asked. 'Not that I've seen Judy White in twenty years. But if you live in Byron Bay that's what happens. People phone. Sometimes if I'm in the mood I'll say, "Come and have some dinner." Othertimes I'll say, "It's great that you know Judy White but I'm a bit busy right now." He laughed. He was in his early forties. Cool-cat good looks just starting to be etched with wrinkles, cropped hair sporadically flecked with grey.

'I don't know that she knows I've been breeding,' he said, turning towards me with a smile; I began to warm to him; but then: 'We've just got to shoot up to my ex-wife's and push back a shed that's blown over in the wind. And pick up my son . . .'

Phil's ex-wife's was a little bungalow up on the sea-view side of the hills. 'My marriage settlement,' laughed Phil, and I began to wonder what kind of a fellow he was. Having dumped his wife on a point of order did he now hang around picking up the skimpy young lovelies that crowded the town?

Whatever, they seemed on the very best of terms. Sheila was thin in all departments: thin figure; thin features; thin dark hair; thin, rather wistful smile. They grumbled jovially about the wind. We flipped the shed back and Phil paced around inspecting it. Yes, it needed a couple of guy ropes here, a weight there. I was starting to feel rather sorry for this beautiful, pensive-looking woman, still dependent for shed-work on her absent, handsome ex.

We pulled Tom, the cherubic blond son, away from *The Lion King* and drove off, a mile or so along the valley to Phil's place, which was a little clapboard mansion. It had been a filmset up the coast and when they'd finished the movie they were selling it so cheap he'd just had to have it. From the bougainvillaea-swamped veranda you could see the turquoise gleam of a long pool. White figures pranced on a tennis court. Far below the sweep of the coast and the sea.

Inside there were polished floorboards, rugs, sofas, a long mirror reflecting an arrangement of dried flowers and a beautiful blonde-curled Melanie in white with matching blue-eyed child. What had happened? Had I strayed into a Buñuel movie? Thank you, Phil. I took a long sip of Yalumba and shook hands with a bald, grizzled Martin who, though no oil-painting and rather camp, was clearly Melanie's 'partner'. He was a set designer from Melbourne, which probably explained it.

Suddenly the lights went out. It was that bloody wind again. We were going to have to eat dinner in darkness. 'There's something for your book,' said Phil, ransacking a storage cupboard by the flame of a cigarette lighter. 'Dinner by candlelight in Byron Bay.' He stood by the open French doors with his hand cupped round a flickering night-light. 'And they're still playing tennis. My sister's crazy – how can she play with a wind like this in the dark?'

Martin was in charge of dinner. In the background he quietly arranged himself a special pair of cooking candles. The tennis party, flushed and jovial, joined us. Phil's sister Meg, her husband Donald and another couple who had to rush off.

Sinking into a leather sofa I quizzed Donald about sharks. He was a builder who dived as a hobby. I told him about the *You'll be right* couple of the morning. How come Aussies could be so blasé about these things?

'They're not really,' he told me. 'It's every Australian's nightmare to be taken by a shark. But you don't think about it. You can't think about it.'

'You've seen them?'

'I've seen them. But, as they say, you never see the shark that gets you.'

But look, there had only been two shark fatalities in Byron Bay in the last twenty years. Both the victims, strangely, had been called Ford. 'I've got a friend,' Donald said, 'whose maiden name was Ford and she won't swim in Byron Bay any more.' He laughed, and I laughed, and then I stopped laughing, for Ford, albeit spelt in a different way, was my mother's maiden name.

Melanie was taking her daughter home. She wasn't the girlfriend of the set designer after all. When she'd gone she became the immediate subject of conversation. She'd recently, Phil told us, 'flicked' the German who'd fathered her child and now she was looking for someone else.

'Not you?' asked Phil's sister.

'I'm not interested,' said Phil.

It turned out that she was something of a Byron Bay *femme fatale*. The German guy had treated her really well. She'd been pregnant by someone else when he met her. He'd hung around while she had a baby that wasn't his. Then they'd had a baby together. 'And now the poor guy's got flushed,' said Phil, taking a long swig of his red wine. 'She says she wants to re-create this great erotic thing we had twelve years ago, but she doesn't really, what she wants is the whole deal.' His eyebrow took in the detail of his painstakingly reconstructed house, his bougainvillaea, his view. 'She's got two kids.' He laughed.

As we sat down to dinner (Martin, it transpired, was the Marco Pierre White of Melbourne: our shellfish soup was decorated with filigree squirls of tomato, the barbecued chicken on couscous came with a mouth-watering stir-fry) we were full-on to relationships and their demise. 'They say,' said Phil, 'that Byron Bay is full of single mothers and bitter men.'

Now it came out. It wasn't he who'd flicked his wife, but his wife who'd flicked him. She was an actress and she'd met this actor. Byron Bay was full of all these alternative therapies and philosophies, and these women (Phil's sister nodded agreement) they're sitting up in the hills with their men and suddenly they do this course or find that therapy and think they can do it all themselves. And then they look at their men and think, 'What do I need with this *appendage*?'

Driving me down into town the next morning we were laughing and swapping disastrous relationship stories. I'd told Phil of my own affair with an actress, a woman who would have taken to Byron Bay like a dolphin to the surf. A mutual friend, also her lover, had described her as 'a spiritual pub crawler'. 'His point,' I said, 'was that she just took the bits she wanted out of all these philosophies and religions . . .'

'*Exactly!*'

'She once had a computer printout done of our mutual astrological compatibility. And she took it *seriously* . . .'

Phil shook his head. His ex-wife had done the same thing. The reason she'd wanted to spend so much time with this *douchebag* actor was that ('Can you get this?') some astrologer guy had told her that they'd been brother and sister *in a past life*. 'So she had to spend more time with him, to work this thing out. She actually said to me at one point, "I just need a couple more months." '

We laughed. 'And all this stuff,' he went on, 'they come up with. The one thing they all find out is that their father's abused them. Christ, there isn't a woman in Byron Bay whose father hasn't given it to her up the arse. Did you read about that poor guy in California? His daughter went to one of these therapists and his life was ruined. Turned out when they got to the bottom of it that she'd been abused by him *in a past life!*'

As I got out of his beautiful reconditioned Holden he smiled and said, 'So anyway, I'm one of Byron Bay's bitter men.'

So I began to spot the single mothers, and became acutely aware of all the tempting things that had changed their lives. In Suppertime Blues, where I went for a chunky vegetarian soup each evening, there was a whole wall plastered with adverts: H'Sing Kung, Palmistry, Tai Chi, Tarot, Massage, Yoga, Authentic Relating, Kirlian Analysis, Vocal Healing, Dynamic Shatso, Thai Kickboxing, Tsubaki (Japanese Catering) . . .

*If all else has failed why not try . . . Japanese Catering . . .*

Byron Bay was indeed humming with the very grooviest of vibes. There was a free magazine called *Fuse*, printed on grey-brown recycled paper. Turning to Editorial you found:

IT'S MAGIC  YOU KNOW
          YOU KNOW
     YEAH?  YEAH
          YEAH

which surely beat that boring double column in the *Australian*.

## The Holy Goat

If Byron was curly, the truly *curved* venue, the location where all this *thang* had started round here, was Nimbin. The hippy town. An old farming settlement that had fallen on hard times and then, after everyone had turned up for the Aquarius Festival of 1973, like ... well ... people had just stayed. And mellowed. And bred. And now it was a tourist attraction. So famous I'd heard about it in London. Shit. How are the funky fallen.

If you were a backpacker (which I now was, having moved out of $43-a-night solo-splendour into a $13 four-bed dorm) the way to go was on a Backpacker Tour; and the best tour, the word was, was the Holy Goat, which spent the morning in Nimbin and the afternoon at the Holy Goat Commune in the nearby hills.

Mick, our guide, had tousled blond curls and sky-blue eyes to match his sky-blue T-shirt (who said Australian men weren't vain?). Though not a hippy himself he was keen to get it across that he was hosting a preddy relaxed day out. As we settled back in our chosen seats he stuck some reggae on the sound system and chucked us over a couple of water-filled plant sprayers. 'This is our organic air-conditioner,' he told us. 'You may want to have a water-fight. We have quite a few water-fights,' he went on, when all of us sat rather boringly not having a water-fight. Encouraged, Steve from Manchester started spraying Ange and Merielle from Narooma. There was some ducking and give-me-that-ing from Heidi from Austria and Rob and Suzi from Liverpool and a *kind* of a fight broke out. Hung from Sydney smiled but, like me, didn't join in.

The Backpacker Tour had a thin tightrope to walk. It had to have enough meat in it to justify the thirty dollars we were all paying out of our cheese-on-toast and bunkbed budgets. On the other hand it couldn't afford to look too much like the kind of boring, grown-up tour our *parents* might go on.

Mick managed it pretty well. In between the granny-type stops (a waterfall, a macadamia-nut farm) he played far-out music and kept us regaled with unarguably right-on patter. 'D'you know what the dope capital of Australia really is?' We shook our backpackery heads. 'Canberra. No, dope is decriminalised in the Capital Territory. All the public servants love their drugs. Like you have all the pollies smoking big fat joints and watching pornography movies. Hypocrites.'

After all the build-up, Nimbin proper was a bit of a disappointment. Just a single street two hundred yards long with shops more touristy than truly hippy. The most authentic was Nimbin Museum, a monument to, and archive of, Nimbin hippy culture.

NO SMOKING ANYTHING IN THE MUSEUM said a sign in the front window and it was clear we weren't talking tobacco. IF WE GET BUSTED AGAIN IT'S CLOSEDOWN TIME said another. Three kaleidoscope-eyed guys with long grey hair and beards nodded at us from the entrance. Inside, there were four rooms, crammed with an extraordinary collection of newspaper clippings, slogan-decorated bits of wood, junk, feathers, dried flowers, you name it.

> European
> settlers come
> chop down trees
> make fences
> bring in cows
> but out of the
> cowshit grows
> the magic
> mushrooms
> eyes open
> trees return
> nature knows

Which I guessed must have been the most wonderful insightful moment for the very-stoned hippy who first scrawled it down.

In the second room a group of ockerish Aussie tourists in shorts were cracked up at the sight of a huge stone penis in a cage. 'Got to make sure we get it all in,' said a guy who was laughing so much he could hardly hold his camera.

The next room was a gloomy purple cave full of skulls. A TV in one corner played a blank blur. GET REAL was written in thick black paint on the screen.

Oh to have been young and free in Nimbin in Christmas '73! Now the streets of the 'people's park' were running with wild, blank-eyed children. One was screaming an endless stream of 'fuck's and 'cunt's, another (ten, maximum) was trying to sell me dope, three others were attacking tourists with water-bombs made from plastic bags. Nobody was telling them off and they all looked bored as hell.

After lunch, Mick was keen to show us what he called 'the positive side of Nimbin'. So we piled down the hill to the RAINBOW POWER COMPANY where a gang of guys with long grey hair framing paradoxically switched-on faces were flogging solar panels, solar-powered water-pumps and other hi-tech alternative technology like there was no tomorrow. (Which for non-sustainable fuels, of course, there wasn't.)

It was time for the highlight of the day – the Holy Goat Commune. But we weren't, Mick told us, as we turned off the little country lane, down a 45-degree slope and into a sudden patch of rainforest, to expect a load of Rastafarians with joints hanging out of the sides of their mouths. The Holy Goat was, besides being vegetarian, both non-smoking and teetotal. 'That kind of shatters most people's image of a commune.' No, despite the tongue-in-cheek name, the Holy Goat was a serious concern.

As soon as we saw Bernie, commune member and our guide for the afternoon, it was clear just how serious. Bernie was German and had that shining-eyed 'at peace' look of the born again. 'We feel,' he told us, 'we've got a few things to share and we like to giff you a bit of inspiration, which is why we do these tours.' Most people knew about the disasters in the world; here at the Holy Goat they liked to talk about some of the more positive things.

One hundred and fifty years ago, white people had come to this part of the country, liked what they saw and, re-creating a European style of agriculture, cut down all the trees. 'But this vass a mistake. This area can get almost the yearly rainfall of England in vun day. In vun day,' Bernie repeated, eyes gleaming.

With the trees gone, the heavy rainfall removed all the topsoil. 'The farmers cut into their own welfare, basically. It took them a few generations to find out.' He chuckled. 'A lot of them still haff to find out. They are still learning their lessons.'

Once the topsoil had been washed away, it was gone for ever. So farmers now depended on chemicals to make things grow. The Holy Goat, by contrast, had taken steps to re-establish the original rainforest. They had been on the site for fourteen years only, 'and look,' Bernie gestured round proudly at the tall rainforest trees, 'how much hass already been a-chieffed. We haff 150 species of birds here now, birds that you don't find on neighbouring properties . . .'

Pausing only to rub his hands and repeat 'Goot, goot!', Bernie led us on. Here we could see how the rainforest was a naturally regenerating ecosystem; the fallen leaves and branches made the compost which fed the soil. Here were the houses they lived in, made of mud bricks, which acted like a natural heating and air-conditioning system. Here was the Peanut Cottage, the centre of the commune, with its two solar-powered showers and open-air bath, propped up on bricks and heated by a wood fire from below. And here, most splendid of all, was the human-powered blender, put together, Heath-Robinson style, from an old exercise bicycle and a broken Kenwood mixer. So even in Paradise they could enjoy fresh-fruit smoothies.

The name for all this, I learnt, was Permaculture: a concept of self-sustainability that had begun in Tasmania in the 1970s and had now spread worldwide. Australia had a network of similar organic farms and if any of us wished to work on one we could become WWOOFERS – Willing Workers on Organic Farms. In return for a few hours' work a day we could stay free on the commune. Indeed Bernie himself had first come to the Holy Goat as a WWOOFER, eight years before.

On the return journey there were no water fights and a very warm feeling in the battered Kombi. The idealistic little valley of the Holy Goat, dreaming in the late-afternoon sunshine, had touched us all and redeemed the disappointment of Nimbin the Sad Tourist Trap.


## Hung

Hung was staying at my Backpackers' hostel so we went out for supper together. Having post-mortemed the tour we laughed about the three spooky oldfellas at the Backpackers'. Hung had noticed them, for sure. The smooth one was James, the German was Tommy and the hippy was Tango. They stayed there and did odd jobs. They always moved in on any girl or pair of girls on their own. Boys they left alone.

Hung didn't believe in 'chatting a girl up' in that way. Some of his friends in Sydney did it, but it seemed to him there was something about the whole idea of 'chatting up' that involved a lie; that didn't allow a woman her dignity as a human being.

Later, we repaired to the noisy Railway Tavern for a few beers with Hung's dorm-mates Steve and Peter, who were both from a village just outside Leeds. The place was packed with young women whose dignity as human beings was being compromised in all sorts of ways.

Steve was an average-looking carrot-top, with the kind

of North Country face that blushes easily; Peter was tall and rather beautiful, with long eyelashes, huge, thoughtful blue eyes and a sweeping mane of blond hair. He was missing his girlfriend, wished he wasn't, wished *in a way* he was single. When he'd planned the trip he'd just split up with another girlfriend and *that* would have been the time to go. But it had taken a long time to save and plan and by the time he was ready to leave he'd met somebody else. He'd been completely faithful to date, despite the endless temptation.

When we got back to the Backpackers', lecherous James was lounging by the entrance to the terrace with a bottle of beer and two pretty girls we hadn't seen before. 'I've got a house two minutes up the beach,' he was telling them. They left *à trois*, giggling.

Hung and Steve and Peter and I played snooker. It was good to have your own gang and I felt rather sorry for the lone Japanese who'd just appeared in my dorm. He was sitting looking petrified on the floor by his bunk reading a newspaper. 'Hello,' I said. He nodded nervously and said nothing. 'You going north?' I asked, returning from the shower. 'Sydney,' he managed. 'I'm coming from Sydney. I'm Japanese,' he added, almost apologetically. Later, he appeared in the common room and plonked himself in the very armchair I'd sat in when I'd arrived three nights before, studying his paperback like a man possessed.

The following afternoon James made his most spectacular entrance yet. He appeared in the middle of the Backpackers' garden on a gleaming black stallion. He dismounted magnificently, the ageing but deeply sexy cynosure of all eyes and proceeded to use the hostel hose to wash down his steed. Various skimpily clad babes of Nordic extraction gathered round to admire and assist. How tragic, I thought, observing the scene from my (now regular) spot in the shade of a coolabah tree. How utterly trag-ic.

That evening, wandering back from Suppertime Blues I

was amused to see Tango hurrying into town, white-faced and lonely. I almost felt sorry for him, when I got back and realised that James and Tommy had deserted him and the three German women he'd been playing chess with so hopefully for the last two days had moved on up the coast. Almost, but not quite.

# 4

# Voiceless
# in Surfers

Was this what I'd come to Australia for? To hear two sparks from Bromley male-bonding with a cabinet-maker from Cranleigh? 'Trouble is yer on the piss every night, trips and shit, soon goes' ... 'Yeah fucken right' ... 'Where you goin' next?' ... 'Bali' ... 'Oh yeah, we was there just before we came here, they won't leave you alone, come up and try and sell you stuff and shit' ...

I was back on the Greyhound, heading north into Queensland up the Pacific Highway. Coming round the bend at Coolangatta you can see Surfers Paradise on the horizon, the long row of high-rises a depressing grey silhouette against the blue sky and sea. In Sydney, people had told me endlessly about this place. 'It's terrible – but you've *got* to see it.' 'The sun sets behind the skyscrapers at three.' 'It's like a honeypot, we like having it there, it keeps the Japs away from the rest of the coast.' And from a man in London: 'If ever there wasn't a paradise – that – is – it.'

At the bus terminal out got: me, two American girls in sex-kitten sawn-off denims, a little Japanese man in a day-glo baseball cap and the Bromley/Cranleigh trio. We crossed the enormous shiny floor to the Backpackers' Advice Centre. (This backpacker business runs like clock-work. When you check out of your hostel at Byron Bay they give you brochures for the next place you're headed, then when you've chosen, they book you in and arrange for you to be met. All for $13 a night. It would be entirely possible to go from Sydney to Cairns without ever once lifting your pack to your back.)

I was picked up by Pete from the Sun 'n' Surf. He was a swarthy Pom – from Manchester – with a ponytail and a huge infectious smile. 'Mark,' he said picking up two of my bags. 'Good to meet you, mate.' On the way to the hostel in the minibus he filled me in: 'Basically, Sun 'n' Surf is a really relaxed hostel. We don't lock you up at 10.30 at night. If you want to scream and shout that's fine. We like noise.'

He showed me to my dorm. It had two Habitat-style pine bunks crammed into what had clearly been, not so long ago, a dingy motel room. Nobody had even bothered to redecorate. The broken phone fitting was still stuck to the wall. 'There's a Puerto Rican bloke and two girls I think. That's your bed, all right, mate.'

There were bras and knickers scattered everywhere. Through the frosted-glass window of a battered sliding door I could see the silhouette of a girl taking a shower. 'I won't be long,' she called. She emerged, wrapped in a towel, long blonde hair dripping, pretty as a Silvikrin ad.

She was Elin from Norway. This was a good-fun hostel and Surfers was okay. No really, it was good fun. She and her friend Margarethe had come for one night, 'just to see it', and ended up staying three. She laughed, grabbed some clothes and went back to the shower.

Came a knock at the door. It was Ross, a Canadian with army-short dark hair. 'Elin,' I called through to my new friend, 'somebody for you.' When she appeared this time it was the *Flake* ad: flowing, knee-length floral.

'Oh hi.'

'You okay?'

'I'm okay, yes.'

'You had breakfast yet?'

'No.'

'I'm making some downstairs.'

'Okay, I'll come.

It had clearly been a long night of passion; now there was the tricky business of making friends in daylight.

I went for a stroll into town. The geography of Surfers wasn't hard to grasp. Three parallel straight lines: the long straight strand of beach; above that the palm trees and luxury high-rises of the Esplanade; three hundred yards back from that, behind a legoland of hotels and apartment blocks, the double-track Gold Coast Highway. At a right angle in the centre was Cavill Avenue Mall where you could sit outside cafés which served flat whites and banana smoothies and sushi and all-day breakfasts (NEW! KEBAB BREAKFAST shouted a sign) or wander into shops which sold Swatches and speedos and Rip Curl boardshorts and Mako, Police and Porsche sunglasses and jewellery and Jeffrey Archer, Sidney Sheldon and the Bob Hawke Memoirs and cameras and real estate and turquoise T-shirts with three embossed gold shells reading SURFERS PARADISE and even, for the home-loving, a turquoise Cron-ulla Pottery teapot or an Original Painting On Queensland Timber. Here was a shop called Condom Kingdom; and here, outside one of the big all-Japanese stores was a giant furry koala: KANGAROO – $300 said the sign round its neck.

Back in the tiny dorm I found the Puerto Rican, lying on his bottom bunk wearing nothing but a black moo-stache and a pair of very tight white scants. He was in his thirties, brown as a walnut, smelling strongly of aftershave. 'Hi,' he said, 'I'm Carlos.' He was from Seed-knee and today he was in a very good moot. He'd just got a job. Just washing up, that sort of thing, at this place called the Hog's Breath Café. 'But it's money,' he chuckled. 'So I can stay a leedle longer with my friends at Surfers.'

I wasn't feeling like a protracted chat so I went down-stairs. It was late afternoon and a merry water-fight was in progress in the pool. Two girls in Sun 'n' Surf T-shirts had been chucked in and were screaming and splashing and oh, *oh*, OH YOU BASTARD!

In the lounge area an Aussie with the kind of physique I've always aimed for but never quite achieved was boring a couple of flirtatious young Kiwis to death. Or rather, he was boring me to death and – astonishingly – fascinating the Kiwis, telling them how easy it was to get work in England. 'You've just got to show you're ready to work hard,' he told them. He'd started by temping, gone on to the trading floor of a Merchant Bank and ended up Just About Running A Recruitment Consultancy.

Upstairs, Carlos had been replaced by – well, well – Margarethe, winningly attired in tight orange hotpants and a not-quite-reaching-your-waist pink top. She had cropped dark hair, huge dark eyes, voluptuous breasts and no sense of humour.

Elin joined us. 'You two coming to the hostel barbecue?' I asked convivially. 'No,' said Elin, 'we're going out for some dinner. Ross and I and Margarethe. You must come with us.' I protested feebly, but she was adamant. It was soon apparent why. I was to take care of Margarethe so she could get cosy with Ross.

We strolled into town down the Gold Coast Highway. They were trying, they really were trying, not to be too giggly, touchy-feely and overwhelmed by lurv – but they just couldn't help it. Margarethe was putting on a brave face, especially as, with the fag-end of the cold that had been with me since my frozen morning hitch-hiking, my voice was deteriorating rapidly from Richard Burton husk to frog croak.

None of them liked the idea of Japanese food which was a bit of a shame as almost all the restaurants were Japanese. Or Chinese, which Ross wasn't keen on either. 'I like to know what I'm eating,' he said. 'Hey, there's a Pizza Hut over there!'

My turn to be difficult. I hadn't come all the way to Surfers Paradise to go to a Pizza Hut. In the end, by that

committee-system of restaurant choosing which guarantees
that you end up in the worst, most expensive place possible,
we settled for a pizza restaurant that wasn't a Pizza Hut
where, budget-conscious all, we ordered a carafe of house
wine and two medium pizzas to share. I was now sounding
like Barry White and wishing I'd stayed at the barbecue.

Then things took a sudden upturn. Margarethe and Elin
had been at the Backpacker Inn in Byron Bay. (I thought
I'd half-recognised them.) And guess who'd befriended
them? James, Tommy and Tango. 'No really,' Margarethe
said, 'James was very nice. He drove us up to Nimbin for
the day.'

I bet he did.

'And he took Elin out on his horse.'

'No?' I croaked.

Elin was laughing, hand over her mouth. 'I'm saying to
him, "I don't want to go on this horse," but he's saying, "I
want to see how you look on this horse." '

'So she goes on this horse,' said Margarethe.

He just had the horse to pick up girls, I said. Of course,
said Elin, but then Tango had his bees. Hives full of them
apparently, at the back of the Backpackers'. 'That's his
thing. All the girls have to get up early to see Tango's bees.'

We laughed; and then, quite suddenly, and for the first
time in my life, I lost my voice. Not a squeak, not a murmur
could I make my vocal chords produce. The Tenterfield
Witch had finally had her revenge. I was forced to sit in
silence as Ross told us in detail about his life back home
in the countryside round Calgary. They did this kind of
country dancing. Like, you know, you hold the girl and
two-step. Elin was rapt; Margarethe's enthusiasm for the
evening was visibly waning. Voiceless, there was no way
of intervening in the Ross monologue, teasing, sending him
up, anything. Eventually I got so desperate I pulled out my
notepad and started writing.

'I've never lost my voice,' Ross was saying.

NOR ME! I scrawled. NOW I KNOW WHAT IT'S LIKE TO
BE DUMB.

'DUMB?' asked Elin, with the look of a kindly nurse.

'Stoopid,' said Ross. 'Now he knows what it's like to be
stoopid.'

*No, no, not that at all.*

DUMB, I wrote frantically, MEANS (I underlined it, twice)
YOU CAN'T TALK.

'Oh right, okay,' said Ross. 'Like, he means, dumb like
he can't talk.'

IT'S TERRIBLE (I wrote). NORMALLY I'M A GREAT
TALKER. SORRY!

Oh dear, oh dear (oh dear). I really can't bring myself to
print out all the things I found scrawled in my notebook
the next day. As I tried, increasingly unsuccessfully, to turn
this sudden handicap into an amusing ploy. They were all
as sweet as anything. Elin had a special whisky mix that
would *definitely* bring my voice back. When that failed, they
all three waited patiently as I scrawled my exponentially
absurd and desperate interventions.

We ended up in a nightclub which was swarming with
every backpacker in town. Over the identical, jostling
youth, I spotted the Bromley lads, handsome Richard going
for broke with a chick in gold culottes while gawky ginger-
nut Dave titted around annoyingly beside him. Nightclubs
are bad enough when your vocal organs are working:
yelled, disjointed conversations over the deafening disco-
beat. Voiceless, I felt like Harpo Marx. I went home.

Carlos was sound asleep as I crept in. Much later there
was semi-suppressed giggling as the girls came crashing
back. Outside, the Sun 'n' Surf party went on and on.
Laughter, chat, shrieks, the occasional 'shsh'. Around five,
just as silence had finally fallen, an incredibly noisy dustbin
lorry arrived to collect rubbish outside. Seemingly for
hours. At 7.18, eventually, I crawled up. Stumbled, brain-dead,
to the Esplanade for a treble espresso and some breakfast.

Returned to find Carlos filling the tiny room with the pong of his anti-perspirant spray. 'Hi Carlos,' I whispered.

'Hi, *Mark*!' Carlos replied in an unneccessarily loud voice. 'You coming to the *surf parade* later. I'm just going to *church* first but then I'm going to the *surf parade*. Just got to catch the 9 o'clock *service*.' He carried on, not seeming to mind that he'd woken the girls, or indeed Ross, who was touchingly curled up with Elin on the lower bunk.

I left in a hurry. When he came down the steps to the pool, 'Are you really going to church?' I asked. I had a notion of going with him, if only to see who on earth went to church in Surfers Paradise.

'No,' he replied. 'But I just like to talk in a loud voice in the morning. Because if they don't res-bect me why should I res-bect them. They come in and out all night. They bring men in there.' He looked directly at me and his eyes flashed fire. 'No *worries*! See whaddimean? They come here for one night and now they're staying three nights but I don't care because I'm *checking out*. Today. This place is too much and I'm *checking out*.'

# 5

## Gossip, Gossip, Gossip . . .

Most of the guys at Surfers were avoiding Brisbane. It was a dump, it was dire, you only went there if you needed to work. The next fun stop up the coast was Fraser Island, where the local Backpackers' organised you into a group of six or eight, hired you a four-wheel-drive and let you head off for three days of uncontrolled adventure on the largest sand island in the world.

If only they knew what they were missing! Here, on 'South Bank', you could sit under a parasol by a miniature canal, sip a strawberry milkshake or a banana smoothie and watch the little *SS Johnstone* chunter gently past with its cargo of bemused-looking senior citizens in sun-visors. You could take a stroll, down the wide steps to the Artificial Beach, with its two pools, its palm trees, its real, if slightly grubby, sand. You could wander into the Nepalese Pagoda and gaze at the wood carvings of Buddha. If you had money you could enter the steamy sanctum of the Gond-wana Rainforest Sanctuary ('Walk With The Animals'). And if you felt like doing something real, you could sit on the low stone wall by the murkily-swirling waters of the Brisbane River, and look across at the extraordinary white and pale-green freeway that swept on stilts along the North Bank, half-obscuring the pillars and porticoes of the old stone buildings that must once have been charmingly, authentically riverside; and a much better bet, you would have thought, for conversion to a Sad Tourist Trap.

Behind, tribute to the prosperous if ultimately corrupt decades of notorious Queensland Premier Joh Bjelke-Petersen (1968–87), rose the glass and concrete facings of the high rises.

Over the clean span of Victoria Bridge, up in central, pedestrianised Queen Street I got used to the reverse of an English winter's day. Central heating turned up too high in the streets, skin-tinglingly cool air in the shops and indoor malls. Of which last there seemed to be any number. All filled with gleaming escalators and squeaky-clean take-away concessions. Were there really enough people in Brisbane to guzzle all these cappuccinos and focaccias? Judging by the swathes of empty chairs there were not.

I phoned the six numbers I'd been given in Sydney and was overwhelmed by Brisbane friendliness. I certainly couldn't continue staying in a hostel, said Graham Foster, before we'd even met. He and his sister Margot had a spare room. 'I'll just have to clear it with her. The only problem may be that we had two Germans last time who came for a couple of days and stayed three months.' Then Peter Gavanagh offered me his couch. Then Moira O'Donnell had faxed back: Had I found somewhere yet; her parents would gladly put me up.

Margot was a dress-designer in her mid-thirties. She had large, black-rimmed glasses and a high, sing-song, slightly little-girly voice. She and Graham lived in the up-and-coming southern suburbs in 'a Queenslander' – one of the traditional old wooden houses built up on stilts with a veranda running all around.

The main room was full of exotic clutter. A stuffed cockerel stood on a table in the corner. A false leg, wearing a pink-glitter shoe, hung from a wall. Marionettes dangled from the ceiling. There were three cats: big Eric, little Eric and Tom, to whom I was introduced in turn. 'D'you like my rooster? I only brought it in here because it made me giggle.'

'You want a beer?' she asked, and slumping back exhausted on her sofa I regaled her with the joys of backpacker life. She raised her eyes to heaven. 'I couldn't do it. I'm sorry, I just couldn't do it. Not any more.'

Graham returned, in a grey suit. He was boyishly blond with a thoughtful wrinkle on his brow. I must come and go exactly as I pleased, but should be careful to lock the front door even when I was in. 'Because of the Aborigines,' he said. 'They're very bold. They just walk in.'

Every day, walking in and out of town, I passed them, sitting under the trees of Musgrave Park with their cans of Castlemaine XXXX and their wine boxes. In the warm morning sunshine there were few and they were quiet. By late afternoon the party would be well under way, a central group under a tree, to one side men and women staggering to and fro like bad actors caricaturing drunks. Children ran unconcernedly around. Little fights kept breaking out. A couple of men would suddenly scramble to their feet and put up their fists. Or a woman would start to scream abuse. 'You fucken fucken this, you fucken fucken that . . .'

One afternoon I decided I would try and talk to them. Go over on some pretext about Land Rights. There had been a recent claim on this very park, and the toilets in the centre were painted in the colours of the Aboriginal flag, half-black, half-red, with a big yellow sun in the centre.

Before I went over, I stopped for a while, watching them from under a tree. Now a woman of indeterminate age detached herself from the group, zig-zagged parodically across the park towards the toilets. Seeing me, she made a mad dash in my direction, ran past, slowed, circled back.

The sun was now setting behind the Greek Community Centre. So the first Aboriginal I spoke to in Australia was dramatically backlit, her long hair a tousled silhouette. She was wearing blue tracksuit bottoms, new trainers and a grubby white sweatshirt that read RIP CURL. With her high cheekbones and long hair she looked more like a Red Indian than any idea I'd had of an Aboriginal.

'Excuse me,' she mumbled.

'Yes?'

'I'm fucken sick.'

'I'm sorry.'

'I just want to lie down.'

'Plenty of room in the park.' I gestured.

'I fucken . . .' She turned, stumbled off and collapsed on her face.

It wasn't the right time, I told myself. They were all way, way gone. I would go back tomorrow.

Margot was back at the house, preparing a 'seafood pigout'. She wasn't sure how many were coming – maybe three, maybe six – so she'd bought two crabs. 'This is Fat Albert and this is Oliver,' she sang in her little-girl-lost voice. 'It seemed such a shame to boil them so I gave them a slow death in the fridge. Normally,' she held up a finger, 'I'd just put a screwdriver through their sternum.'

I told her about my moment in the park. 'It wouldn't be a problem if I went over and talked to them, would it?' I asked. She thought I was 'jack-crackers' even to consider it. 'I suppose I'm a bit paranoid,' she said, 'but we've had them in here. I got bailed up by three of them.'

'Bailed up?'

'They pushed me against this wall. "Give us what you've got! Give us what you've got!" I told them my father was just coming and he was a big man. I was just bluffing, telling them anything, but it was weird, at that moment my father arrived in his car and they ran off out the back. But I've been jumped on in Queen Street too. And there were two British tourists who were beaten up in town last year.'

Her friend Lisa arrived and the subject, in best Australian fashion, was dropped completely as Lisa was introduced to the crabs. 'This is Fat Albert and this is Oliver. Did you watch *Reservoir Dogs* last night?'

'Ah yes.'

'How did it take you when he cut his ear off and was dancing around to "Stuck in the Middle with You"?'

'Ah well I got my period about six o'clock and then I was quite sick, so not too well actually.'

We drank 'champagne' and I asked them where I could find a wig for Friday's forthcoming 'Hair Ball', to which Peter Gavanagh had invited me, sight unseen. Lisa had two wigs. A dark one and a long blonde one. 'A piece, you know, goes right down to your waist, but you can't borrow them, 'cause I use them.'

'When?'

'Out.'

'And nobody notices?'

'No, they're very good. I've done the Wild Thing in the blonde one.'

'The Wild Thing?'

Margot was laughing. 'You know,' said Lisa, 'the Wild Thing.'

'Sex,' said Margot.

The other guests drifted in. A dark-haired Megan, then a woman with white-blonde hair and a beaky nose, Edwina, who'd just dropped in and wouldn't stay, all right she'd stay for a glass of champagne. With a slam of the front door Graham was back and into the shower. 'Alive!' he murmured as he switched it off.

Megan's husband Don was late because he was having an affair with Rita, his tennis partner. 'Oh sh-sh,' said Megan, giggling, when we heard him at the door, 'otherwise he'll think I'm going on about it.'

The champagne-fuelled pigout formed a great energetic arc of hilarity, the women screaming with laughter about their friends and/or sex, the men, in a cross-current, alternating between a barrage of jokes and sudden adult seriousness about Big Issues. 'Why's a woman like a cyclone, Mark?' 'They start off by blowing you and end up taking your house!' But then: Joh Bjelke-Petersen was not, no he wasn't, a crook, as I'd been told, and read. He'd run the only state in Australia that had ended up debt free. 'I could have run Queensland if I'd been left a balance sheet like that,' said Graham. Wayne Goss, the new Labour Premier, was busy stuffing it up of course.

Across us, the women were choking with mirth about Don's tennis partner. 'Does she have a decent shitter?' asked Lisa. 'What's that supposed to mean?' 'Her arse.'

Halfway through the evening I had a sudden profound realisation. Australian women didn't say 'Na-ow', as I'd thought. They said 'Nye'. *Nye, nye, nye.*

Someone had referred to Lisa as 'a cum-guzzling harlot'. 'But I'm a Catholic!' she cried.

Peter Gavanagh turned out to be tall, dark and, in characteristic Brisbane fashion, exceedingly laid-back. He had the same gently curving inclusive smile I'd noticed on the Brisbanites I'd met in Sydney, and a habit of adding 'yeah' about five seconds after he'd said something, as if to remind himself that he'd just said it.

Ah look, he said, as we mellowed through a Chinese meal together, if I was interested in the Aborigines a good person to talk to might be Mrs Donovan, the mother of a mate of his, who'd been running a single men's boarding house right on Musgrave Park for twenty years, and now refused to take them as lodgers.

It was a long, one-storey building surrounded by a low palisade fence and a well-kept garden. Inside, there were single rooms off a gloomy wood-panelled corridor; a strong smell of lone, elderly male permeated throughout.

Mrs Donovan was a sweet Mrs Tiggywinkle of a woman. At the far end of the corridor her kitchen was the very model of spic and spanness, with a neat little calendar by the kettle. I envied her her schedule: *Tuesday October 4th –*

*French dressing*, it read. She had to stay by the phone today, she had a room to let.

Once we'd got the cups of tea in front of us and were over the polite preliminaries Mrs Donovan was very keen to stress that, despite her ban on Aborigines, she wasn't a racist. 'I've got nothing against coloureds,' she told me. Being a Kiwi, she'd been brought up with Maoris in New Zealand. 'The Maori you always respected.' They were very artistic, musical. Then she'd taught for years in Fiji and she loved the Fijians.

But there was something about the Aborigines. 'They're very dour, very anti-white.'

Look, she'd had black Africans in the boarding house. 'As black as your hat.' She'd had all the Islanders. 'They're all clean and pleasant and pay their rent, which is all you can expect.' She laughed. 'I've even got an Eskimo at the moment.'

But there was something about the Aborigines. 'Poor bugger, he just doesn't get his act together. If they've got a quid they'll drink it. I don't know,' she nodded in the direction of the park, 'possibly most of these people are only part Aborigine.'

'I don't know what it is, it's like they've got this awful chip on their shoulder. It's like a resentment they've got. All the years I've been around here, you never get them telling you about their legends and customs, like the Eskimos.'

'They never stop to talk to you?'

'Except to abuse you. You know, what are you looking at, you white effing c.' She laughed. 'You know, if you just look up while you're gardening.'

'So you've given up having them to stay here?'

'Yes. I've had these guilt trips and tried again on occasion, but every time I've been knocked back.'

Mostly they'd been drunks. 'Another guy, excuse the language, he shit his pants, and I don't see why I should bother with that. Then I had a young lad, he got given an apprenticeship in the city and this was at a difficult time, in the recession, so it was quite a thing to have. But he got involved in drugs and had to give it up.

'What comes to my mind is a fair degree of slyness. They don't seem to be a very secure race. I feel sorry for them and then angry with them. It's certainly true they've no ability to control grog.

'They do all right if they've had a European upbringing. That girl who just won the Olympic race. Well obviously it was the father who was the motivating force there. Same with the Goolagong girl.

'They're a phenomenon to me. I'm totally fascinated by them. It fascinates me that a race of people can have been on this continent for thirty or forty thousand years and during that time they don't seem to have made a road or put up a monument. They've got these Aboriginal cave-paintings but . . .' she shrugged. 'The Maoris have built wonderful villages . . .'

As she saw me to the front gate she laughed and said, 'Anyway, you won't be interested in my opinion. I'm just a little Aussie battler.'

On the phone, Moira O'Connor had described herself as wearing a brown skirt, a pink top and high heels. 'In fact I'm looking quite posh today.'

Seeing her, I liked her immediately. She had tight dark curls and a face straight out of a Roddy Doyle movie. Irish humour too. As we walked up Queen Street we laughed about all the malls and coffee shops.

'People in Brisbane hadn't heard of cappuccino till four years ago – so naturally we're all crazy for them now.'

'It's amazing there are enough people to drink them.'

'We want *more* malls, *more* coffee shops.'

We were going for a bee-yah with this guy Damien who was down from a huge cattle station in Far North Queensland. 'Effin Q' as they called it. His cousin had committed suicide and the whole family were in Brisbane for the funeral.

We swept up to the ninth floor of a swanky, tube-shaped hotel, sat watching the sun set, in a sub-tropical blaze of orange, over the glinting snake of the Brisbane River. Damien was a surprise: courteous, gentle, almost diffident, far from the Foster's advert ocker I'd immediately pictured. His mother Susan joined us, then a wiry fellow called Stephen who was a professional stockman. 'Come and stay,' said Susan, before the first drink was over. 'If you want to see the outback, come and stay. I shan't be there for a fortnight, but Geraldine can look after you.'

Then Damien and I were in Moira's car, whisking out in the darkness to the suburbs. 'They put up a statue to a footballer in this city,' laughed Moira, 'that's the sort of city it is.'

'He was a good footballer,' said Damien.

Having picked up an ice-cold pack of Toohey's COLD from one of those great Aussie institutions, a drive-through off-licence, we arrived at a large clapboard Queenslander, where we met Rita, whose place it was, and Bruce, who was a carpenter, and Moira's mate Roberta who was a slim lawyer with a chalk-white face and an amused, lipstick-crimsoned smile. 'You see that thing,' she said, as we waited in the garden for Bruce to bring the beers down. She was pointing at one of those whirligig clothes dryers, looming out of the darkness. 'That's an Australian institution – the Hills Hoist? Every home has one? They're supposed to be really convenient, but in fact they take up half your lawn?'

When I first meet strangers I'm still naive enough to fall into the trap of assuming, if they're doing something cosy like having a meal together on a Wednesday evening, that they're all the best of friends. It took me a good half-hour now to realise that I'd stumbled into a little hornet's nest of sexual jealousy.

Rita was a broad-hipped blonde who did Marlene Dietrich poses on the long flight of wooden steps up to the kitchen. Bruce, whom I'd assumed from the intimacy of their banter to be her boyfriend, had black curls scalped above the ears, a broad white toothy smile, a pigskin-wallet tan, and a terrible (and endless) line in jokes.

So there I sat, lips to the cold mouth of a Castlemaine stubby, thinking: Isn't this great, that here, in good old egalitarian Oz, the following people can sit round a table together: the son of a large landowner, a carpenter, a civil servant, a woman who works for a road construction company and a lawyer; and there isn't even a *smidgeon* of that class tiresomeness that would, inevitably, despite the best efforts of everybody, be present at home.

Rita was leafing through a brochure for the new top-of-the-range Honda NSX. 'Isn't it just *gorgeous!*' she cried, half-serious, half-sending herself up as camp, flirtatious funny-woman. The car was just the thing for a *single girl* like her. But could she afford it? 'I spoke to my aunt,' she said, 'and she was pointing out that all this materialistic *anxiety* about a car wasn't the right way to go for personal happiness. But I said, "Wait till you *drive* it!" '

Liking Moira, I was doing my best to like her friends Rita and Bruce. Then, with a sudden crinkling of the brows, Moira ran off upstairs. When Bruce, then Rita, went after her, Roberta enlightened me. Bruce was Moira's brand-new boyfriend; Rita was Bruce's ex-girlfriend; and the problem was that Rita wouldn't let go of Bruce and worse, Bruce wouldn't let go of Rita. Moira was doing her best to be friends with Rita, but, but . . .

'Wasn't she awful?' Roberta said, as she drove Damien and me home.

'She wasn't *that* bad,' I said.

'The way she kept asking Damien about whether he knew all the right people up North,' said Roberta.

'Who lived where, did I know the Macdonalds?' said Damien.

'Private-school educated city-country girl,' said Roberta. 'Ugh!'

'I thought this was supposed to be a classless society,' I said.

They laughed.

Two thirds of the surnames I'd been given were Irish; the other third were Italian. Elisa Gambaro's dad was a restaurateur, who'd started after the war with a stall selling seafood. Now the Trattoria Gambaro was Brisbane's largest fish restaurant and they owned a big house on one of the finest stretches of the river.

Inside there were grey marble floors, arches and white walls decorated only with the graduation photos of the four children. A replica of Michelangelo's David stood on a pillar; on top of the enormous telly, Romulus and Remus.

Elisa, blonde and Australian, was laughing warmly about it all. 'A friend came round and said, "D'you guys buy these statues in bulk?" '

'It is very Italian,' I said, 'with the marble floors and everything . . .'

'And the arches,' said Elisa, completely laid-back about her parents' alien taste. 'Arches everywhere.'

But then, in a very European way, she insisted on putting a linen tablecloth on the outside table and bringing me wine and a snack of salami and cheese and thin rye biscuits. Her family, she said, was from the Italian South. Calabria. They'd come over after World War Two. Because they'd broken away from the tight Italian family structure to make it on their own, there was, she thought, a tremendous pressure on them to succeed. And they were very singleminded about making it and not squandering what they'd made. 'The mentality was: "Save, save, save. Invest in land. Stay at home. Don't spend money." ' Whereas the biggest handicap for a lot of Australians to making it was this sort of, 'Spend, spend, spend, live for now' attitude. Gambling was a big Australian thing. But Elisa couldn't imagine her father ever gambling. Maybe there were some Italians in Australia who gambled, but she didn't know of any.

Back in England I'd read a certain amount about both pre- and post-war Italian immigration. The difficulties the New Australians had faced. Some had said that 'you Italian bastard', 'bloody New Australians' and variations on this theme had been the first words they'd ever heard in Australia. One had said, 'When I could understand English well and I knew what they were saying, it was much worse than before.' Many had returned home, often under pressure from their wives. (In 1902–1904 the figure for returning immigrants was an astounding ninety-five per cent.) But even that hadn't proved simple. New habits learned in Australia (wearing miniskirts was one example) were not tolerated at home. Some came back. One returnee had grown so homesick for Australia that he'd taken to hanging around forlornly outside the Australian Embassy in Rome, always with a broad-brimmed felt hat on the back of his head. He would call out to passers-by in authentic Australian accents, 'G'day mate, how're ya *goin*?'

Elisa's father was more than happy to talk to me about his early years. Unfortunately, I have no Italian and his accent was still so thick I found it hard to understand him. I just about gathered that he'd come over in 1948 to join his father; that he'd started out making *terrazzo* then owned a corner store before hitting the jackpot with the seafood stall. But when I asked him if anyone had ever been rude to him on account of his being Italian, he shrugged, smiled broadly and threw up his hands. 'Naturally you fine in every country there are people where they got no manners where they no understanda we should be loving this world one with the other . . .'

So what should I see that was quintessentially *of* Brisbane, I asked everyone. Ah look, they said, the thing about Brisbane was it was just a big country town. Although since Expo it was more like a city. I'd seen South Bank, well, they laughed, there was always . . . the Koala Sanctuary.

Perhaps I should do the tour of the Castlemaine XXXX

factory. You know, the one pictured on the cans? Right next to the factory on the road was this huge copy of the picture on the tin? With a giant arrow pointing at the original factory?

A big thing in Brisbane, someone said, was drinking beer at home.

One thing that was new in Brisbane, said someone else, was that people were staying in town for the weekend; going out for coffee.

Ah look, of course, said someone else, I must go to Brekky Creek for a steak. On a Friday lunchtime. That was a Brisbane institution. Sitting in the sun all afternoon with the best steak in Australia. Unfortunately on the Friday I went it was pouring with rain.

I decided to stop trying to be analytical and just abandon myself to the ever hospitable Brisbane flow.

Judge Brackenbury had invited me to a concert of Schumann at Parliament House. 'The Premier will be there,' he'd told me. I hadn't realised that Wayne Goss would be sitting in the same row and I'd be shaking his hand in the interval. 'I hear you're stuffing up the economy,' was what I didn't say. In the same ten minutes I met the Speaker of the House, the Vice Chancellor of the University of Queensland, and the judge's formidable American wife, Miriam. 'What aspict?' they all asked.

Hoping that neither the Premier nor Miriam had noticed that the plastic bag I was carrying contained a long, curly-blonde wig I sped in a cab to the 'kiosk' in New Farm Park, where against a wondrous backdrop of blossoming jacarandas and cherries the Hair Ball was in full, thundering swing. Peter Gavanagh was Dr Johnson; Graham Foster was Bob Marley; Elisa Gambaro was Dolly Parton; and for the third time that day I heard that if you hadn't started revising for your exams by the time the jacaranda was in bloom, you were in serious trouble.

Gossip, gossip, gossip went the people of Brisbane. I'd only been here a week and already I felt as if I knew half the people in the city. And what they were up to. 'In Brisbane,' said Peter Gavanagh, 'if you fart your mother knows about it the next day.'

It wasn't just what they were up to – it's what they'd been up to, last month, the year before, forever. 'People have very long memories in Brisbane,' Roberta told me with a wicked smile, 'and they don't forget.'

*The things I could tell you . . . No I really shouldn't . . . Well, the thing is . . .* Ah look, I could see myself settling happily in Brisbane for a while. Rent myself a little Queenslander, sit out on the veranda and read and write, pop into town for a coffee and chat at the Bar Merlo . . .

But Moira has been working hard on my case. My original plan, to go up the coast to Cairns, would be thoroughly predictable and boring. Everybody did that, and all I'd see was turtles on Fraser Island and a thousand more back-packers. Damien's father, Mr Dale, was driving back to his station in FNQ on Thursday. 'You've got to see it,' Moira said. 'That's the real Australia.'

It's all fixed. I'm to spend a day and a half in a car with a man I've never met. 'He's like a patriarch,' says Moira. 'Up there what he says goes.'

# 6

## The Patriarch

On the crowded, early-morning freeway out of town the Patriarch veered wildly through the traffic, swearing cheerfully at the bar-stards overtaking on the inside lane. Cities clearly weren't his thing. Twice we took the wrong turning and ended up speeding merrily back into central Brisbane.

Then at last we were out, heading west on the Warrego Highway. We climbed the dry hills of the Dividing Range to Toowoomba.

'Normally it'd be a bit greener here, I'd imagine,' I ventured.

'Yeahp,' the Patriarch replied (half 'yeah', half 'yip'). 'Dry as a billy goat's bum at the moment.'

He was a big man, with the belly of a serious eater below a farmer's rough red face. Above was a thatch of thick grey hair; below, he had a neck like an old bull, rippling down from his chin. On the left-hand side of his throat a new square of skin had been grafted in, a darker pink, like the patch on an old rug. He had an endearing way of turning from the wheel, fixing you with his right eye (his left was lazy), spitting out a dry remark, then smiling. Every other sentence ended in 'eh?'

Politically he was on the right. 'Old Joh' (Bjelke-Petersen) had been the man. To get things done. Old Joh, he didn't ask too many questions. 'If some bugger wanted to come here to Queensland and start a business Old Joh wasn't too bothered about whether it'd make the kookaburra cough, what it'd do to the cane toads, eh? The mouthless moth, that's the latest one. Can't put that factory there because it'll destroy the habitat for the mouthless moth.' He turned and gave me the sideways smile. The trouble with Wayne Goss was that he couldn't make a decision. 'Old Wayne has to form a *committee* for everything. There's a problem about the mouthless moth, Old Wayne'll form a committee. The *committee*'ll make the decision. That's the way old Wayne operates.'

On we drove, across the endless flat plain of yellow grass and scattered eucalypts under the vast blue sky. Every two hundred kilometres or so we'd come to a little one-street town. Dalby, Roma, Augathella. Clapboard houses and English gardens, roses by the palisade fences. Then we'd be through and the countdown to the next place would begin – 110, 100, 90. Every now and then a tiny white dot would come shimmering out of the mirage puddles of the heat-hazy horizon. A road train: a great snub-nosed beast with three, four, five containers behind, sitting bang in the middle of the tarmac, so you'd be forced to skitter off onto the dirt as it thundered past. 'So,' I asked, after a while, 'is this the outback yet?'

The Patriarch shook his head.

'Pretty flat round here,' I ventured.

'This is *hilly*.' He chuckled.

Around 9.30 (it felt like a late lunchtime) we stopped at a petrol station café for 'smoko'. Outside the air-conditioned car it was already oven-hot; a cool shiver ran down my spine as the sweat prickles began.

'You get a good feed here,' said the Patriarch. So we had 'a drink of tea' and two rounds of toasted sandwiches. (I liked the fact that, in the Patriarch's language, there was no distinction between humans, cattle and kangaroos. What they put in their mouths was all 'feed'.)

Driving on, I took the wheel and we lurched onto the subject of the Royals. 'I'll tell you what,' said the Patriarch.

'The antics of this current lot have damn near turned me into a Republican. I've heard of the man that wanted to be king. But whoever heard of the king that wanted to be a tampon?

'That Anne,' he went on, 'she'd have a bit of backbone I'd imagine. But I bet she'd be a tough old bitch to deal with. As for Andrew, they say he'd take er, whatsername back...'

'Fergie.'

'Fergie. What's all that about, eh? Should have backhanded the bitch.' He shook his head and gave me the smile. 'Take her *back*. And that last one – what's he called?'

'Edward.'

'Edward. Don't think they're going to get much breeding out of him. I'd say there's more than a bit of the limp wrist about him, eh? What d'you reckon? Whereas the Queen, now there's an impressive woman. Of all the public figures in the world she must be one of the ones to have best stood the test of time. Eh?'

The other public figure he was well impressed by was Nelson Mandela. 'He's quite a feller, eh? But how long can he last? He's eighty or something. They need to stuff the bar-stard I reckon, hold him together with safety pins.'

Aboriginals, none the less, were still 'abos'. Or 'coons'. Or 'murris'. Their women 'gins'. The story (which by now I'd come to think of as The Story) was much the same, if more frankly expressed, as I'd heard everywhere I'd been so far. The 'full bloods' were terrific, they had a morality, they had a dignity, they had an instinct with cattle; it was the mixed-bloods, the half-bloods, (what an old lady I'd met in Sydney had called 'the creamies') that caused all the trouble. Now all the Aborigines got everything on welfare: house, food, drinking money. It was gutless of 'those socialists in Canberra' to give them all these grants. 'I know twenty old Abos who could butcher a cow quicker than most butchers. Yet they fly the meat across from Cairns for them. And those old gins could bake bread if they had to . . .'

A little later he said, 'I'll tell you something, Mark. In every country in the world they should make a rule. That no laws can be made on account of colour. That's what I reckon. To judge a man by the colour of his skin, just that, that doesn't make sense to me. You've got these blackfellas here now, they're getting paid by the Government to do nothing. House provided. Get their kids' school fees paid. They even get an allowance to *encourage* them to get their kids to school. It's true. They get that kid to go to school, they get fifty dollars. Down the road you've got some poor white guy, he doesn't get that allowance, he's slaving away extra hours to get his kids to school. It's no wonder they end up hating them, eh?'

Around six we arrived at Longreach, the regional centre, and checked into the Jumbuck Motel. Peter (I'd stopped thinking of him as the Patriarch now) explained that he was halfway through a big cattle sale and the agent, Don Fisher, might join us for dinner. In the end he didn't make it till 9.30, by which time I was in bed. I fell asleep listening to them negotiating through the thin wooden wall that divided the bedroom units.

Coming down for breakfast at seven I found them both tucked into huge fry-ups. Peter was having The Drover's Breakfast: bacon, eggs, steak, sausages, tomatoes, chopped liver, potatoes. Don was watching his weight with The Shearer's Breakfast: bacon, eggs, liver, sausages and tomatoes. Despite having the crimson nose of a heavy drinker, he was a good-looking cowboy style of fellow, late forties or so, with blond hair that kissed the lobes of his ears, jeans tucked into knee-high leather boots, only the suggestion of a belly.

I sipped my tea and listened to them talking cattle. A buyer had been found. The cows had to be mustered, sorted, dipped and transported before the sale was considered done. This number of trucks would be needed, with this number of decks and, of course, a chopper for Sunday.

Business over, Don relaxed and told me the story of the agent and the old widow of R—— Station. Every year the agent would go up there to sort out a price for her cattle and it'd be the same routine. They'd haggle and disagree. 'My price or your price?' he'd say and the old widow would stick to her price. Then they'd have dinner and after dinner, the same as every year, the agent would go to bed with her. 'My price or your price?' he'd say. 'Your price,' the widow would gasp. 'She used to wait all year for that one root!' Don laughed.

We drove on, coming sometime after smoko to a sign that read ENJOY MATILDA COUNTRY. 'This is the closest town to the billabong where the old swagman drowned,' said Peter. 'A swagman's just someone who's carrying his swag, his bedroll, his Matilda on his back. Waltzing Matilda, eh?' Suddenly he swerved left off the road and drove me across country on dirt for a mere hour or two till we came to it, a thirty-foot waterhole in the middle of nowhere.

I'd never really listened properly to the words of the famous song, but it was, Peter explained, a simple tale of police brutality. There'd been a big shearers' strike in 1894–5 and a couple of sheds got burnt down. 'Bullets were fired at the station manager and so on. When the police got there they went and rounded up the suspects, and down by this waterhole they found this old swagman who they thought was the bloke who'd thrown the match in the shed. And rather than be captured by them he jumped in the waterhole and drowned. At least that was their story. Although there's nothing to say the police didn't hit the poor bastard on the head and throw him in there. He didn't have a horse. They'd have had to ride back two hundred miles to the nearest civilisation. Charge him and try him. Those were hard days, eh?'

'Would you call this the outback now?' I asked as we drove back on dirt across the infinity of bleached-blonde grass. Peter smiled. 'Yes, I reckon you could call this the outback now.'

'You know,' he said, a little later, 'my father used to refer to England as home. Home. That's what he called it, eh? As if he'd been bloody camping out here for four generations. He'd never been to England in his life. But he still called it home.

'So you see, these old blokes, in the war, didn't think they were fighting *for* England. As another country. They were fighting for England as their own country. Home, eh?' He chuckled.

'And then, when they changed the passports so that if you went to England you were treated just like anyone else, had to queue just like a bloody Frenchman, some of those old folks didn't like that much, eh?'

Finally, in late afternoon, we arrived at Victoria Creek, the local town, a mere two hundred kilometres short of the homestead. It was one street: a garage, a pub, and a string of shops. And yes, a couple of men were crossing the road in broad-brimmed, green Aussie hats.

In Peter's club we knocked back ice-cold beer from tiny 7-ounce glasses, which were kept, as always in Oz, in the fridge, opaquely frosted. Round the table with us were the local agent and the local truckie sorting out final details of the dipping and transporting. They were all mates together, even though Peter owned a station up the road the size of Yorkshire and was probably the major employer of both of them.

Six stubbies later it emerged that *I* was driving the final stretch, on dirt, in the gathering dusk, a gleaming-eyed gauntlet of five-foot kangaroos and three-foot wallabies, any one of which, if hit, could bounce off the 'roo bar' up front and come flying through the windscreen. Peter was not a good passenger. He knew the road like the back of his hand. 'Watch out, mate!' he cried, as I swerved to avoid yet another stalled marsupial. Then: 'There's a little bend before the next gate. Some bar-stard had too many drinks in town, came round here a bit too fast, smashed into the gatepost and wrote off thirty thousand dollars' worth of Toyota. You want to know who that bar-stard was? Me.'

In the morning I took stock of the homestead. It wasn't huge. A wooden oblong surrounded on all sides by a broad veranda. On the ground floor at one end was a book-lined dining room, at the other the veranda became a big open room with battered chairs and sofas grouped around a TV. There were no windows, just trellis and taut wire mosquito net. It was altogether too hot for glass.

Upstairs the bedrooms were inadequately cooled by slowly revolving, heavy wooden fans. The privilege of actually being cold was only given to Peter and the guest who occupied the other air-conditioned outbuilding on the lawn out front. In a couple of days that would be me. But Don was bringing the buyer up tomorrow so I was making do with a perch on the veranda.

Damien, the eldest son I'd met in Brisbane, had his own station a hundred kilometres or so to the north, so in and out of this Chekhovian set wandered the following cast: David and Eric, the second and third sons, stockmen; Geraldine, the turning-thirty daughter, cook and temporary mother-replacement; John and Michael, nineteen- and seventeen-year-old stockmen; Mr B, the shuffling elderly 'gardener'; and last, but in no way least, Alison the backpacker, kitchen skivvy and general cleaner, who had been recruited from a noticeboard in Cairns, originated from Grimsby, *spork laike thatt*, and had more than a few sharp opinions about life at Clara Downs. But she was thrilled to see *me*. 'I'm fed up of being the only Pom round here,' she told me.

It was Saturday night, so we were driving a paltry eighty kilometres to the next-door station for a barbie. The place was owned by Peter's younger brother Robert who'd built a new mudbrick house for himself over the creek and left the old, falling-down homestead to the mercy of his young jack- and jillaroo employees. They were from all over. Hunky Tim was from South Australia, big-thighed Kelly was from Melbourne, scruffy blonde Carol was a Kiwi, and caramel-skinned Rocky, most exotically, was an American Indian from Montana.

We sat in a sprawling group around the long outdoor wooden table, Robert's wife Belinda and her little boy and girl at the centre. The children were dressed up, he in neat black jeans and white shirt, she in a flowing red dress and matching floppy hat, because their teacher from the Mt Isa School of the Air was visiting. He was Simon, a gentle fellow with curly ginger hair and a non-stop toothy grin. The kids in his class only got into town a couple of times a year, he told me, so he liked to come out to the stations and visit in his own time. What a nice guy, I thought.

But where was Merielle the governess? 'She's dolling herself up,' said Kelly. 'Probably spending a good half-hour in front of the mirror so she'll come out looking stunning.'

'But she knows everybody,' said Mother. Simon studied the dirt.

Merielle made her entrance. Black curly hair, cropped; mascara-framed black eyes; a fat splash of crimson lipstick; full, low-cut blue top; bulky white shorts. She sat down next to me and told me she'd heard I was a writer.

Through the bush the sun set. Mother and the kids went home. The barbecue was piled with dry branches, soaked with diesel and lit.

Alison the backpacker and Kiwi Carol were shrieking with laughter to one side. They were both fed up with their jobs and their families. 'No, it's great out here,' said Alison, 'but they're all so stupid, these Australians. That's why Carol and I stick together, isn't it Carol?' 'Yes, Pom,' said Carol. 'You know what Mr Dale said when I arrived,' Alison went on, ' "The last one was ugly, but she was efficient." I mean, Jesus!' *Next* weekend they were going to go into town and show them. 'Aren't we Carol? We – are – going

– to – *show* – them. Put on our high heels and skimpy tops. We are going to take Victoria Creek by storm.'

'By storm,' Carol agreed.

They went in to get another bottle and I sat gazing up at the super-bright stars. In the warm darkness the ex-homestead looked like a filmset, so clear-cut, so glowing, almost, were its edges. Broken stained-glass windows in pink and yellow ran round the outside. One of the frames had half-fallen off the first floor onto the edge of the cylindrical water-tank. Beyond the white palisade fence, the still eucalypts faded ghost-like into the darkness.

I was joined by wide-thighed Kelly, bubbling suddenly with party enthusiasm. She told me about jillarooing (such a contrast to her life in Melbourne), her trips overseas. Then Merielle had come over, then Geraldine, and Kelly had suddenly gone quiet.

'You all right?' asked Geraldine.

'I'm *mad*!' shouted Kelly. She stood up abruptly and chucked her wine in Geraldine's face, then stormed off, slamming the homestead door theatrically behind her.

'What was that all about?' asked Geraldine.

Merielle shrugged. Kelly fancied Damien, but Damien was now flirting with Kiwi Carol. Or something. 'I'll go and see if she's all right,' said Merielle, running inside.

We ate, we drank, we danced. Kelly came back, sat rather sheepishly at the far end of the table. Rocky got drunk and boisterous. 'You should see him when he gets really drunk,' said Carol. 'He thinks he's a dog. No really, he goes round on all fours barking. Tim chained him up once. It's funny but it's awful.'

Then Simon and Merielle were having an intense heart-to-heart in the kitchen. Then they were dancing, then they'd vanished.

Damien and Kiwi Carol had been dancing too. It was past midnight. 'D'you want to go?' Damien asked me. 'I don't mind,' I said. 'Oh stay,' said Carol, throwing her arms round his neck. 'There's plenty of bedrooms here. Why don't you all stay?'

Merielle reappeared, looking flushed. I went inside to get a beer. When I returned Merielle and Damien were having a stand-up slanging match. Later Alison explained that Damien had said, 'What d'you want to root an imbecile like that for?' As I came out, Merielle was saying, ' – he's actually a gentleman and we were dancing, if you must know.'

'Hm,' said Damien, with a chuckle.

There was a long pause, then she rounded on him, her dark eyes flashing. 'You think you're so great, Damien Dale, don't you? You just think you're the big stud of the Gulf. Any young girl who comes out here you think you can just drive over and have a look at, but all you want to do is root us. But we don't want to root you, Damien Dale, because – because – we don't want to. You think you're so great – but you're actually – actually you're a waste of space.' Trembling with anger, she outlined his body shape with her hands. 'You are a waste of *this – much – space*. You think you're a man, but you're not a man . . .'

Damien, drunk and hurt, was taking her seriously. 'Okay then, okay, if I'm not a man, what am I, eh?'

'You think you're a man, but you're not a man. You're an apology for a man. You're a pathetic piss-poor apology for a man. You're a wimp.'

'No,' said Damien, waving his finger slowly at her. 'I am *not* a wimp.'

'You're a wimp.'

'Call me what you like, but I'm not a wimp, no.'

'You are a wimp. That's what you are – a wimp.' This might have gone on indefinitely, had not Rocky reappeared. He was very drunk now, surely just about to get on his knees and start barking. He lurched towards poor besieged Damien. 'You thing yer bedder than me,' he shouted. 'You thing yer higher class because yer white.'

'Rocky,' said Damien slowly. 'I do not think I'm better than you.'

'Yer do,' shouted Rocky. 'Yer all do. Yer all thing yer bedder.'

'You've got a chip on your shoulder, we don't think – '

'You *give* me the chip,' Rocky shouted. 'You whites give me the chip, you shits. You fucken arseholes give me the chip.'

'We don't give you the chip. You give yourself the chip.'

Rocky snorted, truly like a dog, turned towards Carol. 'Hey you, you cumman dance.'

'Rocky, I don't want to dance at the moment.'

Across this, Damien: 'Hey Merielle, we're mates, aren't we? Merielle?' Kiwi Carol had long since removed her arms from Damien's neck. 'He just thinks he can go to bed with us,' she was telling me, shaking her head angrily. 'Just because he's Damien Dale. But we're not like that. We don't *want* that.'

The muster had started. It was late the next morning (nine) and I was going up in the chopper. If Dick the pilot could just get the engine started. 'She'll be right, mate,' he told me with a wink. 'Just give her a jump start, no worries.' He wandered off across the yard to fetch the Landrover.

'She' was a little plastic bubble with two bucket seats and open sides. Above were three flimsy white blades and an insubstantial white pipe leading to an even flimsier-looking rear propellor. What was I doing? I'm not crazy about flying at the best of times. I knew that heli-mustering was so dangerous that pilots couldn't get insurance.

Dick had got the jump leads on and the blades were whirring. He gestured for me to get in, showed me how to use the headset intercom. 'You'll need these two, mate,' came his crackling voice, pointing at a belt and a shoulder strap. 'Shouldn't fall out then.' He grinned, sucked hard at his drooping roll-up, gave me the thumbs-up, and –

*Oh shit.*

With a stomach-lurching whoosh we're up in the air, coasting along about a hundred feet or so above the red earth, the little green wattle trees, the bleached stick-trunks of dead eucalypts, the tiny dots that are anthills –

*· Oh shi-it.*

Dick has seen a cluster of cows. He banks sharply sideways so I'm suspended by my shoulder straps at a 45-degree angle, nothing between me and the far-below ground –

*Oh shi-i-it.*

He dives. Towards the little, not-so-little, suddenly big trees. The leaves fly, the cows dance out of the airstream. 'Just got to get 'em up against that long fence over there, mate, see. Then we push 'em up that track and into the paddock.' Before he's even finished speaking –

*WHOOSH!*

We're off up again, in a giant curve, tilting over his side this time. I'm aware I'm biting my tongue, clutching the edge of the plastic bubble (there isn't even a *handle*), my body an arc of tension, my mind repeating, This isn't so bad, this is actually quite fu-u-un –

*Oh shi-i-i-i-t.*

The roller coaster takes another dive, we're right in among the trees again, cattle dancing, dust flying, one moment a hundred, the next four feet off the ground.

And that's how it's done. Up to spot the stragglers, down to swoop behind them like a giant mechanical hawk, chasing them through the treetrunks till they're safely in the herd. Later, over a beer, Dick muses on why the cows respond so instantly to the helicopter: 'It's something primeval in them; whether a big bird used to prey on them centuries ago, I don't know.' Thirty years ago, this mustering was done much more slowly by ringers on horseback (Aboriginals many of them) but then this crazy Vietnam veteran turned up, a Yank, used to wear a red headband they say, and now, Australia-wide, the horses are a quaint extra and flying choppers is what every head stockman aspires to do.

Up in the air I'm sort of getting used to it. It's almost boring after a while, if you can be bored and scared stiff at the same time. The first stage, getting the bulk of the herd up against the fence on the long straight dirt track to the paddock, is achieved remarkably quickly. Then we get to the stragglers, the reluctant, recalcitrant ones. Dick has great fun with these.

After two hours we land for a minute and I make an excuse to join Eric in the Toyota. 'Just want to see what it looks like from the ground,' I say, fooling neither of them. And what it looks like from the ground is – *horribly* dangerous. I can hardly believe I've been up there in that mad little dancing white bubble.

Eric inches forward. 'Come on you old bitch!' he shouts, honking at a straggler. The cow sits down behind a tree. Eric jumps out, claps his hands, chucks little dry logs at her till she leaps up and lollops off. I'm still transfixed by the chopper, one moment noisily right above us, the next a distant white dot in the blue.

'Do these guys ever get their motors stopping?' I ask Eric.

'Yeah. But if they're high enough they can land. The propellor keeps on going, they can bring her down.'

'And if it isn't high enough?' Dick is swooping about twenty feet above us now. 'If his motor stopped now,' Eric shouts, 'he'd be duckshit.'

Back at the homestead, Geraldine and Alison kept the meals coming. Breakfast at five was mince, bread, steak, tea. Smoko at nine was tea and cake; a good half-hour break which the sons came back from the yard for, sat around with any spare truckies or pilots yarning away. ('I told him he should backhand the bitch, next day *he* came back, black and blue' – 'Fair *dink*um.') Lunch, around noon, was more meat. From twelve-thirty to two, in the broiling heat of the day, there would be a snoring silence as everyone had a 'camp', then they'd be back out to the yard and paddock again.

Glad to be on the ground and alive, I sat in the shade at the end of the house, watching the plump, wobbly-necked cane toads hopping over the lawn under the sprinklers. A riot of bougainvillaea tumbled down from the upper veranda to smother an orange-flowered oleander beneath. There was a flaming African tulip, a blossoming pear, a bahinia, filigree-fronded pepper trees, a big white flowering bush that not even old Mr B knew the name of. Beyond the fence at the bottom of the lawn, the grass reverted from lush green to khaki as the bush sloped away gently to the half-empty creek. In Brisbane, everyone had told me knowingly that up in FNQ I'd 'really see the effects of the drought' but it turned out this was just city-know-all stuff. Clara Downs was north of the drought; there hadn't been a huge amount of rain, but enough.

I leafed contentedly through books and newspapers. According to the *North Queensland Register*'s resident satirist, THE CROCODILE, Paul Keating was 'the bloke who reckoned the best thing about North Queensland was flying over it at 35,000 feet in a Jumbo jet *en route* to Paris'. Keating's fondness for foreign travel was well known up here; as was the socialist millionaire's taste for classical music and penchant for expensive antiques and neo-classical art. He wasn't popular in FNQ.

Around four there'd be a cry from Peter. 'Mark, come for a drive, mate.' We'd head out in the air-conditioned Toyota to check fences and gauge the state of the cows. Peter was concerned that he'd got a good price for what seemed basically to be a job lot of the scraggiest of his cattle.

Along the way we had yet more rambling discussions about politics, race, religion, morality, history. With years of long country evenings behind him, Peter was better read than many a London chatterer. He quoted verbatim from Gibbon and Macaulay, knew the geography of London, which he'd never seen, down to street-names, its history in quirky detail. His big plan was to take his wife Susan to Europe. They'd been meaning to do the trip for years, but next winter they were going. 'What d'you reckon would be the best months to travel, Mark?' he kept asking. Then: 'I'm not worried about England, but those French, they've got to be some of the rudest bar-stards in the world, wouldn't you reckon?' 'He does this every year,' said Geraldine, as the maps were brought down and studied. 'They'll never go.'

Around six, the sons would return from the cattle yards and, showered and changed, we'd all sit round having a Castlemaine XXXX. Straight from the stack of cans in the cold room where the meat carcasses hung. Then dinner, another meat meal. By 8.30 they'd be in bed, reading; by nine asleep.

After a couple of days I said to Peter, 'With all your sons out working every day I feel a bit of a useless Pom, just sitting around reading on the veranda.'

'We need a useless Pom round here sometimes just to keep a conversation going,' he replied.

On Monday evening Don Fisher the agent choppered in, dapper as ever, bringing Roger the buyer, who looked more like the Missing Link than the multi-millionaire cattle-whizz he was reputed to be.

His jeans and T-shirt were filthy. His hair was long and lank. His lower lip drooped. He ran the back of his hand over his face like an ape. 'Christ, but he's an ugly bastard isn't he?' said Eric, when he'd gone off to shower. 'But you should see how many wives he's had,' said Geraldine. Roger had no problems with the ladies apparently, the best looking in Brisbane flocked to him. 'Why?' 'Because he's rich,' said Geraldine. 'I can't see any other reason, can you?'

Poor old Fisher, by contrast, was the one you felt should have been rich. He had the style: the hair, the boots, the deep, lilting, musical voice. And here he was, the seat-of-the-pants man, yarning away, keeping the two big cattle-men sweet for a mere thirteen grand's commission.

Because Roger was staying the night, the dining room table had been laid and there was wine for dinner. In his honour, there'd been a 'kill' earlier, which meant a treat of 'fresh meat'. 'Don't eat too much,' Geraldine told me. 'It'll make you sick tomorrow.' It made me quite sick that night. The ribs were tough in the sense that the flesh hadn't relaxed, and the blood, dripping down your chin, tasted as fresh as blood from a cut in your hand.

The men stood round the barbie, yarning away, munching on the burnt, crimson ribs. 'So would you reckon I could drive in Paris, eh Don?' Peter was asking the well-travelled agent.

In the morning we're up before light. Sausages and cold steak for breakfast in the kitchen as the pink and orange of dawn trickles along the blue horizon. Then off and away, bumping along the dirt road to 'the yard' where the cattle are to be drafted. They're herded from a long corral into another, smaller enclosure, then another, then a pen that leads into the polygonal drafting ring – 'the pound' – with its four clanging steel gates out into four more yards.

David, as head stockman, sits up on the rail above the pound, shouting out 'Dry!', 'Wet!', 'Weaner!', 'Heifer!', as each wide-eyed beast comes galloping through. I'm working the 'dry' gate. At every call of 'Dry!' I have to swing open my gate for the dry cow to thunder through, then slam it sharpish before the next one arrives. Woe betide me if I screw up. 'Christ Michael you're a sleepy cunt!' shouts David as the teenager doesn't get his gate shut fast enough and lets a heifer into the weaners' yard. In the old days, Damien tells me later, a jackaroo who made that mistake would have to go into the herd and retrieve the animal himself.

The sorting process proceeds in waves, under the watchful gaze of Roger the buyer. Last night, at dinner, he was so tired and well oiled that his head slumped over his food until it was virtually in his plate; today he is beady as a hawk, with a critical eye for every beast that runs before him. Don Fisher stands to one side, trying hard to look jovial; he doesn't get his thirteen grand till the cows are dipped and beyond the inspectors at Victoria Creek.

Once one batch has gone, the jackaroos run into the long yard and chase up a new lot, moving in a ragged line, waving their big hats in the air, jumping up and down yelling 'Oy! Oy! Oy!' till the animals stampede and the air is thick with orange dust. Eric and David carry long whips which they crack high into the air. The others have thick black polythene pipes which they rap across the buttocks or face of any beast daring to run back. Eric, whom I'd picked as the sensitive son, lying reading in his bed on the veranda till well after nine, now reveals a new aggressive side. Whacking out at the animals just for the hell of it. 'Get in there you stupid bitch!' he cries. 'Go o-on!' 'Act your *age*!'

Batch, sort, batch, sort. On and on we go, as the sun gets warmer and the jokes start to flow. 'You are a waste of *this – much – space*,' Eric teases Damien. 'I was called a wimp so many times I started to think I was one,' Damien laughs. It feels like lunchtime but it's only 8.15. Eventually, eventually, the job is done and we're back after lunch but no camp to find three huge road trains. The cows are shouted up a walkway by the jackaroos, then prodded up a ramp into the trucks with bright yellow electric-shock prongs.

Up on the top deck one of the drivers is trying to get a difficult cow from one end to the other. He's limping, having been kicked, now jabs at the terrified animal with his yellow electrode. She kicks him, hard, on his wounded leg and he grits his teeth in anger and stabs back with the electrode. 'Get in there, you fucking *bar-stard*,' he screams.

Later, I share a beer with the Patriarch. 'I just wanted to get you out there so you could see what goes on,' he said. 'Otherwise you might get the impression that all we do is sit around yarning and drinking beer. But it's hard work like that every day of the year.' He gulped at his Castlemaine and waxed philosophical. 'The trouble is, Mark, in the world today, there's too many lawyers and politicians and other bar-stards ... But for every one of them, at the end of the day, someone has to dig the hole, or muster the cattle ...'

'Peter,' I said eventually, 'you sound more like a Marxist than a devoted supporter of old Joh.'

'You reckon?' he said, and cocked his humorous, unlazy eye at me.

# 7

# The
# Never-Never

Over the road, under the awning of a neat blue clapboard house, sat a group of four or five Aboriginals drinking in the shade. Suddenly two of the men got up and started fighting. An old guy with a mop of grey hair and a beard, and a younger, musclier fellow with a matt-black torso over pale-blue denims. They dodged around each other, sparring. Then one of the young fellow's punches had connected and the old guy was flat on his back. The young fellow punched the air and let him get up, then knocked him flat again. Another bloke sprang up and, like the third Scouser in the Harry Enfield sketch, started by separating them, ended by chucking his own punch at the younger guy. A desultory non-fight followed, the old bloke was led away, tottering down the street in that now-familiar caricature of drunkenness.

I was in Normanton, a one-street town 150 kilometres or so north of Clara Downs, sitting outside 'the Purple Pub', sipping a frozen XXXX in the broiling heat of the early afternoon. At eleven this morning, when Peter and I had driven into town, it had presented a theatrical spectacle. The traditional outback hotel, painted in vivid hues of violet and mauve, hung from veranda to street with partying blackfellas.

Now they'd vanished. All that was left was the exhausted-looking white barlady and a mixed couple: a haggard whitefella and his black girlfriend who looked, with her tattered flowery dress, wild hair and stick-thin legs, like nothing so much as a rag doll. It was Thursday, welfare payday, 'pension day'. Every now and then a taxi would draw up, driven by a white. The blacks in the back would run into the pub and return with a twelve-pack of Castlemaine or a couple of wine boxes. Then the taxi would speed off.

The motel down the road, by contrast, was truly, at last, the lager-advert cliché. They wore wide-brimmed felt hats. They made loud jokes about 'poofters'. They capped each others' yarns by saying 'fair *dink*um'. Surely the dunny out back would contain a huge, grinning spider.

The ebony-coiffed barlady was a splendid specimen of Aussie womanhood who had every single one of her male customers eating out of her hand. Once, she told the respectful circle of hats, she'd worked with this poofter in Brisbane? One day she'd run her hand up his leg and – *ooh how he'd jumped!* This kept the guys chuckling into their stubbies for a good ten minutes.

A tottering whitefella in a fluorescent orange baseball cap came in and ordered a beer. 'You can only have a takeaway,' she told him briskly.

'Why mate?'

'Because you're drunk, mate.'

Then an Aboriginal trio appeared. A slick-haired husband, his rag-doll wife and a large-eyed child with bare feet and a snotty nose. He was greeted politely, his cheque was cashed, he was loaded up with enough beer and wine for a party of thirty. The codger next to me on the bar mumbled that he was okay, this one, not a dole-bludger but a stockman. 'Some of 'em work, you know, eh?'

In the Purple Pub, and elsewhere, the pension-day party had resumed. Laughter – interspersed with the occasional squeal – rang out in the cricket-chattering night.

In the morning Martin and I flew north. He was Peter's

brother-in-law, manager of a station a mere five hundred kilometres out of town. 'If you think this is the outback,' Peter had laughed, 'you should see Coniston Plains.' That was truly the Never-Never.

The little aircraft wobbled slightly as it inched forward high above the vast brown plain. Far below were countless dots of trees, each with its tiny shadow; then a swirling abstract of blue-grey river and pale ochre sand; then, through the haze on the left, the washed-out aquamarine of the Gulf of Carpentaria, merging at some indefinable point with the sky.

Martin sat at the controls reading the *Cairns News*. Peter had told me that he was a Pom and I'd be wise to keep off the subject of the Republic, so I'd cornily conjured up a straight-backed, white-haired fellow with a little moustache who offered you a g. and t. before dinner and spoke in clipped colonial tones. But Martin wore jeans and was only ten or so years older than me. He reminded me of one of the nicer house-prefects at school: square-shouldered, decent, more of a loner, perhaps, than one of the lads. He'd come out to Australia in his late teens, jackarooing, and had liked it so much he'd stayed.

Coming in to land we passed a bush fire. Martin banked the plane round to get a close look at it. He swallowed visibly before muttering, 'Bloody blackfellas.'

'Somebody started that fire this morning,' he added.

'Why?

'Oh, just to help them catch a wallaby or something. They don't care that it'll burn a hundred acres of ground. I've got fields of seedlings I've put down just near there.'

There was a bumpy dirt airstrip, and towering above the little white gate into the homestead garden a tall, chestnut-like tree (nobody knew its name) which had dropped a magnificent carpet of yellow blossoms onto the lush green of the lawn.

There was a whole new cast of station characters to get acquainted with. In the kitchen was Karen, the camp cook, with cropped black hair over worried eyes, and a near-fatal case of questionmark inflection. She was from Brisbane but loved it up here? People just were what they were? There was nothing artificial about them? It had totally changed her and her values? In Brisbane she'd always been so shy and awkward? Now she could talk to anybody? Next year she was probably going overseas? She cooked for the seven stockmen and the one jillaroo, who were out on horseback today, mustering?

Coming in from the garden was Martin's wife Christine, slim, boyishly pretty, with short dark hair and a toothy smile that frequently became a delightfully infectious laugh. She was a writer too, with a weekly column about Coniston life in the *North Queensland Register*.

In the little schoolroom to the right of the main house was Lucy, the Alice-in-Wonderland-like seven-year-old daughter and her governess, Miss Emma, of Polish extraction, from Melbourne. Fiddling with one of the trucks in the yard was Craig, late twenties, balding and moustachioed, son of some friends from the East Coast. He'd come for a bit of fishing and ended up staying and doing odd jobs.

And down behind the banana trees, lumbering about among the bushes with an axe, was Vince, 'the gardener' – with a fund of yarns and titbits to keep you occupied for your entire stay – if not your entire life. Despite his enormous girth he had, with his bushy Victorian sideburns, such a striking facial resemblance to Michael Palin as a Monty Python character that it was impossible to take him entirely seriously. Not that he did himself; his stories being interrupted frequently with a laugh that sounded like the last gurgle of the bath running out. 'Ha ha ha!' he'd begin; 'eugh eugh eugh!' he'd end, tears in his eyes, shaking his head extravagantly from side to side.

'So what kind of work d'you do?' he asked now, as I sat under the vine on the patio catching up with my notes. When I told him, he lowered himself slowly and weightily onto the bench opposite. 'So you'd be doing something like that James A. Michener?' Unfortunately, I said, I'd never read any James A. Michener. Not read any James A. Michener! Vince's head swung back and forth in disbelief. '*Alaska*'s a good one. *Texas*, that's another good one.' *Alaska* was over a thousand pages long but Vince hadn't been able to put it down. He read a lot, did Vince. A hundred books so far this year, he reckoned.

He'd been a shearer originally. From age fourteen. In Queensland to start with, though he'd soon realised that he could double his pay over the border. 'No point in working for boy's wages in Queensland when I could get man's wages for doing the same job in New South Wales.'

They'd shear 180 sheep a day. Some did 300. In two-hour stints. 'You'd do two hours, then half an hour's smoko, then two hours, then lunch, then two hours . . .'

He'd had an accident and had to give shearing away. He'd run a pub, with a mate, over on the Atherton Tablelands, this side of Cairns. That'd been put paid to by the RBT, the Random Breath Testing. Their takings were cut in half. Ten thousand dollars on a Friday night dropped to five thousand and they couldn't survive. He'd moved to Victoria Creek, an alcoholic.

He'd given up drinking one Christmas Day. His house had always been a place where people dropped in, stayed the night, whatever. That afternoon he'd been there, watching these idiots. 'One was fighting his shadow on the wall. Two others were lying flat on their backs with their mouths open. I just looked at them and thought, "I don't want to be like that." And I gave it up. Never had a drink since.' Before that, he'd been getting through four flagons of wine and a bottle of rum *a day*. 'Ha ha ha! Eugh, eugh, eugh!'

## Bull-Catching

At dawn, Martin and I set off in the bulltruck, a converted ute with big chunky tyres and a ferocious arrangement of thick steel bars mounted in front of the radiator. (With its cracked windscreen and battered khaki paint it looked like something out of M.A.S.H.)

A huge crimson sun rose behind the blue-grey eucalypts. Silhouettes of horses and riders shifted in the billowing brown dust against the orange-streaked sky. Five young white jackaroos, one raven-haired jillaroo, two hunched Aboriginal stockmen trotted in a rough circle, the cattle-herd moving slowly between them. A gentler, more old-fashioned kind of mustering, I was thinking, as I rode behind with Martin in the bulltruck, than at Clara Downs.

My first shock comes as an errant heifer is wrestled to the ground by the head stockman. He's off his horse, now tying the cow's kicking rear legs together with a tight leather strap, then she's chained to the back of the bulltruck and dragged over the rough ground till her hide is rubbed raw and crimson. The stockman runs over to the bulltruck, grabs a small sickle-shaped saw and sitting astride her, dehorns her. From a tiny hole at the centre of each stump red blood spurts like a fountain, runs down to matt the skin on her neck.

'D'you do that to punish her?' I ask Martin. He shrugs. 'It'll hurt her. Maybe she'll remember.'

My second shock is the bull-chase. Over the radio there's a sudden cry of 'Bull!' and Martin, who's been idling along behind the herd, is gunning the truck over the rough ground, knocking down small trees and saplings, swerving to dodge larger ones, crashing down into gullies, in pursuit of the galloping white bull.

'The bastard,' he mutters, teeth clenched as he crashes on. From the other side the helicopter swoops in. The bull wheels, sees us, panics, charges straight at us. Martin accelerates and rams him full on. The bull's astonished face is framed by the cracked front windscreen. Martin swerves and batters him again, this time from the side. And again, till he falls. Martin drives right up on top of him, pins him down under the truck, then reverses off. Two stockmen, right behind us, are off their horses and onto him, strapping his thick, kicking back legs together. He squats there stunned, eyes wide, flaring nostrils splashed crimson with blood.

'You gave him a fair belly-bashing there, mate,' comes the crackling, chuckling heli-pilot's voice over the intercom.

Now the bull's front legs are strapped, too, then he's dragged twenty yards on a chain. A rope is tied round his horns, the other end to the trunk of a tree. The straps and chain are removed and he's left in the hot sun, head tossing angrily, to exhaust himself.

They're 'cleanskin bulls', Martin tells me, rogue males who've slipped through the mustering net several years running and are now, effectively, wild animals. By mid-morning we've found, chased, battered and caught seven. One got his horns under the front-bumper of the bulltruck, lifted us an alarming foot or so into the air; another charged a stockman and gashed his horse; another, a huge golden-brown beast ('the yeller feller'), put up a terrific fight, halfway through which the bulltruck's clutch went, and for twenty seconds, impotent, I thought we were in serious trouble.

In a lull between fights Martin and I talked about England. His father had worked in London, commuted every day. 'He did that for thirty years of his life. Getting up at 6.30 to get the seven-something from Haslemere to Waterloo. No, I don't think I could lead that kind of life . . .' 'Bull!' came the cry over the intercom. With a gleam in his eye Martin was off.

Robbie, the head stockman, who'd abandoned his horse and flown heavenwards on one of the choppers, had now reappeared in a big white cattle truck. It was time to collect up the wounded bulls. To meet the crucial American meat-safety standards, and therefore be worth their $600 each, they had to be brought in alive.

The lorry is driven near to each tied-up bull. Depending on the fight the animal puts up, he's either knocked over again by the bulltruck, or wrestled down by Robbie, whose short-sleeved shirt is now drenched with sweat, foam and bull-blood. The straps are reapplied to front and rear legs, the chain strung round the neck; then the wretched beast, quelled, half-strangled, is dragged up a ramp into the back of the lorry. His eyes widen a little as the wire noose tightens.

In the back of the truck the chain is removed and he's pushed and pulled to his feet. The third bull won't stand. I hold his tail while Martin rubs it bloody between two sticks. 'Bit of pain should get him up,' he says. The bull springs up, stumbles down to join his roped-up fellows at the far end.

Back at the homestead, Lucy was chasing one of the white peacocks across the lawn and Christine and Miss Emma were sitting with cups of tea watching a big black pig truffling in the billabong.

'What an ideal life,' said Christine, laughing. Vince appeared, leaning picturesquely on his axe, told us the story of the last pig, Sara, who'd unfortunately chosen to build a nest for her piglets right under the tree inhabited by the fish eagles. 'Poor old Sara,' he gurgled. 'Those eagles just thought they had a supermarket down there. Every time she waddled off they'd have another piglet. In the end she had none left and she used to go up behind the house and sit staring sadly at Alice's piglets through the fence. Thought they were hers. Ha ha ha!' he began. 'Eugh eugh eugh!' he ended, shaking his head.

Many yarns later (Christine had gone inside) we got onto immigrants. In Vince's opinion they'd *made* Australia. Particularly the Italians. 'Those dagos. They're the best bloody immigrants we ever had.' Before, your average Australian had expected to poke around for eight hours and get paid for two days' work. 'No, those Italians got us into gear, I reckon. A lot of 'em come from Calabria, those Southern parts. They were willing to be deprived, that was the point.' The Australians were *never* prepared to be deprived. The other thing was, the dagos'd help each other. Families would help each other. Build up one farm and move on. 'Before ten years is out they've got all the bloody farms.'

Somehow we got onto Sir Les Patterson. Some Australians, Vince said, hadn't liked that portrayal, because Barry Humphries had made Australians out to be lazy, disgusting bastards. 'But I reckon, if we look at what we are, rather than what we'd like to be, he's right – we *are* lazy disgusting bastards. Ha ha ha! Eugh eugh eugh!' he gurgled.

## The Town that God Forgot

The next-door property, Mapangoola, was an Aboriginal community. Coming round the long bend in the rough dirt road and over the cattle-grid, my first impression was that it resembled a South African township. The smell of woodsmoke, litter everywhere, dogs, dirt yards, little black kids running around. I soon noticed some essential differences. The roads were tarred and well maintained. The houses were bigger and built from proper materials. Yet the whole place was in terrible repair. Nobody was building anything, nobody was selling anything. Many of the women were in a dreadful state: dirty, unkempt, scowling. Contrast, the women of, say, Soweto-on-Sea in Port Elizabeth, who would emerge from the tiniest shack with broad grins and clean, generally ironed, clothes.

First stop was Archie, the travel agent – and yet another Pom. He had a neat black beard, heavy-rimmed black glasses and a preserved-in-aspic South London accent.

Christine had told me that he was 'terribly irreverent' and 'a scream'. She'd laughed as she'd put the phone down to him. 'Does he know he'll be talking to a racist?' he'd joked. But now, confronted with a fellow Englishman with a note-book, he was clearly on best, unquotable behaviour.

There were about 1200 people in Mapangoola, he told me as we drove slowly along the spanking new main road in his neat little white lorry. Around thirty would be non-Aboriginal: schoolteachers, carpenters, administrators, mechanics. 'Those sorts of jobs for which Aborigines have not yet got skills,' he said diplomatically.

Originally Mapangoola had been an Anglican mission. In those days many of the Aborigines had lived in cabbage-leaf 'humpies'. Then the Government had taken over and the humpies had been replaced, as I could see, with proper housing.

So what about all the derelict and boarded-up houses, I asked.

The council were renovating those, Archie explained. It was cheaper, obviously, to redo the older houses than build new ones. They would be given to the 'more, shall we say, traditional Aborigines, who, to be politically correct, don't do quite as much housework as you or me'.

As we drove on, this political correctness of Archie's began to slip slightly. Pausing outside the school he told me that attendance was a terrible problem. He didn't know the exact figures. But you'd never get more than thirty or forty per cent of kids in at a given time. 'A lot of that's got to do with alcohol abuse among the parents. Because the kids haven't got a bellyfull of food they're not inclined to go to school.'

The swimming pool was closed, which was 'a jolly shame'. 'The poor old plumber couldn't keep up the main-tenance. They used to break in and smash things.'

The biggest building in the place, as central as a church, was the Canteen. It was closed today, Monday. 'But you come here on Thursday when the social security cheques come through. You know, "I'm just a social drinker, when I get my social, I drink it." '

The sad fact was that they just didn't want to work. Although, he added hurriedly, here in Mapangoola they now had the Community Development Employment Programme – the CDEP – which meant they had to do some work for their dole, picking up leaves or beercans, sweeping, that sort of thing. A single man had to do two days a week, a married man four.

Pulling to a halt outside his little shop he turned to me and said, 'They're in limbo, the Aborigines, that's the trouble. They're between cultures. I mean, if you were to have a competition, grab a kid off the street and find out who knew more Aboriginal words, I'd win hands down.'

Inside his shop a little boy was buying a can of Coke from Archie's assistant. 'Why aren't you in school?' Archie shouted at him, genially enough. 'That nice Mr Keating's given you your Land Rights, why don't you go to school?' The kid laughed and ran away. The phone rang. 'Jurassic Park,' Archie answered, 'the town that God forgot.'

I'd come to Mapangoola at a bad (if somewhat symbolic) time. The council offices were deserted; 'the powers that be' were all away at a Land Rights conference. As for the rest of the community, they were mostly tied up with a funeral. A young man had died the night before. Some said of heart failure, some said of drink. He'd been twenty-three years old.

Looking for some kind of optimistic note, I headed off to the school. The buildings were modern and in good nick. There were photocopiers, word-processors, computers. But Eleanor, the Scottish headmistress, looked tense and exhausted.

Mapangoola had not, it turned out, been her chosen destination. Her husband was a Torres Strait Islander and she'd applied for a posting in the islands, but nothing was available so they'd come here instead. She was staying for two years. 'Maybe they'll get a third out of me,' she said wearily. 'Maybe.'

Between us, on the wall of her office, was a wooden cabinet full of fine Aboriginal craftwork. Raffia mats, intricately woven bags and baskets, beautifully decorated boomerangs and woomeras. Every Tuesday morning, she told me, the elders of the community came in to school and taught the kids the traditional skills. How to gather the raffia, make the dye, do the weaving. 'Look at that basket,' she said. 'Look at the intricacies in that basket. I wouldn't know where to start.'

On her desk there was a sweet photo of her and her family. She, white; her husband, black; her three cheerfully grinning brown children in between.

I slung all the whitefella criticisms I'd heard at her and one by one she rebuffed them.

Of course there were problems here, this was a poor area. No, they didn't all drink. Of course not. There were plenty of teetotal Aboriginals in Mapangoola. And anyway, what about Troppo's, the bar where the whites drank every night. It was all so hypocritical, a lot of this.

'A young girl phoned me up about a job the other day. From Brisbane. "How safe is it?" she asked. But in Brisbane I wouldn't go down the Valley in the evening.' Of course if you were walking around the backstreets of Mapangoola when the Canteen was in full swing and it was dark you might get into trouble. But you might get into trouble anywhere.

'And if that was you, and you were living here and you had nothing much to do of an evening, where would you go? Would you stay in your overcrowded house? Or would you go over to the Canteen where there's light and music and this warm atmosphere emanating?'

Yes, it was true that a lot of the houses had smashed windows. 'Well maybe we should think about that. How must it feel to be in one of those bessabrick houses with twenty or thirty other people at night? Particularly when the nights are as hot as they are at the moment. We say these things, but all of us Europeans have air-conditioning.'

Yes, it was true that school attendances were not as high as they could be. 'But you've got to *walk* with people, you can't just expect them to be able to do everything immediately.' As for that myth that Aboriginal parents got extra money for getting their kids to school: 1) there'd never been such a scheme for primary schoolchildren, and 2) for secondary students, what little money there was was means-tested. 'In any case,' she added, 'they don't all claim it. I'm not sure how many of them are aware of their rights.'

'Here's something else,' she went on. 'Where do all the white people round here get their food? From Woolworth's in Cairns. Where do the black people? At the store. Have you been into that store? Just go and look at the use-by dates in that store.'

Just down the road, in the Tertiary and Further Education Centre (TAFE) I met another well-meaning white person, David Pillsworth, who showed me round the well-equipped workshop (where a blackfella in a blue boiler suit toiled alone) and gave me a sheaf of brightly coloured copies of the *Mapangoola Community News*. It was full of magnificently upbeat headlines: NEW LOGO FOR MAPAN-GOOLA, MAPANGOOLA GIRL IN NATIONAL QUEST etc. They'd started it, he explained, because the community had been getting such bad press. (It was produced by a PR firm in Townsville called John Crook Enterprises.)

The headline of the latest edition read: COUNCIL BUDGET ACCEPTED. Underneath were a few figures. While $506,000 was to be received in grants for housing-related projects, public housing in total had an expected expenditure for the coming year of $2.067 million. An estimated $200,000 would go to 'youth and recreation activities'; Education and Training would soak up $588,800; Public Transport (in a town about two kilometres long) $33,800; Land and National Resources $347,600; Roads $629,700 . . . The list went on. (All this money was over and above the Social Security payments to individuals.)

Dancing up and down the veranda of Mapangoola's little police station were three or four Aboriginal kids dressed in miniature police outfits, complete with flat caps and arm bands with the motto of the Queensland force: AUTHORITY THROUGH TOLERANCE.

Mick the duty officer had only recently been seconded to Mapangoola from Brisbane. He told me enthusiastically about all the new anti-crime programmes they were launching. A number of tribal elders had recently become community policemen (with powers of detention, not arrest). Then there was the Juvenile Crime Initiative. They'd set up Justice Groups, again with the elders; the idea was to use traditional tribal methods of dealing with young offenders. So far it had been remarkably successful.

'If you talk to some of these old guys,' said Mick, 'you'll find that they think the white man's law is weak, compared to Aboriginal Law.' There were plenty of Aboriginal fellows who'd rather be dealt with under white man's law.

Whether it was the strength of their law, the novelty, or something else entirely, wasn't clear, but Mick seemed thoroughly excited about his new life in Mapangoola. Part of the problem, he told me, was that there were three tribes in the one place. 'Six months ago, if you'd asked me, I wouldn't have known that Aborigines had tribes.' Now he'd been adopted into one. Gilbert was his new name. His family name was Whistleduck. He smiled proudly.

I paced across the dirt looking for elders who might talk to me. Two of the three whose names I'd been given were not at home. The house of the third was full of wailing mourners. The funeral was in full swing. But, backing out in some embarrassment, I was pursued by the old man I'd come looking for, Banjo Patterson. 'Sorry to interrupt your ceremony,' I said. He shrugged. 'We like to keep our traditional ways, as much as we can.' We agreed to talk the following morning.

'You came back alive,' said Vince, gurgling through the gloaming towards me. 'Didn't get captured by any spinifex fairies.'

'Spinifex fairies?'

'Aboriginal ladies.' He raised a Pythonesque eyebrow. 'Watch out when you're down in South Australia. They've got the Nullarbor nymphs.'

I told him about my day. 'I'll tell you what, though,' he said. 'The people in this part of Queensland are some of the most racist in Australia.'

'You think?'

'Oh *yes*.'

But the Aborigines were a terrible problem, whichever way you looked at it. 'Nobody knows what to do about it. Nobody. So they just throw money at it and hope it'll go away. It's all conscience money, of course. They treat them all right now but they treated them pretty bad in the old days. Queensland pudding. That originated round here. They used to make a poisoned fruit pudding and feed it to the Aborigines. Flour and whatever and fruit. Boiled up into a big pudding. Like a plum duff. Add a liberal lacing of strychnine. Cook for three and a half hours and serve to the nearest Aboriginal community. With gusto!'

At nine in the morning Banjo Patterson wasn't at home. Over in his shop Archie tapped at his calculator. 'Mapangoola Mean Time,' he chuckled. 'Mean time you wait.'

Another old man was walking past. 'You could talk to 'im,' Archie said. 'Not a bad old bloke. Still goes hunting, courtesy of the traditional fourwheel drive and the traditional high-powered shotgun.'

Eventually, around ten, Banjo returned. There'd been a delay at the hospital.

We sat, facing each other at one of those pub-style

wooden tables in the shade of a tree right outside his little house. He puffed thoughtfully at a pipe, spoke slowly. In the background, outside his front door, sat his two women, sewing, respectfully silent.

'Some time,' he began, 'people are pretty bad here. Young people don't respect the elders. They don't want to take it from the past. When we die, when we old people go away, they won't know what to do. They've already forgotten the culture. They think that's all in the past. But you've got to keep our culture up. Our culture should balance us both ways.'

'What d'you mean?'

'Both ways. Balance it. Make it equal.'

I still didn't follow. 'We've got to *cooperate* together,' said Banjo. 'Young and old, you got it? Black and white, we got to balance it. When you start to cooperate together everything go fine, everything run smooth. I learned white man's way. I learned my way. Should be possible for the two to live together.'

Yes, there was too much drinking in young people. They didn't know when they'd had enough. He met my eye. 'I never touched it. Since 1960 you've been allowed to vote, you've been allowed to drink. Young people today, they're born free. Soon as they turn eighteen they're in the pub and they don't know when to stop. They want to drink everything. Hot spirit – they want to drink more and more.

'They're getting the money too easy. They waste a lot of money on grog. They're not getting food.'

His sons came to *him* to eat. He shrugged. 'I can't say to them, "You're not getting any feed here." In my heart I got to make it equal. Although they're man enough now, they're all big boys now.'

His sons were thirty-four, thirty, twenty-three and twenty-two.

Women were drinking too. But 'women should be at home sometime'. Now they're at the Canteen, they all mixed at the Canteen. He gestured at his wife. 'I should be able to say to her, "If you've got a beer at home you should be satisfied." '

As if to illustrate his point a woman in a tattered dress wandered past, wailing, clearly drunk at 10.30 in the morning. 'Look what he's done to me!' she yelled at us several times. Banjo ignored her. Did I know who that was? She was the girlfriend of one of Martin's stockmen. Banjo shook his head wearily. 'When he's home she's quiet as a lamb. When he's away she drinks like a fish.'

'And you've told him that?'

'No, I don't like carding the yarn to him. Don't want to get into trouble.'

I asked him about the Juvenile Crime Initiative and he smiled. Yes, they were trying to make it good for the younger people. An example: twenty young boys had recently broken into the Canteen and taken two kegs of beer. 'The police called upon the elders. The police got the boys together and the elders beat them. Yes, hit them on the hands with a fighting stick. I hit one bloke over the head – because he's the leader. "You've been in jail," I told him. "You should have more sense." '

A flicker of a smile crossed his face. 'Me and my mate we got into them. We got into them until we're sick and tired of belting them. The police sergeant was very pleased about that. They're not robbing white people or anything. That's our Canteen. They're robbing ourselves. I told them: "Next time I take the blood off your head." So they're too proud to do it now.'

'Proud,' I queried. 'You mean "frightened"?'

'Yeah, they're frightened of us. And proud of us. They won't do that again now. You've got to do the right thing. If we do bodily harm we'll squash it between us. Rather than send them up to the big jail, we'll keep them here. We're trying to make them do the right thing.'

I returned to the police station to ask about Banjo's role in the Juvenile Crime Initiative. The sergeant, Bruce, a young, rather *sportif*-looking blond shot a glance at Mick and they exchanged a slight smile. 'He told you that?' 'Yes.' 'The elders approach us,' he said with a shrug. After all the fuss about Deaths in Custody, the Aborigines now had a right to see their elders in their cells. 'So we allow them to see the prisoners. We don't monitor them. We leave them alone.'

'An elder'd be one of the family,' said Mick. 'We don't interfere with that.'

Mapangoola's problem, Bruce went on, was simple enough. The grog. The majority of offences were drink related.

'You should see this place on weekends,' said Mick. 'It's beautiful. There's no grog. It's quiet. Without the grog we wouldn't know what to do with ourselves.'

The whole system, Bruce thought, was too paternalistic. There was no reason for them to get off their arses and do anything. It wasn't as if there was nothing to do. 'Have you seen the rivers? We've got a beautiful system of rivers here, running off from the Tablelands. They could be growing mangoes, farming barramundi in pens, growing oysters, there's no shortage of stuff they could be doing.'

Before I left, driving out past the mural that read, MAPAN-GOOLA – MANAGING TOMORROW'S RESOURCES TODAY, I did as Eleanor the headmistress had suggested and visited the store. Most of the goods had USE BY dates well into '95. But there were plenty of June and August '94s too. And on one very dusty shelf I found a row of Peek's Gourmet Devilled Ham Spread tins, with 01:89 stamped on them.

Outside, at the single pump, a coffee-coloured gentleman called Randolph served me petrol. I didn't ask for his opinion, but he gave it me anyway. 'All the young ones, that's all they want to fucken do. Soon as they turn eighteen they reckon that's the life. Sitting in the pub drinking cold beer.'

The council were all out of town chasing Land Rights.

'But they don't need any more land. They got enough fucken land. Too much fucken land if you ask me. What they need to do is get out there and make it fucken work. But they don't want to do that.

'Nothing'll change it,' he concluded. 'That's the way it's gonna be for the next two thousand fucken years.'

Randolph, Christine told me later, was the child of an Aboriginal woman and an American fighter pilot who'd crash-landed over the area at the end of World War Two.

Everybody turned out, the following day, for the end of the muster. The dust rose from the huge gathered herd of cows. The stockmen shouted and whooped on their horses. Craig circled on the motorbike, chasing stragglers. Little Lucy, heels kicking fearlessly, chased a runaway 'poddy' calf on her grey pony.

Truck and ute horns hooted. The choppers circled in the sky behind. The sad, baggy eyes of a captured cleanskin bull gazed over the white rim of the cattletruck. Miss Emma sat beside me in the ute. 'Vince'll be having a feast,' she laughed. 'Nobody's at the house.'

Later I found Craig, his arms, hands and trousers drenched in blood. 'You missed the kill,' he said, grinning under his moustache. A fat bullock had been shot and hacked up and now lay in quivering bloody pieces on a bed of willow leaves in the back of the ute. Lucy and Karen were standing together admiring the spread. 'That's dinner,' she said, pointing at the hacked carcass. 'Ribs. They're favourite.'

Robbie and two of the stockmen were unloading the lumps of meat and hanging them on hooks in the cold room. Martin was sawing up ribs with an electric saw. 'I-can-see clearly now the rain-has-gone,' he sang.

It was my last night. A lift to the East Coast had materialised. With an ex-policeman from Mapangoola, who'd been up for a few days for a spot of fishing.

## Confessions of a Policeman

We left at five, in the dark. John was a big man with a black beard, dark glasses and a bush hat. 'D'you have a cook?' he asked me.

'A cook?' (How well off did he think I was?)

'A wife,' he elucidated.

Inevitably, as we drove west through the dawn, we got talking about Mapangoola. He'd been the constable there for four years before resigning. It had got to him, eventually. The violence. He had felt himself changing inside and it had scared him.

I'd told him I was a writer and every now and then it was as if he were checking himself, thinking, He's a writer, he's going to put this all down. But he seemed to have a need to talk, to tell me how it was; for him, and the people on the ground, who actually had to do the job.

The point was: it was one thing for the politicians in Canberra to come up with their rules and regulations, but they were completely out of touch. After four years day-and-night experience in Mapangoola there was one thing you had to understand. The murris only respected you if you were tough. Look, that's how they treated each other.

Yes, John had used violence to control the blackfellas. He'd given this one a hiding, thumped that one on the jaw, knocked that one down. *But that was all they respected!*

Take an example. There was this big murri called Jimmy ... Now John's sergeant had been a very different type from him: non-drinking, non-smoking, strict Methodist, never laid a finger on anyone. One day this big Jimmy had punched this sergeant smack in the face. In John's view that wasn't on. Something had to be done, otherwise Jimmy would be going round town telling all his mates that he was the one who'd smashed the sergeant.

John's chance came when he was called to the Canteen to stop a fight. It was Jimmy who'd started it. 'I went up to him – Christ I was nervous, mate – and I said, "You, outside, now!" Jimmy looked slowly at me and said, "I've got a jug of beer here and I'm going to finish it." I said, "Outside – now!" Jimmy refused. So I got hold of his right arm – that was the hand he'd have used if he wanted a fight – and I took him outside and when we were outside I said, "Jimmy, if you want a fight we can have one now." And Jimmy stood there and looked at me – but he didn't fight. Then he got into the cart. And when he was in the cart, he was shouting, through the wire mesh, You fucken this and I'll fucken fight you and . . . All the murris standing round knew that he'd had his chance and hadn't taken it, so they were laughing at him.'

After that, John had had no more trouble from Jimmy. And that was the point, that's how they were. That's what they understood.

John gave me several more graphic examples, then told me how, when it had finally been time for him to leave Mapangoola, a group of murris had invited him and his wife to the Canteen. 'I didn't go on my last night. If anything unpleasant was going to happen, I wanted it to happen a few days before so I had time to do something about it. Anyway, I went in there that night with my wife, and this one old murri comes up to her and was touching her on the arm, and she was moving away and he said, "No, no. I want to tell you, that I respect your husband. I respect your husband because he's strong."

'Then they got this chair and they wanted me to stand on it. Obviously, I wasn't that keen. Alone with my wife in that place. But in the end I got up on it, and what they wanted to do was sing me into their tribe. So that's what they did, they sang me into their tribe.' John turned to me with a smile; his eyes shone with pride.

It was a six-hour drive on rough dirt, past a million dried-up *eucalyptus roadsideanas*. Every hour or so we'd pass a landmark. 'That's a famous place,' John would say, and I'd find myself gazing at a creek, a waterhole, a tiny farm.

At one point we saw a group of black feral pigs, snout

deep in the blonde bush grass. John slammed on the brakes. Grabbing a big hunting knife from the dashboard-compartment he ran off after them with his brand-new pig-dog. 'Follow me in the car,' he shouted.

But the dog wasn't up to it. As, bumping uncertainly through the trackless bush, I caught up with him, he was swearing at his disappointing new pet. 'Fucken dog,' he shouted. 'Bloke who sold him to me said he was a good pig-dog.'

Approaching Mossman the landscape changed. There were little farms dotted here and there in a landscape of fruit-trees and vivid green sugar cane. Behind, a low range of hills. 'What are those hills called?' I asked. John smiled. 'I don't know. It's just a fucken range of hills.'

# 8

# Of Psychedelic Fish
# and Other
# Natural Wonders . . .

CURRENCY EXCHANGE. HAPPY HOURS. DONUT KING. A
KABAB. Oh dear, I was back in the Twentieth Century. With
a vengeance. A man with a shaved head and a chandelier-
sized mobile hanging from his nose sauntered groovily
past. Then a whitefella with dreadlocks. Then a crowd of
Japanese, giggling as they snapped each other against a
poster of a yellow and purple fish. There were backpackers
everywhere, loudly comparing notes on the myriad leaflets
offering diving trips to the Reef.

In the morning 'the Esplanade' had shrunk to a tawdry
strip of dead neon at one end of the true Esplanade: which
was revealed as a long sweep of luxury hotels fronted by
a grassy strip of promenade, lush with palms and figs, with
splendid views out over the sparkling – yes, I'm afraid so
– mudflats.

I'd always imagined Cairns as sand, but it was as
'Gateway to the Reef' that the old port had come to promin-
ence, not for any particular beauty of its own. Still, the
rainforested mountains provided a dramatic backdrop, and
the place played host to a fabulous assortment of birds:
wheeling, standing, scuttling everywhere, chirpy in the
knowledge that no Japanese could follow them – shutters
whirring – out onto the squelchy sheen.

It was Tuesday the 1st of November, the day of the
famous Melbourne Cup. 'The whole of Australia stops for

the Melbourne Cup,' I'd heard more than just a few times. So I decided to test the truth of the assertion by taking a boat out to the reef. Not the expensive Outer Reef, to which the shops along the Esplanade offered upmarket catamaran rides or costly seven-day scuba courses, but the low-budget, day trippers' bit of the reef – Green Island.

Our hosts on the packed Sea Cat were of course members of that ubiquitous Australian brotherhood – the 'humorous' tour guide. Showing us how to put on a snorkel they told us not to make the strap too tight or, 'it'll cut off the oxygen supply and you'll end up like one of our crew members'. And as Green Island loomed up: 'The right side of the jetty's the boating channel, so if you go swimming *there* you'll have a *rather* unusual haircut by the middle of the afternoon.'

To be honest, I was only visiting the reef because I felt I had to. Coloured fish. Really, I could take 'em or leave 'em. I'd seen the postcards, very pretty, yes, yes – but so what?

But once down there, with the soft coral (I didn't know coral could be soft) swaying gently to and fro, and the psychedelic wonders shimmying past below you, round you, above you, the jadedness I'd been feeling since I set foot in Cairns melted away and I became an inspired apostate. Such colours! Such shapes! Such miraculous absurdity! If God did create the world this was the day He was on acid! The *Priscilla* costumes paled into blandness. Vivienne Westwood – *pff!!* Would even she risk that purple with that yellow?

It didn't matter that this was the cheapest cruise; that there were three or four other big dayboats tied up, motors running, just the other side of the jetty; that when you lifted your head above water you heard the *oki-noki-chawa* chatter of Japanese honeymooners taking yet more snaps of each other; that thirty yards away a party of Germans, knee deep in the wrong place, were grumbling at the seaweed – no, once under the water you were in Wonderland.

On the island itself I found a stack of brochures for the

spanking new 5-star Green Island Resort. They featured a handsome young couple gazing adoringly at the sunset. The reality, of course, was a long line of American geriatrics, each with regulation sun-visor and white shoes, shuffling in a queue towards a tepid barbecue lunch. Mantovani played softly from the surrounding canopy of tall rainforest trees. 'Ticket number 92,' called a soothing voice, 'your coffin is ready.'

There were just ten minutes to go before the Melbourne Cup and this tiny part of Australia (the Green Island Food Court) had not even *paused*. However, up by the pool at Reflections Bar, Narelle had got hold of a portable TV and five or six of the Aussie staff were waiting for the off. 'You've just got to be at Flemington on the first Tuesday in November,' a formidably fashionable Sydney PR had informed me. 'Anyone who's anyone's there.' I scanned the crowd for her, but she clearly wasn't as photogenic as the lovely Tonia Todman, who'd been plucked by the interviewer to tell us that she'd covered her hat with just *layers* and *layers* of chiffon . . .

Only half-watching the galloping hooves, Narelle was more concerned about a chaffinch chick that she'd rescued, fallen from its nest onto the grassy pool-surround. Now the fluffy little sweetie was tamely walking over her hand.

'You've got a friend there Narelle,' said one of the waitresses.

'Finally,' Narelle replied.

'This is the trophy they're all after, the most famous trophy in Australian sport,' screamed the commentator as the horses thundered to the line. 'Glory, not to mention about one-point-three million dollars for the winner . . .'

Beyond us, unconcerned, a Japanese couple in full scuba gear were led into the pool by their instructor. Beside them, I was glad to see, was another hi-tech individual in rubber – their underwater video cameraman.

## Out of his Tree

Forty minutes or so to the north-west of Cairns in the mountains was the little village of Karunda. Once a genuine hippy hangout, it had now become, like Nimbin, a Sad Tourist Trap, full of shops with names like Rainforest Magic, and with a 'famous market' selling all the usual junk.

If not by bus, the tourist's way to get there was on the old railway, which cut neatly through the rainforest and offered splendid views. Now, though, a rival was planned – Skyrail ('Simply the World's Most Beautiful Rainforest Experience'). 'Skyrail has been developed on environmentally sustainable, impact-free principles so that you can be sure that your visit is also helping to protect this sensitive and precious environment,' lied the glossy brochure. For of course, in order to get the pylons up in the first place, ancient trees were going to have to be removed, huge holes dug and so on. The development was Cairns's big issue of the moment, and camped out in the forest blocking the sinking of the first crucial pylon was a large group of greens, hippies and others who objected passionately enough to camp without facilities.

The most celebrated was Manfred, who'd been living up a hundred-foot-high quandong for ninety days. No Luddite he. He had a laptop, modem and mobile phone on his rickety perch.

At the treetrunk's foot sat a threesome whom you would never dare invent, even for the most caricatured New Age sitcom. A teenager with tumbling blond curls squeezed oranges into a gourd. Another, older guy hacked moodily at a coconut. Behind them a girl with tousled ginger hair, a Nordic accent and a long Earthmother dress strummed idly at a guitar.

*Dappled sunlight plays over the little clearing.*
COCONUT GUY: They're destroying our forest, mate. This

is just one phase of it, the ecotourist side of it. Down south they're selling the forest for woodchips to Japan. So it's all connected, the whole forests of Australia, mate, they're all continuous, you know ...

NORDIC GIRL: It's a real ... it's a real ... it's true, yeah ...

COCONUT GUY: The whole of the Coffs Harbour area is being totally degraded, for the Japanese especially. I've seen maps of the whole Coffs Harbour area written in Japanese, with all the designated golf courses and developments and airports and stuff like that. It's being destroyed, mate ...

ANGELIC BLOND: *(nodding)* Global materialism ...

NORDIC GIRL: Is that World Heritage land as well?

COCONUT GUY: Well it's never been logged. Pristine rainforest.

ANGELIC BLOND: The whole world's World Heritage really ...

NORDIC GIRL: *(starting to sing)* The world belongs to the world ... and I am not of it ...

ANGELIC BLOND: The Immortals ...

NORDIC GIRL: *(half-sings)* I am already in it ... but not of it ...

COCONUT GUY: *(seriously)* So that's what's happening. The North East Forest Alliance has been working to save a lot of the forest and they've been in direct confrontation with the police and BORAL and the State Forest for about the last five years, 'cause there's only three more years of old growth logging left and it'll all be destroyed then ...

ANGELIC BLOND: D'you want an orange juice at all, mate?

MARK: *(groovily)* Why not? Take what I can.

ANGELIC BLOND: There you go, mate. Tree-picked this morning.

NORDIG GIRL: *(smiling and strumming)* Enjoy the feast.

We looked up. Way above us, on Manfred's little platform, a tall guy in black was fitting himself onto the Heath Robinson rope harness which was the only way up the towering tree. Manfred was just visible against the bright light beyond. He had long grey hair and a huge beard.

'I'd say be very careful if you go up there,' said the Coconut Guy. 'A bloke broke his back last week. It's extremely dangerous.'

Slowly the tall man lowered himself to the ground. He was Hurse, a professional tree-climber from Cairns whose name hardly reassured me. His regular job was to go round 'harvesting' tropical fruit from trees in tourist locations, so they didn't fall and give visitors brain damage. (No joke. A German had recently sued Cairns Town Council after being knocked unconscious by a falling coconut in the Esplanade.)

I was now seriously worried about going up to talk to Manfred. 'You'll be right,' said Hurse, reassuringly. He was a professional; he'd stick around and supervise the hoist.

Taking a very deep breath indeed I strapped myself into the harness. Hurse and Manfred began pulling, each from their different ends. I started to climb.

It was a long, long way up. The foursome on the ground got tinier and tinier. 'Hey, stop!' I cried suddenly. 'I'm going to come down.'

'You'll be right. We've both got you.'

'No really, I want to come down. No, no *really*,' I shouted, embarrassment overcome by rising panic. 'I can't handle it.'

Ignominiously I was lowered down. 'Shout up your questions,' came Manfred's faraway voice. So I lay on the blue tarpaulin and tried a long-distance interview. But with a hundred feet between us, and Manfred's face, let alone reactions, barely visible, it wasn't easy to get that necessary intimacy. Quite apart from which I couldn't think of one question I wanted to *shout*, especially with my silent New Age audience.

'Look Manfred,' I yelled up eventually. 'I'll go back to Cairns and call you on the mobile.'

But hey, there was movement from above. The Great Hippy was lowering himself over the edge. Slowly, slowly, down he came through the branches, chuckling to himself and shaking his head as he approached. 'Wow!' he said, looking round in a stoned manner, 'I'm out of my tree.'

He hung four feet above me, swaying gently from side to side. Now there was no need for questions. His thoughts came out in a stream. It was, in so far as I could follow it, the same message as Bernie from the Holy Goat's. Permaculture was the answer. Trucking food around the planet was insane when you could grow it at home. We should learn to live on local resources and not destroy the wilderness. It would all be possible if it wasn't for the slavemasters, the slavery system . . .

'When you say the slavery system,' I asked, after he'd repeated this concept three or four times, 'what d'you mean by that?'

There was a long pause.

'Well, erm, what we're sucked into,' Manfred replied. 'Like basically you got Adam and Eve. You got the Tree of Knowledge. If you start pickin' off the knowledge, like, "What's going on here?" asking the question, it's like saying, "Up there is a fruit, and it's really nice and sunny up there so it's really nice and sweet, and over here it never gets any sun, it's quite bitter and stuff, so everyone's gone all over the place, and um, it's just er, we *know* it all now, there's no *need* for us, it's the *time* for us, like the Bible states, it's the end of time, we don't *need* to think, it's on your wrist or it's in your head . . .'

Forty-five minutes later I left him, only a little bit the wiser. Driving past the rest of the protestors' tents and vans I met Michael Daunt, the switched-on leader of the local Greens. He was pacing back up the forest track to organise a photo of the entire protest group, together with some members of the local Aboriginal people, the Tjapukai, who'd just pitched up at the camp. They were making a Land Rights claim on the entire area.

'I'm going to send the photo to the Skyrail people,' he told me. 'Just so they know what they're up against.'

The land the protest was on belonged to Mr Marshall, who owned the little farmhouse down the road. He was a white-haired gent sitting neatly on his lawn tractor as the scraggily dressed hippies trailed past. 'Oh yes,' he said, 'it's open go for them. But no Sky-Rail. They want to put a winding station here. With our blessing they could get the stuff they need up by road. Without our blessing they can only bring it in by chopper, which is going to be *very* costly.'

He nodded at his unlikely allies. 'They call them ferals now. Twenty years ago they were hippies. In those days they were nearly all dropouts. They belonged to good wealthy families and they got the dole. Now they're just like the backpackers. They have a code. They tell each other where the protests are. Some come up on their holidays. One fellow just went back to Port Macquarie. He's got a regular job. They're not all bums.

'Things are pretty bad for young people now. It all boils down to who you are. Who your connections are. If you don't have the right connections it's a pretty hopeless case.'

Back in Kuranda I looked for Rhonda Duffin, the spokesperson of the Aboriginal group who were making the Land Rights claim. I was directed to a house with smashed windows, little barefoot black kids running in and out, grinning like Africans. Rhonda, they said, was at the museum, where she worked.

I was not alone on this particular trail. Another whitefella was already there, just emerging from the museum's front door, bowing slightly and grinning ever-so-friendlily, as whitefellas do when they've just got the information they require. 'I'm a step ahead of you mate,' he said with cheery Aussie frankness as Rhonda's face remained straight, brows knotted. Brett was a teacher from Trinity Beach, doing a project on the rainforest.

Rhonda had clearly had enough. No, she didn't want to discuss the Land Claim with me, even if I was writing a book. She looked me levelly in the eye and said, 'Our rights have been completely ignored. We don't need a court or a judge to tell us this is our land. We know it's our land.'

In an echo of Banjo Patterson, her friend Andy added, 'We're coming to a point where we're losing all our old people. Once we lose that we'll have nothing to pass on.'

'Without that,' said Rhonda, wincing and turning away, 'we're nothing.'

## A Royalist

Steve Dmitriou, who lived in the hills on the other side of Kuranda, was the editor of *Cannabis News*, a publication which he described, with a Manfred-style cackle as, 'new, fresh, and surprisingly non-dangerous'.

The aim of the newspaper, now on its fourteenth edition, was to get the drug legalised; in Queensland, as in South Australia and the Australian Capital Territory. 'And it also gives you,' Steve told me, 'the view of someone experienced in it, experienced with the people in it, you know, experienced with the total allure of it. Simply because, as we say in the *Cannabis News* often enough, we're a product of history. You know, it's ridiculous to go to someone who's been a cannabis consumer all his life and expect him to, erm, not use cannabis. For whatever reason they use it, and say, "Now you've got to conform and be just like the rest of us." '

Cannabis consumers, he continued, were discriminated against, 'just as much as, say, if they were discriminated against by racism, or by feminism, I mean er, sexism, or ageism, or whatever other "ism" you want to put. I think the prejudice against cannabis consumers is akin to, and parallel with—'

'Cut it short, darling,' interrupted Judy, his beautiful if rather haunted-looking life partner. Her long dark hair matched Steve's deep sunken eyes almost perfectly. Until now she'd been sitting at one end of the rough kitchen table in silence, doodling spooky faces on a pad.

'Cut it short!' echoed Steve. 'No, I'm sure the man wants to know as much as he . . .' He tailed off, having apparently lost his thread mid-sentence. Then: 'Who knows?' he said, and after another ruminative pause, 'What, you think he might rip off our idea?' He cackled loudly. 'Ha ha ha ha agh-agh-agh!'

'Don't worry,' I said, trying to defuse the situation, 'I can always edit.'

'He'll edit,' said Steve, nodding with heavy meaning at his life partner. 'He'll edit and pick out what he wants . . .'

It turned out that Steve had long planned to be a journalist. He had indeed, many years before, started a journalism degree at Adelaide University. 'I've always believed,' he told me with some solemnity, 'there was no such thing as a small newspaper, just small newspaper men.' He cackled. 'You know I plagiarised that from somewhere in my college days.'

Now, with his own paper, his ambition had been realised. Every Saturday he sat at the entrance to Rusty's Bazaar, the famous hippy market in Cairns, wearing a top hat with PRESS written on it. At intervals he rang a bell and shouted, 'Let Freedom Ring! It's the *Cannabis News*!'

It hadn't been easy getting to this position. During his forty-five-odd years Steve Dmitriou had had many tribulations and persecutions. He'd been a newcomer and a have-not almost everywhere he'd been. He'd been in jail (for possessing a hundred plants). Most hurtful of all had been having the first newspaper that he'd started, the *Kuranda Community News*, stolen from him. If only I had the space I would print this terrible tale. As it is I must refer you to *Cannabis News* issues 1 to 13 where, between campaigning articles and poems by Steve Dmitriou, Alison

Dmitriou, and 'Special Writer SD', you can find the numerous details.

Driven beyond frustration by those who had hounded and persecuted him, Steve had now decided to appeal over the heads of the Kuranda Council, the Queensland Government of Wayne Goss, and the Federal Government of Paul Keating, direct to the highest authority in (or rather, out of) the land, Her Majesty the Queen.

What had he said, I asked.

'I protested against certain conditions. I protested to her about the theft of my newspaper, how Her Majesty's Regional Director of Education and Her Majesty's Headmaster of Her Majesty's school were involved in the theft of our publications, which they have now, by sleight of hand, changed its name to the *Kuranda Paper.*'

'So you're a royalist?' I said.

'I'm in a difficult position there,' Steve replied, 'because I like to think of myself as a Christian. In that regard I am a royalist, yeah, and my King is Jesus.'

If ever, I thought, as I bumped down the drive away from his pretty little hilltop house, there was a living advertisment for the magical, mindbending effects of marijuana on the human brain, it was Steve Dmitriou, the persecuted but unrelenting editor of *Cannabis News*.


## Flying

From 7000 feet the landscape is a crumpled brown blanket, stained with green-grey smudges of forests. Here and there you see a station, a tiny white dot of settlement on the empty vastness. Mt Isa looms up, a child's model of industrial intrusion, with toy-factory chimneys above toy-car scattered streets. Approaching the Centre the vegetation is sprinkled more sparsely and beneath the burnt brown is the deep red of Mediterranean tiles. The McDonnell Ranges appear, a long thin ridge on the horizon.

*In the beginning the world was a bare, flat plain, devoid of all features and all forms of life. Then came a time when the supernatural beings known as the Ancestors woke from their eternal sleep under the surface of the plain. The sacred sites where they emerged turned into waterholes, creeks, salt lakes, mountains ...*

*Now each Ancestor was invisibly linked with one particular animal or plant. So though, say, a Kangaroo Ancestor would generally move about in human form, He could turn into a Kangaroo as and when it suited.*

*From this Man/Kangaroo the kangaroos of the district were descended, as well as the human beings conceived there. These humans were regarded as reincarnations of the Kangaroo Ancestor. So a man belonging to the Kangaroo totem would never kill or eat a kangaroo since he believed that both he and they were descended from the same Ancestor. Likewise emus, goannas, honey-ants, spinifex and so on.*

*The Ancestors wandered around the world, singing it into Creation, and having adventures described in the sacred Aboriginal tales that the white Australians refer to as 'dreaming stories' ('dreamtime' being the coinage of a white anthropologist, the translation of an Aboriginal word which refers to this mythical period of creation, but also to the present, and the future). The routes that they travelled were known as 'songlines'.*

*Having finished their journeys and their work they either returned to the earth or were changed into sacred rocks, trees, hills and so on. They slept again, as they'd done always.*

*But they retained their power to send down rain, and to fill the earth with plants or animals of their own totem, whenever they were summoned by magic increase rites, in which their human reincarnations intoned the sacred verses that they themselves had first sung during their own labours of creation.\**

---

\* I have used various sources here, notably T.G.H. Strehlow, 'The Art of Circle, Line and Square' in *Australian Aboriginal Art* (Ure and Smith, Sydney 1964).

# 9

# Waiting for Emily

In Alice Springs – a grid of scorching streets where tourists and backpackers in skimpy flourescent clothes were forever milling in and out of air-conditioned Aboriginal artefact galleries – I walked into the Arunta Bookshop and asked the grey-haired old lady behind the desk whether this was indeed the place that had been the setting for that amusing scene in Chapter Six of Bruce Chatwin's *Songlines*.

She smiled.

'Yes,' she replied.

'And are you the – the – '

'Yes.'

*She was an Old Territorian in her late sixties. Her nose and chin were excessively pointed; her hair was auburn, from the bottle. She wore two pairs of spectacles on chains . . .*

'Was it all true?' I asked, looking at her really quite normal nose and chin.

'Oh, he changed some things. As you see, my hair isn't dyed and I don't have any chains on my glasses – but otherwise, yes.'

*I had already spent a couple of hours in the Bookstore . . .*

'He was here for – oh weeks,' she went on. 'He used to sit over there and read for hours.' She gestured to where I'd been squatting, on the single, rather grubby yellow stool. *In the room that served as an art gallery, she had two easy chairs for customers. 'Read as much as you like,' she'd say . . .*

'He had Rushdie with him.'

'*Salman* Rushdie?' (I'd always been under the impression that Chatwin had been gloriously alone.)

'Yes. He was writing articles for the English newspapers.'

Two American tourists had now come into the shop. They fingered through the titles.

*The customers were a couple of American tourists, who were deciding which of two colour-plate books to buy . . .*

Was I about to be treated to a real-live replay of the same scene? This would surely be something for post-modern literary historians to get their teeth into. But no – they looked around and went out.

I browsed for a while. It wasn't just *The Songlines*. There were so many books about Aboriginals and Aboriginal Art. *Mysteries of the Dreamtime; Voices of the First Day; Reaching Back; Aboriginal Health and History; I, The Aboriginal* etc. And outside in the brick-paved, pedestrianised centre of town there were no less than thirty-two Aboriginal Art galleries. The Leaping Lizard, the Australian Aboriginal Dreamtime, Central Australian Artefacts . . . As well as the paintings you could buy 'Dreaming' tea-towels, 'Captured Spirit' T-shirts, dot-decorated boomerangs, fighting sticks, music sticks, didgeridoos . . .

I realised there'd been an Aboriginal Art explosion recently. I had no clear idea why. The answer was simple. 'Dot-painting' – in its portable, saleable form at any rate – was a decade younger than I was, not yet twenty-five years old.

Previously, of course, there'd been the centuries-old rock and cave paintings: simply drawn animals and spirits *à la* Lascaux (though, it had recently been estimated, twice as old). Then there was the more elaborate work on bark, woodshields, spearthrowers, boomerangs and shells (known to Europeans since 1878). Then in the 1930s and '40s, at the Hermannsburg Lutheran Mission, there'd been the work of Albert Namatjira, his associates and sons,

known as the Hermannsburg School; these were representational landscape watercolours of Central Australian
scenes, ghost gums against red mountains and so on, but
in an essentially European style. There'd been other off-
shoots: the Birrundudu drawings on brown paper, the
pastels by children at the Carrolup School, which had led
to the stylised naturalistic adult work of Revel Cooper. But
the dot-paintings (as they'd become known) had only been
around since 1970, when an art teacher at Papunya
Aboriginal settlement, Geoffrey Bardon, had encouraged
Aboriginals to paint permanent, public versions of the
secret-sacred drawings they'd previously done on skin or
earth with ochre, blood and featherdown, on canvas, with
acrylics.

It was a simple three-part process. On the primed white
canvas the artist laid down a dark even ground, red ochre
or black to mimic the original earth or skin. Then the 'story'
was painted on, in a series of symbols. A horseshoe would
represent a person, a series of concentric circles a waterhole.
The painting might depict something as simple as a number
of people gathering for an increase ceremony (known to
whitefellas as corroborees) or it might tell one of the
dreaming stories of the Aboriginal totemic ancestors. (In
that the stories related to local features of landscape, often
providing explanations for those features, the painting
would also be like a map.) The third element was the
famous dots. These were just infilling and had no significance at all, though some white interpreters liked to say
that they represented spinifex or mulga. Though they gave
their artists acrylic paint, Bardon and subsequent white
advisers at Papunya had limited them to the 'traditional'
colours – burnt sienna, burnt umber, white, black, two
yellows and an orange.

These Papunya paintings, which to the untutored looked
like elaborate and beautiful mosaics, had rapidly become
popular with both punters and critics: they were accessible
abstracts, pretty enough with their concentric circles, horse-

shoes and controlled-palette coloured dots for any Sydney or Melbourne wall. And with titles like 'The Myth of the Two Possum Men' or 'Bush Plum Dreaming' they had that mysterious Aboriginal extra; there was a secret story in there, and even if you didn't *quite* understand what a 'dreaming' was, it sounded, well, both mysterious and profound ... And it was all to do with sacred Aboriginal beliefs about the land, beliefs that in the 1970s and '80s, with the emergence of the Greens, were beginning to make sense to progress-weary Europeans. So it was pretty, and a talking point, and it made you look both radical and informed – what more could you want?

The success of the Papunya paintings had led to a proliferation. Realising that whitefellas were prepared to hand over good money for these things, Aboriginal artists had sprung up at many of the little communities that scattered the Western Desert. At Balgo, Utopia, Napperby.

Initially they had stuck to straightforward representations of the dreaming stories; but then, some artists had started going off in different directions. Undoubtedly the most celebrated of these was an old lady in the community at Utopia, Emily Kame Kngwarreye, whose paintings now hung in all the major Australian public galleries, and were on sale at substantial prices, not just in Sydney or Melbourne, but in New York, Frankfurt, Paris and London. Shortly before I'd left England, I'd seen her work at a gallery in Cork Street, the very epicentre of London's art world. (Two doors down, there'd been a dead sheep in formaldehyde.)

In Australia, her biggest dealer was a cattle farmer whose property was adjacent to Utopia, and, it was rumoured, now made more money out of Aboriginal art than he did out of cattle. His name was Bill Partridge.

From what I'd heard of him, I'd imagined something of a dapper smoothie, not the tall, rather shambling blond who approached me now, through the dazzling noon sunshine up the steps of Alice Post Office.

'I'm going to leave you with a couple of girls for the afternoon,' he told me, when we'd made our introductions. 'If you don't mind helping them doing a bit of loading, then we'll be off in the evening.' He gave me a rapid, rather forced smile and his blue eyes swerved away.

The 'girls' were waiting at his parents' bungalow on the edge of town. Julie was Australian, dark, tallish and pretty in black singlet and blue jeans. She was a journalism graduate, had answered an advert in Canberra to become Bill's 'Art Secretary', but seemed to have ended up (she laughed, in that laid-back Australian way) as a general-purpose dogsbody. Jane was English, shorter and plumper, a backpacker from Yorkshire. In her late twenties, taking nine months off to travel between jobs, she'd seen a postcard in a Backpackers' in Alice offering work as a cook and general help. She wasn't enjoying herself *at all*.

'The first day was enough,' she said, in her strong North Country accent. 'You definitely know your place out there. You're staff and don't you forget it with those two.'

They were quite a contrast. Julie the Aussie, upbeat and making the best of things, bantering cheerily with the guys in the wholesalers as we went round loading up the ute with goods for Bill's Aboriginal store; Jane the Pom, her mouth set in a downward curve, quietly bubbling with resentment. (If she didn't look so pink and cross, I thought, she'd be rather attractive.)

At five we met up with Bill. He was staying late. I was to go ahead with Julie in the loaded ute; Jane was to follow, driving the secondhand car Bill had bought for one of his Aboriginal artists.

Fifty kilometres or so off tar we skidded across the dirt road and came to a juddering halt just short of a gumtree. Shit. So nearly had I found myself in yet another Australian cliché. It was a flat tyre, and the spare was under all the roped-on boxes. Laboriously, we unpacked everything, found the jack, with difficulty changed the wheel. Julie was worried that Bill was going to catch up with us, tell us off. 'For what?' I said. 'It's his tyre,' said Julie.

Driving on into the sunset, the landscape was as eerily beautiful as you could have hoped, the tile-red earth glimmering with crimson light from the big sinking bloodball of a sun, the countless bushes and trees casting long deep blue shadows.

As we arrived at Murray Hills, round the corner into the dirt yard in the gloaming, I caught a glimpse of Bill's wife Carol, by the till in the store, lit from the side, looking haggard and exhausted. By the time we'd got out of the ute she'd gone. We unloaded the boxes, walked round the back of the homestead to a couple of tables under a spreading cedar-berry tree by a swimming pool. Julie brought me an ice-cold beer and Carol emerged, now made-up and welcoming. She was tall and skinny, with thick-rimmed black glasses over a narrow, pale face. Her hair fell long and flat and dark on either side.

She would show me the art in the morning, she said. Basically the whole house was the gallery. She laughed. One day they'd get round to building a proper separate gallery, but until then . . . well, their art and their lives were intertwined.

We sat in the darkness, drinking and talking. About the Aboriginals. What Carol and Bill were doing for them. The wonderful art; but then, the shocking crooks that existed in the artworld. Dealers from Sydney or Melbourne who drove up to Alice, then out to Utopia with fistfuls of dollars, found Emily, got her to paint something, put her name to something, regardless of the quality. 'They're just car-salesmen types,' Carol said, repeatedly pushing her hair up and letting it fall again, 'but there's nothing we can do to stop it.'

Bill arrived. No longer the brisk businessman he was a different person, friendly and forthcoming. 'Want a beer,

Mark?' he asked, pouring himself a long frothing Coke and draining it almost instantly.

It was eleven o'clock and Julie was worried about Jane, who still hadn't arrived in the battered secondhand car. 'I passed her,' Bill told us. 'She'll be right.' But by midnight there was still no sign. Bill appeared briskly from the house. 'This girl still hasn't turned up. We'll have to go looking for her.'

So we were off again, racing down the narrow dirt road so fast that surely, I thought, we'd skid and crash ourselves. 'In these situations,' said Bill, eyes bright, hands tight on the wheel, 'your imagination goes wild, doesn't it?'

'Yes,' said Julie quietly. She was squashed in between us, worriedly scouring the dark bush for an overturned car.

'Of course,' said Bill, as we drove further and further, 'if something has gone wrong, we can have the flying doctor out here in minutes.'

Eventually, about eighty kilometres from the house we found her, stalled in the middle of the dirt road, lights on.

'Going our way?' said Bill cheerily.

'Yes,' Jane replied through her teeth. She was so puce I thought she might explode.

'Are you right?' asked Julie.

'Don't expect me to talk about this till *much* later,' muttered Jane.

The problem was found, jump leads were applied, and we set off in convoy, Julie and Jane rattling along in the secondhand car, Bill and I behind in the Landcruiser.

In the morning, Bill was too busy on the phone to show me any art. Nor was there any sign of Emily. It was Thursday, pension day, so it was unlikely, Julie said, that she'd show up. She generally came when her relatives were short of money.

Down at the store, Carol was flat out cashing the social security cheques. All morning the Aboriginals arrived, in their battered or not-so-battered vehicles, up the road from the Utopia Community. They signed their cheques, got their money, loaded up with provisions from the store, left.

Like the Victorian lady of the manor with the villagers, Carol knew all their names and circumstances. 'Sandy, yours is here.' 'Where's Elizabeth? You need to get Elizabeth here, she's got more than you.'

She showed me some of the forms sent down by the Government. One was a Pension Concession Card for the old ladies. *Carry your PCC at all times when you travel*, it read. Carol raised her eyebrows. 'What do we do with this? We can either go through it all with them for something they'll never use, or we can chuck it in the bin.' She raised her eyebrows. 'So we chuck it in the bin.'

When the Aboriginals got really low on cash they got potatoes and onions and meat and put it together with a pack of soup and made themselves a stew; the stockmen remembered this from their days on the camps. 'We're very conscious about their diet,' Carol told me. The worst two problems were obesity and diabetes. 'So you try and help them, whichever way you can, to limit sugar.'

None the less, the store was full of sweets and Coke and ice-cream. 'I hate it that some of them might be getting too much,' Carol said. 'But whatever you do, it's going to be there.' In any case, they'd only started the store because the Utopia folk had asked them to.

Not so long ago, all they'd had was rations. The station owners would hand out so much sugar and flour and so on. It was when social security had come in that the whole ball-game had changed. 'Suddenly we're selling them things, not handing them out.' She smiled. 'I think in some ways they're lucky they've got us here.'

(And what did the Aboriginals think, I wondered, as they sat around in the yard laughing and chatting and eating ice-cream while Carol rushed hither and thither, making money out of them certainly, but essentially at their beck and call, providing goods from faraway Alice.)

Jane, meanwhile, padded around in her maroon T-shirt

and tight grey shorts, obediently cleaning, sweeping, cooking, serving, and building up steam like a pressure cooker. 'They're the rudest, most ignorant people I've ever encountered in my life,' she murmured to me, as I made myself a coffee in the kitchen. 'It's a real eye-opener working here. We do the canvases you know.' She laughed. 'Julie and I. We stretch them and paint them black and they put the dots on them. I don't mind abstract art, but you want to feel that the artist has put his heart and soul into it. Don't you? This is just a bloody production line.'

She puffed off with a coffee for Bill and came back. 'They're on best behaviour at the moment, because you're here. You know that, don't you?'

The next day there was bad news. The wife of one of the old fellows I'd met in the store had died. 'How?' 'Oh, alcohol probably,' said Carol. 'Or maybe she was hit in a fight.' It could well have been a domestic thing; or possibly, since the old fellow's brother was the traditional killer, appointed by the tribe to bump off malefactors . . . 'No,' she mused, finger on lip. 'I don't think he'd kill his sister-in-law.' Whatever. The community would have to go through with the traditional 'sorry business'. Emily was one of the family. It was unlikely she'd be coming up to paint for at least a couple of days.

Just as I was wondering whether I should stay (Julie was taking the ute into Alice the following morning; after that, there'd be no trip till next week) Bill appeared. He was in cheerful and charming mood again. 'D'you want to come and have a look at some art?'

At the end of a corridor just off the main, open-plan living area was a strongroom chock full of rolled-up canvases. We dragged some out, rolled them flat on the living-room floor. Bill was trying to put together an exhibition, for a gallery in Paris. 'When I go overseas,' he told me, 'I have to go on a very quick learning curve to find out the best places to show – that's important.'

'We're basically collectors,' he continued, as we surveyed the colourful splendour on the floor. 'We keep the best and sell the rest. In Melbourne or Sydney or overseas. We don't sell much in Alice Springs because it's basically just tourist art there.'

There were over a hundred artists in Utopia, and they, he reckoned, had the pick of the crop. The paintings varied from the most traditional old Papunya style, with significant symbols that told a story, surrounded by white and ochre dots against a dark-brown background, through to the latest, most abstract stuff, pioneered by the remarkable Emily. In these, the background 'in-filling' dots had expanded and taken over completely. And the traditional palette of four ochres had been replaced by bright pinks, purples, greens, and, in one bizarre series of paintings, blacks.

'The way she uses colour now,' Bill said, 'it's really fascinating.'

She'd had, he told me, three distinct phases. You could see the early stuff as primitive, the middle range as pretty. 'Now I guess she's doing altogether more,' he paused, seeking the right word, '*challenging* work.' He shook his blond head and grinned. 'The market's going bananas over this abstract stuff.'

Carol had joined us, was perched on the little sofa by the door to the kitchen.

'So the symbols have completely gone,' I said, gazing at a mass of pink splodges haphazardly arranged on a white ground.

'No,' Carol cut in. 'They're there, underneath. People are so odd. They say, "Where's the dreaming?" It's there, underneath.'

I must have looked puzzled, as I scoured the imbroglio for symbols, because she continued, 'She's used that traditional background and moved on from it. She's made the connection.'

'Emily,' Bill elaborated, 'has gone from being a good local

artist, to being a national artist, to becoming an international artist. Like Picasso, she's going on and on through
different phases. We've had professors of art from
Melbourne and Sydney up here, pointing out how she's
changing.'

I was keener than ever to see Emily at work now. There
was no doubting that her early work, where she'd stuck to
telling the stories, had a precision and quality about it that
many of the more slapdash efforts I'd seen on the walls of
galleries in Alice did not. It was easy to see how she could
have emerged as a star. And the paintings of her middle,
'pretty' period, where the symbols had begun to be sub-
merged by larger, non-traditionally coloured dots, had, in
addition to their originality, something powerful and
beautiful about them too. Bill's comparisons with Monet
were perhaps a bit over-the-top, yet you could see what he
was driving at. But the recent stuff, which looked for all
the world as if someone had jabbed randomly at a black
canvas with an old brush – no, I couldn't see it.

Friday came, and Saturday, and still no Emily. In the
evening, Bill appeared. 'I'm off to feed a few calves,' he
said. 'Come along.' So we loaded up one of the utes with
lick and food pellets and headed out across the dry bush
to the waterholes.

Bill's twelve-year-old son David sat in the back with his
gun. Every now and then there'd be a shout, the ute would
stop, and encouraged noisily by his father, David would
shoot down a galah. (Though the sight of this lovely pink
and grey bird falling lifeless to the ground didn't seem to
bring him any obvious pleasure.)

'They need thinning out,' Bill explained. 'They've been
breeding up.'

We spotted two roos, lolloping away through the evening
light. The truck stopped abruptly. From the back David
was levelling his gun. 'Go for the head,' shouted Bill. 'Do

a headshot. Right between the eyes, just under the ears.' He turned to me with a shrug. 'I know it's a gruesome business,' he said, 'but it teaches 'em a lot of things in life. Teaches 'em confidence.'

With one crack the roo was felled. It lay half-dead on the ground. Dad picked up an iron bar. 'Finish it off, David,' he shouted. 'That's it, one shot to the head.' But it wasn't enough. Bill bludgeoned the head with his bar, then father and son dragged the roo back across the dirt by its tail. Purple blood spilled from the broken line of its mouth onto the orange-red dirt. Bill chucked it in the ute, splattering blood all over his shirt, the truck and his son.

He reached into its belly and pulled out a semi-opaque pink plastic model of a roo. 'See this,' he said. 'The foetus. If it had hair on it we'd rear it.' But the unfortunate junior was bald. With a flick of the wrist Bill cracked it dead against the side of the ute.

The next stop was a bogged cow. She was in a wet slurry of mud up to her neck. Her eyes were crazed with fear. So it was the old chain treatment, noosed round her neck and tied to the truck as she was dragged out. She lay, covered in mud, too weak to get up. 'Hey David,' shouted Bill, 'come and look at this.' He poked the cow's eye with his finger. It didn't spring out – so she was dead. He shoved his boot on her side and pumped. This brought her round briefly; for a flickering moment the eye showed life again.

Bill and David tried to drag her to her feet. 'There, David, take the ear, pull.' But she was too weak to stand, rolling onto her side and expiring before us. 'What'll happen to her?' I asked. 'Oh we'll drag her off to be burnt when she's dried. Could use her for dingo bait, but I've left my knives behind.' He turned to me with his most concerned frown. 'This is the worst side of the cattle industry, Mark. Not nice, not nice at all.'

They hadn't had a proper Wet since 1983. His cattle were hungry, weak, dying on their feet. This was the traditional time for the Build-Up – and there wasn't a cloud in sight.

If there was no rain before Christmas he could lose a million dollars' worth of cattle. He smiled. If it wasn't for the art, they'd be finished.

We dropped off the dead roo with Bill's Aboriginal stockman, Birdie. He was tall and distinguished looking, his black beard flecked with grey. Like every other Aboriginal I'd met to date, he looked away as he shook my hand. ('Oppression, degradation and loss of self-esteem, the legacy of hard and tragic encounters with European Australians,' I'd read, in one of the many glossy Aboriginal art books, 'have taught many Aboriginals to avoid eye contact, the stare of white society.')

He'd cook the roo the traditional way. Dig a pit, put hot coals in it, drop in the roo, top up with more hot coals, leave for several hours.

After dinner, Bill was keen we return for a taste. In the bright moonlight, Birdie and his wife were getting ready to sleep, their double bed standing out in the bush beneath the stars. The roo wasn't yet done, so we picked at a section of the tail, which snapped off easily, and tasted like fatty ox-tail.

In the morning a miracle! The weather had changed. The sky was an English blanket of grey. By the old tennis court beyond the pool the wind-chimes jangled. The heat was muggy, thundery.

'Rain?' I asked.

'It's just teasing,' Bill replied, holding out a hand. 'This can go on for weeks. I tell you, Mark, the worst thing is if it builds up like this and then rains on your neighbour's property. That's when you feel like going out and shooting a few galahs.'

Julie appeared. 'Emily's here,' she said. The great painter was sitting under a tree outside the store, as tiny and old and wizened as she'd appeared in the blown-up photos I'd seen of her in Cork Street. She was wearing a pink T-shirt that said SATURDAY'S BLUES and a bright orange headscarf.

There were two younger women with her, and a gaggle of screaming kids. They were all painters, but as yet none of them was painting. 'Got to go gently,' Bill said, 'with this sorry business.' None the less, Julie was set to work priming canvases.

A tiny plane flew over. 'The aeroplane's here! The aeroplane's here!' shrieked Bill's nine-year-old, Charlotte, running past in her latest (pink frilly) dress.

An important gallery owner from Melbourne was arriving, and Charlotte had been sternly warned not to make any reference to the fact that he looked rather like Rowan Atkinson's famous comic creation Mr Bean.

Oh dear. William Mora (of the top Melbourne gallery William Mora) *did* look like Mr Bean, albeit a dapper, urban sophisticate Mr Bean. A whiff of cologne joined the pungent scent of rain on parched earth.

We proceeded in a solemn threesome towards the seated cluster of Aboriginals, who went silent, then shy, one of the younger women ducking behind Emily.

'This is Emily and Lily,' said Bill, 'and Camilla's hiding.'

Mr Bean nodded and smiled. Emily just nodded briskly and carried on chewing, not bothering with a smile.

We retreated to the living room to consider the canvases. Mr Bean was impressed. But a lot of the most recent ones had a clumsily scrawled 'Emily' on the bottom left-hand corner. Mr Bean stroked his chin with his fingers. 'I think it'll look a lot better without the signature,' he said. Bill was clearly put out. 'Good, good,' he said. 'We'd like your opinion on that.'

Julie was beckoning at me through the sliding door. I hurried off. Sure enough, Emily, having moved from the tree to the shelter of a corrugated-iron-roofed shed, was – at last – painting. She had a three-foot by four-foot canvas, primed matt black, on the ground in front of her. To her left, five little pots of bright acrylic paint: two orange, one yellow, one red, one white. In her hand she clutched a half-inch camel-hair brush.

This was her technique: She dipped the brush into the orange pot, then out onto the black canvas, splosh, splosh, splosh in a line of orange that gradually decreased in brightness. Then, without pausing at all, the brush would be back in the paintpot, the yellow one this time, so as she brought brush back to canvas the line of orange sploshes would gradually turn yellow, till the progression was yellow with a lingering tinge of orange. Then, not stopping for anything as mundane as a washing of the brush, she switched to a white pot. Jab, jab, jab, went her brush on the canvas, the yellow, orange and white mixing haphazardly as she proceeded down the line.

Bill and Mr Bean had appeared, stood quietly behind me. 'Basically,' said Mr Bean, having watched for a while, 'it's not a hard technique to imitate – but it's the *choice* of colour.'

Emily ploughed on regardless down the row, barely seeming to notice the watching whitefellas. 'Turn 'im a bit,' she muttered to Lily and Camilla, who were working at their own, traditional, paintings in the background. The canvas was turned. Emily ploughed on across the rapidly decreasing area of black.

'How does she choose her colours?' mused Mr Bean.

'She picks them out,' said Bill. 'You see, she's sick to death of white now so she starts on red again.' He told a story about the Australian abstract artist Melvin Ramsden; half at us, half at Emily (who took no notice). 'You know, he reckons, between each brushstroke, he needs to stand back for a while, have a beer maybe, think about it. And he came out here and saw the speed with which Emily works,' Bill chuckled and shook his head. 'He couldn't believe it.'

'My mother's an artist,' said Mr Bean, raising his voice to attract Emily's attention. 'A very well-known artist in Melbourne.'

'An old woman, just like you,' said Bill.

Emily barely looked up. She just raised her eyebrows fractionally and grunted.

'When we were little,' said Mr Bean, 'we used to sit and watch her, like this. I can't paint at all – wish I could.'

'Nor can I,' laughed Bill.

Behind Emily, the two other ladies were proceeding more slowly. Having drawn in 'the story' in a series of deep-red-ochre horseshoes and circles (each horseshoe was a person, each circle a waterhole) they were now outlining the horseshoes with tiny white dots. It was a careful process, working with a little match-sized stick, slightly chewed at one end.

Emily had finished. She sat back, swigging at her can of Lemon Crush SOLO. An inchoate mass of orange, yellow and white splodges lay before us.

'That's a nice little painting,' said Mr Bean. 'You could call it, "Before the Rain".' He turned to me. 'It's beautiful, isn't it?'

Despite her exertions, Emily was immediately ready for another masterpiece. A canvas was fetched. Julie and Jane had neglected their duties and this one was only half-primed. No matter. It was put before her. 'She obviously can't say "no",' said Mr Bean.

'You right for paint?' Bill asked. 'You right for colours?' Emily grunted. Away she went, marching off down the side of the black canvas with a new row of colourful splodges.

Bill went back to the house; I sat watching with Mr Bean. 'Wonderful activity this,' he said. 'When you think that ten years ago they had nothing to do.'

'What would one of these fetch in Melbourne?' I asked.

He shrugged. 'Oh, around $30,000.' (Later, Julie told me that Emily got a few hundred dollars a painting.)

'It's only in the last ten or fifteen years,' he went on, 'that Australia has discovered the incredibly rich artistic heritage it has. When I was younger, art students all wanted to go to Europe. Now when they leave art school they all want to head north.'

Half an hour later Emily had all-but finished another painting. Bill stood over us, rubbing his hands. 'This is where you start to get nervous,' he said. 'If she goes on too long she just loses it.'

'It's a beauty,' said Mr Bean. 'It's looking lovely, Emily.'

Emily wasn't listening. 'Bloody whitefella,' joked Mr Bean. 'What would he know?'

'Okay Emily,' said Bill. 'We'll go and do some shopping now.' He led the old lady off towards the store, followed by a gaggle of children. I was left alone with Lily and Camilla.

'How do you choose which colour to use?' I asked, as Lily filled in the dots around the symbols.

Lily chuckled. 'Just put on anywhere,' she said.

I caught Camilla's eye. 'D'you think you'll ever paint like that?' I gestured at Emily's painting. Her glance flicked over and back again. She covered her mouth with her hand and laughed.

Emily was back, surrounded by happy grandchildren. Ellory was struggling with the cellophane wrapper of a bright orange and green CAR KILLER. Roxeanne had a doll. Tom had a super pop gun that fired yellow balls. Emily's fierce mask of concentration had softened totally. She sat, rocking on her backside, watching the children play, her huge lower lip pushed out in a contented smile.

'You ladies should be as fast as Emily,' Bill joked at Lily and Camilla.

'Too slow!' Emily laughed. 'Too slow!'

Camilla was blacking out the whole of her painting.

'Starting again?' asked Mr Bean.

'No good,' she muttered.

'It looked all right to me.'

'No, no,' said the artist, shaking her head.

That night it rained. Proper, hard rain, splashing off the corrugated-iron rooftops, drenching the baked earth, making big puddles in the ruts. Bill was in the very best of moods. William loved the paintings, and the rain, if it persisted, would save him a million dollars.

# 10

# Ritual Secrets

It did persist. Back in Alice the cloud was so low it had smudged out the tops of the ring of red-orange hills that surrounded the little town. The scent of eucalyptus and drenched parched earth was exhilarating.

The hundred-yard-wide bed of the Todd River was still dry, though; and wild-haired Aboriginals were still to be seen tottering, shouting, fighting, slumping finally under one of the many tall trees that grew there. They drank in a bar right at the top of Todd Mall, not just known as, but actually called on the sign – ANIMAL BAR.

In the daytime there would always be a sprinkling of dishevelled blackfellas among the shifting crowds of tourists. A little fight would break out, or a barefoot woman in a stained, torn, floral dress would suddenly let out a wild high-pitched scream of abuse, fucken-this, fucken-that, alarming the tourists as they went about the serious business of snapping up indigenous art bargains.

At the Lutheran Mission in Gap Road I met Philip, a priest who'd spent most of his life in the desert working with the people he called 'traditional Aboriginals'. As a child on Hermannsburg Mission he'd learnt the local language (Western Arrarnta) and spoke it fluently. None the less, he was wary of claiming to know 'what Aboriginals thought'. 'I think,' he said, 'you could only really understand the full dynamics if you lived in that culture and gave up your own. I have a level of understanding, from a white man's point of view, that's probably reasonable, but imagine the reverse, how could you say you understood white society unless you lived in it?'

His central point was simple. The problems were all too obvious. But the solutions being put forward by Government did not account properly for the vast cultural differences between traditional Aboriginals and white Australians.

The traditional Aboriginal had a very different understanding of how the world worked. They believed, as I knew, that the world had been created by totemic Ancestors. More important, from the point of view of white misunderstanding, was their confidence that they could still enter into the creative activity of the Ancestors. When they staged their ceremonies (corroborees) the Aboriginals understood that they were *creating* the food and meat and water which they needed to live. This ritual was what they classified as work.

They then hunted or collected what they'd created. For the traditional Aboriginals of the desert, this sort of perception was still very much alive. It was this, more than anything else, that made it so difficult for Aboriginal and white Australians to understand each other.

Since the status quo was the result of ritual, when a traditional Aboriginal looked at the white man, what he saw was superior ritual. The work a white man did, his job, came in the same category as the Aboriginal's 'collecting'. So what the Aboriginals wanted to know was: what was the ritual we used, first of all, to create what we collect.

Indeed, Philip said, some Aboriginals even harboured feelings of ill-will towards whites because they believed that whites were deliberately not letting them into the full secret by which they produced their obvious wealth of food, houses, cars and money.

Many Aboriginals believed that more recently the white man had been starting to let them in on some of their ritual secrets, like the forms which can be filled in at the social security office. Done correctly, this yielded a fortnightly cheque. Then there were those meetings where you could make applications for houses, tractors, Land Cruisers. Yet another secret was royalties from mining operations. But obviously, the whites were still keeping quite a lot of things to themselves – how else could you explain the visible disparity in standard of living?

The difference in the way these 'traditional Aboriginals' looked at the world extended beyond the economic. Take health, for example, one of the central concerns of Government, not to mention the international agencies. For Aboriginals, Philip said, ill health and death came from other than natural causes. Contact with taboo places, inappropriate behaviour which offended spirit beings, or the deliberate manipulation of the spirit world by one individual to cause another harm. If someone died of cancer, for example, the question asked by the traditional Aboriginal was: Who caused that person to get sick with cancer in the first place?

Now the white man pitched up with his understandable concerns about the dreadful Aboriginal health levels. He would, of course, expect the Aboriginal to be grateful, and so forth. But the reality was that the white man's very concern made the Aboriginals see their ill health as the white man's problem. 'Because it's a big problem for us,' Philip explained, 'because we're badgering them all the time to do something about their health, they say, "Well, you reckon you want to do something about it, then you can fix it. But don't expect me to put in any of my effort or my money." '

He gave me an example. 'This actually happened. A bloke from out bush came into town in his own motorcar because he wanted to do some business, this was on a Wednesday. On the Friday he had to be back in town for a medical appointment – he had his leg in plaster – but now it was the Government's business to bring him in. Because it was Government business to fix his leg. Not his business. "You've made yourself responsible for my leg, you fix it." '

'So,' I asked, still a little puzzled, 'this traditional Aboriginal thinks: We abandon our primitive ways of looking after ourselves and tap into the white man's superior way of doing things?'

'Yes and no,' said Philip. 'They'll use both systems. They reckon that if the problem of the ill health, whatever it is, is caused by Aboriginal factors, then it's really only an Aboriginal traditional healer that can fix it. If it's caused by something that the white man has done, or comes through the white man's system, it can only be fixed that way.'

Another example: Some years before, a violent hailstorm had hit various Hermannsburg outstations, in some cases unroofing and demolishing shelters. The reason for this, according to the Aboriginals, was that a small hill connected to the hailstone totem had been desecrated by a gang of road builders removing gravel. White, meteorological explanations were completely irrelevant.

These were problems of understanding. When you moved on and tried to put solutions into action there was a whole new set of problems.

For a start, the current Government definition of an Aboriginal Australian was: a person descended from the original inhabitants of Australia who chooses to identify as an Aboriginal. Aboriginality was thus a matter of race, not culture.

Contrast the definition of traditional Aboriginals. They saw an Aboriginal as one who knew his own Aboriginal traditions and lived by them. For them, Aboriginality was a matter of culture, not race. And surely, Philip argued, that was a more sensible way of defining people. The difference between a traditional Aboriginal living in the desert and someone of mixed descent living in suburban Australia was vast. In reality, the two had nothing in common with each other 'except some vague, socially irrelevant thing called race'.

And yet, under current Government thinking, it was this latter group of Aboriginals who would happily speak on behalf of all Aboriginal people. A group who by and large had no knowledge of traditional Aboriginal culture had effectively succeeded in setting the whole agenda for relations between whites and Aboriginals.

It was these people who ran and operated the numerous Aboriginal organisations on whose advice the Government relied, and through which Government dispersed funds: the Aboriginal and Torres Strait Islander Commission (ATSIC), the Land Councils and so on. 'But these,' Philip said, 'are not grassroots organisations. They're Western in orientation and they have Western solutions. The evidence for that is that all the money they're pouring in is going nowhere.'

They were elected and operated on non-traditional lines and therefore were not controlled by the people they were supposed to represent, nor were they accountable to them.

The whole idea of traditional Aboriginals getting together in such organisations was highly problematic in any case, because of the nature of their social organisation, particularly their kinship system. Philip got to his feet and led me to a blackboard where he sketched out the basics of the hugely complex Arrarnta classificatory system, which places everyone at birth into one of eight classes, which then define a person's rights and responsibilities towards everyone he comes in contact with for the rest of his life.

The point being that whereas he, as a non-Aboriginal, could have a boss at work who was, say, on a committee of which he, Philip, was chairman in his spare time, this sort of hat changing just wasn't possible for traditional Aboriginals. Their relationship to each other, and consequent obligations, was fixed for life. 'Even if you're running a store,' said Philip, 'and you're a relative of mine,

I can't say, "You can't have it." If, that is, you have a right, through the classificatory system, of demanding it from me.'

The central problem, as Philip saw it, was how to bring a real understanding of the white way of doing things to the world out there in the desert; by the same token, to get the white community to stop approaching the question of Aboriginal disadvantage from their own ideological preconceptions and start working around the cultural realities.

## Hay Arse Rock

My Backpackers' hostel was swarming with the usual Euro-happy crowd, swapping travelling experiences in upbeat, broken, tragically unironic English-as-a-foreign-language. Kink's Canyon. The All-Gas. Hay Arse Rock. These were the natural splendours they were trailing around like so many fluorescent ants. There were any number of tours available, ranging from the basic coach ride with Greyhound through to a 5-star adventure where you drank champagne at sunset by the Rock and met real live Aboriginals who told you dreamtime stories.

With sinking heart I contemplated the brochures. *You will need: a hat, flynet, sturdy walking shoes . . . Be prepared to have fun!* Oh god. There would be forced treks, jolly fireside moments, relentless green-shorted members of the Guild of Humorous Aussie Tour Guides. I wanted a clean experience. Just the Rock and Me. But there wasn't anywhere in Alice that would rent you a car for a day. It was two days minimum, which made it $165 plus petrol – altogether too much. I was all set to give in and take a tour when I saw the note attached to the hostel noticeboard. Was anyone driving to the Rock? Two German girls, Steffi and Christine, would share costs.

If I'd been hoping for a cross between *Priscilla* and *Thelma and Louise* I was to be disappointed. After the initial backpackerish exchange of home-details (they came from the countryside, just outside Munich) the girls barely spoke. We sped south, purring along the streak of black tarmac through the gently undulating bush.

It turned out that they didn't want to see the Rock at all. They'd already been there, climbed it, done that. Afterwards they'd met some Australian guys who were working as builders at the Ayer's Rock Resort (Yulara, to give it its Aboriginal name). It was the builders they wanted, and – ho, ho! – they hadn't informed them of their arrival. 'We want to giff them a bick Sir Price,' said Steffi, who, with her round face, scattering of spots and thick glasses looked like a friendly but shortsighted currant bun.

*Oh god.* I knew what was going to happen. Steffi and Christine were going to head cheerfully into the pub, rucksacks-a-dangle, only to find – *Sir Price! Sir Price!* – they'd been supplanted in the builders' affections by Trudi and Ingeborg from Norway. I would then be stuck with two weeping adolescent German females with nowhere to stay.

Yulara turned out to be a tasteful cluster of low-rise hotels, discreetly bedded in the desert nineteen kilometres away from the reason for its existence. At its centre was a pink-bricked shopping square known conveniently as Shopping Square. Here there was a Tavern, a bottle shop, a bank, a newsagent, and a supermarket.

Buying – no, not champagne, that would be a bit tragic on my own – two beers for the sunset I waited while a tall blond German was politely ticked off for trying to buy a twelve-pack for some loitering Aboriginals. 'I did not real ice this vassn't a prop lemm,' he was telling the manager. 'If I do not giff it to him he'll scratch my car I'm thinking.'

It was a more than mildly ironic scene. Having been kicked off the area in the last century, the local Aboriginals, the Anangu, had then been given back the Rock as part of the Petermann Aboriginal Reserve; in 1958, a National Park that included both Rock and Olgas had been excised from the Reserve; finally, in 1985, the Hawke Government, with much ceremony, had given 'Uluru' back to the Anangu, who were then immediately required to lease it back for nine years to the Australian Government. So it was now, technically, owned by the Aboriginals; or some Aboriginals, (there being an ongoing controversy over whether the right Aboriginals had got title). The fact that individual blackfellas were barred from buying drink at the off-licence and were removed from the Tavern by security guards at six o'clock was just one of those things. (Anyway, as the manager was now explaining to the German, it was at the behest of the Anangu elders that these rules were enforced.)

The sun was sinking in the sky. I paid ten dollars for my pass onto 'Aboriginal land' and purred down the beautifully smooth tarmac road towards the giant orange postcard-subject itself. Against the empty waste of mulga and spinifex there were any number of helpful signs. NO PARKING ON ROADSIDE FOR NEXT 3KM. SUNSET VIEWING AREA – COACHES ONLY. SUNSET VIEWING AREA – CARS ONLY. SUNSET VIEWING AREA – DISABLED CARS ONLY. Ah, to be in the great Australian wilderness!

Gosse, the first white man to have seen the Rock, described it famously as 'an immense pebble rising abruptly from the plain'. Which is good, though sadly dated. Now it would have to be 'an immense pebble rising abruptly from the tourist coaches'. But the metaphor works because the excitement – and there is, despite everything, an excitement – is one of scale. The Rock is so smooth, and the vertical ripples down its sides are so huge that it really does look like a vast model of something smaller. Perhaps not a pebble, on second thoughts, because a pebble suggests something straightforwardly rounded; if anything Uluru's ripples make it look squeezed or moulded, like a giant splurge of orange toothpaste, or one of those jellies (generally rabbit-shaped) we used to make as children.

Finally it towers above you and you are at the least-steep end, the point where The Climb begins. Here there is a sign telling you that as it is a sacred site the Traditional Owners would prefer you not to climb it. Then, in case you still fancy the idea, there are a series of plaques commemorating those who have either died of heart attacks on the climb or fallen off. My favourite was:

```
IN MEMORY OF
LESLIE ARTHUR THWAITES
OF NEWCASTLE N.S.W.
WHO DIED ON TOP OF THIS ROCK
ON 15TH JUNE 1972
AGED 63 YEARS
THE CLIMBING OF AYERS ROCK WAS
ONE OF HIS LIFE LONG AMBITIONS
```

Half an hour before sunset, the SUNSET VIEWING AREA – CARS ONLY was already three-quarters full. A hundred vehicles in a line – and this was the off-season. I slid into a space next to a terminally beaten-up Kombi full of hippies playing the Grateful Dead at top volume. A little further along, a couple sat on their crimson bonnet eating strawberries; their vibe was the Brandenburg Concertos. Others strolled up and down expectantly, cameras and videos at the ready. Japanese, American, Australian, French, German, Lancashire accents mixed and mingled. 'Of course her maternity leave's been extended now . . .' 'Flying directly to Singapore . . .' Behind, the famous monolith glowed ever more crimson.

And then, right at the end, just as everyone had got their tripods and loved ones lined up for the moment of maximum rubescence, the sun disappeared behind a long, low streak of cloud. The Rock just sat there, a dull orangey-brown, the sunset-viewing party rendered utterly, as opposed to slightly, ridiculous in front of it. Oh well, we'd all just have to buy postcards.

Back at Yulara, Wednesday night was staff party night. The tourists were all safely bedded down in their hotels getting some kip before the Sunrise Viewing (or Climb) and in the Tavern in Shopping Square the chambermaids and barmen and waiters and porters were letting rip. They were mostly backpackers who'd run out of money, Alison from Blackburn told me. She and her friend Kirsty were down to their last $30. They didn't want to phone home, they wanted to do this thing on their own, so they were being chambermaids for a while, saving up for the rest of the Big Trip.

Across the crowded floor I saw Steffi and Christine, at the centre of a group of hilarious blokes with tattoos. Christine looked well gone, mascara'd eyelids down, vermilioned lips on the rim of a florescent green cocktail. Steffi's head was thrown back, laughing extravagantly. I left them to it.

In the morning they looked shattered. As I drove back, at speed, through the weird and wonderful orange-earthed wastes, they slept like babies, snoring sporadically.

# 11

# Going Troppo

Everybody had told me that Darwin would be unbearable. November was the transition from the Dry to the Wet – the Build-Up. It was as hot and humid as a sauna. People became violent, committed suicide, succumbed to 'mango madness', 'went troppo'.

But as I stepped nervously out of the gleaming-white, air-conditioned oblong that was Darwin's spanking new International Airport, it was clear that this was just the usual traveller's tale. It was warm, sure, and moist, and within fifteen seconds my arms were covered with tiny beads of sweat – but no way was it *as hot as a sauna.*

Central Darwin wasn't huge, a rectangular grid of streets behind the Esplanade, which row of luxury hotels looked not onto a curve of sand, nor even a sweep of mudflats, but over steep grassy cliffs to the milky-blue horizon of the Timor Sea. At one corner of the promontory a twisting lane led steeply down to the harbour; the other was marked white on the map – MILITARY AREA. The Royal Australian Air Force were billeted here, protecting the exposed north of the continent; it had been here that the Japanese had launched their bombing raids in 1942, killing over a thousand and flattening the city almost as effectively as Nature had done in the famous cyclones of 1897 and 1937.

Darwin's fourth Fury – Cyclone Tracy – had come thirty years later, on Christmas Day 1974. Now the municipal

buildings squatted butch and reinforced, rarely rising
above two or three storeys, as if daring Nature to have
another go.

20 YEARS SINCE TRACY read the banners in the central
mall, and between them – weird as anything for a displaced
Pom – were the Christmas decorations, big red and silver
bells glinting against the clear blue sky. I was used to frosty
nights and overcoats, minced pies and mulled wine, not
frangipani trees in bloom, at night the rumbling of thunder
and a dazzling overhead light show.

## The Marranunggu

In a bubble bath in the luxurious Plaza Hotel I pondered
the ironies of travel writing. Here I was, Free of Charge,
with a gratis whisky in my hand and the prospect of a
lonely but complimentary meal in the 'Fine Dining' Iguana
Restaurant downstairs with a French waiter who would
fawn on me and offer me three different types of garlic
butter. Why? Because I was writing two travel pieces for
English newspapers. And what, of all the glamorous Aussie
subjects I'd put before them, had those English newspapers
both, independently, been interested in? Why, Aboriginals.
Specifically, a new holiday in which you the reader could
go out to one of those large pale orange sections of the map
and live, for a while, alongside genuine indigenous folk.

*Every day is different* (said the brochure) *as you join in with
the MARRANUNGGU in their foraging and fishing trips. The
day to day lifestyle changes with the seasons and the MAR-
RANUNGGU live as close to nature as possible. They change
and adapt lifestyles to work in harmony with nature.*

When I'd arranged to do this back in England I'd
imagined it would be a little extra; the book would boast
altogether more authentic encounters. Now it seemed like
a godsend. A visit to the Northern Territory Land Council
had made it clear that getting out to Aboriginal land wasn't

just a matter of hiring a four-wheel-drive and going. You had to apply for permission to Traditional Owners, justify why you wanted to go, wait for their response etc. etc. It would probably take six weeks at least, I was told.

'It's the same as coming into my home or my garden,' said Yvonne, their charming (white) spokesperson. 'You ask my permission. It's just that some people's gardens are slightly bigger.'

Well quite. In the case of, say, the Arnhemland garden several hundred thousand square kilometres bigger.

I could completely see the Land Council's point. Originally the whole of Australia had been Aboriginal land. Shouldn't there now, in this vast and empty continent, be areas where Aboriginals could get on with whatever life they wanted, traditional or otherwise, without some bloody anthropologist or journo popping out from behind a tree and asking them to tell them a dreaming story, oh please, just for me, my Ph.D/article/book will be so much better if you do.

On the other hand I could also see the point of the bearded bloke with the tattoo I'd met at the bar of Darwin's Railway Club. Did I know, he'd said, that the Abos comprised a quarter of the population of the Territory and owned half the land. *Half the land!* And now, with this bloody Mabo legislation . . .

Private ownership of huge tracts of land is one thing. It may irritate in theory, to think that a person is arrogant enough to believe that they actually possess a hillside, a wood, a stream; but in practice, if you can drive and walk across it, picnic and camp on it, this irritation is containable; someone has to maintain the land, and the difference between 'owner' and 'guardian' is perhaps just a matter of semantics. But refusing access to all except the owners is a different thing, guaranteed to infuriate the adventurous. I couldn't think of another place in the Free World where such a large area was literally *out of bounds*.

This quasi-apartheid had another side-effect, put well by

Bill Harney, the first ranger at Ayer's Rock, writing about Aboriginals over thirty years ago: 'The traveller only sees the ones on the roadway, for should he want to visit one of the Aboriginal Reserves he has to go through a wall of red tape. Thus is the best side of Aboriginal life hidden and the worst exposed to our view.'

There were four takers in the air-conditioned Landcruiser, all Americans. Up front, a quiet, fifty-something couple, John and Dorothy. Next to me at the back was Ned, late seventies, thinning white hair, prominent pink hearing aid, one of those grizzled old timers who Tells-a-Story. 'I'll tell you *whad*,' he begins, fixing you inescapably with his still-beady brown eyes. His companion, Sherry, was young, wide-eyed and enthoosiastic. She had very long pink legs, very short white shorts, huge red-rimmed glasses and a goofy face. At first I'd taken her for an adventurous lone traveller, but as the 'we's' started creeping into her monologue it dawned on me that she must be with Ned. His youngest daughter, I assumed; possibly his granddaughter. It was only when Ned reached out, and with a gnarled, liver-spotted finger touched her leg, that I realised she was his *wife*.

We bumped off the smooth tarmac onto dirt. The bush had rapidly given way to thick eucalypt woods, knee-deep with lush green speargrass. 'You get pythons round here,' shouted Chris, our bearded guide, from the front. 'You got Dolly Python?' said Ned, chuckling loudly at his own joke. Then he doubled up, groaning; a fly had landed on his hearing aid. 'Jeez!' he cried, when he'd finally located and brushed off the intruder. 'I'm going to have to use some of that *Rid*, that fly was buzzin' right *arn* there.'

The road became a narrow grassy track. We passed the battered wooden sign telling us that this was ABORIGINAL LAND and we could only go on it with a permit from a Traditional Owner. Then we were out of the woods and onto a huge empty plain, across which an army of gravestones appeared to be marching. 'Boy!' gasped Sherry. They were weirdly formed termite mounds, Chris explained. We all piled out excitedly and took the same photograph.

The camp was in a clearing by a waterlily-covered billabong. The Marranunggu (all four of them) were waiting for us by the camp fire. Only Doug was black. Margi and Jason were the colour of milky coffee, Shane was almost as white as I am.

I went for a row on the billabong with Dick, newly appointed Aboriginal Tourism Officer for the Northern Territory, who was out researching and monitoring the product he had to promote. It was beautiful out there: the waterlilies in flower; overhead a thundery sunset sky; the eucalypt trunks, lit orange by the sun, reflected in the still water. But Dick wasn't troubled with this; he wanted to know exactly how much I knew about Aboriginal Tourism. What Aboriginal Holidays had I come across in Australia besides this one?

Dark grey clouds raced up from the horizon. A sudden breeze puckered the surface of the water. 'D'you think we should go back?' I asked. (I was trying to remember whether being in a boat on a lake in a thunderstorm was the safest or the least safe place to be.) 'Their experience is dispossession,' Dick was shouting. 'Until 1967 they weren't even *citizens*. They couldn't even vote and . . .' A gust had carried his sentence away. 'A powerful *cultural* experience . . .' I caught. 'Not the experience of . . . guy with . . . *didgeridoo*. We're trying to present . . . Aborigines as they are now, not some *mythical* idea . . . how they *should be* . . .'

Back at camp the wind had dropped. A few fat raindrops had moistened the earth but the camp fires blazed brightly. At one, Margi was cooking turtle and wild goose; at the other I found Sherry, eyes shining with excitement. 'This is great,' she said. 'But it's not what we expected at all. My husband thought there'd be a village near by.' (I didn't have the heart to tell her that the whole point about Aboriginals was that they'd been nomads.)

Ned lumbered over. Now would have been the time for a Welcome Sherry – or even a Welcome Double Brandy – as Ned regaled us with Tales of Colorado Hay-Broking. But grog was banned out here, for guests as well as Marranunggu.

Though Doug and Shane had now joined us round the fire, the conversation remained firmly on international issues. John was the Director of an American National Park and he and Dick were now improvising a list of the World's Best National Parks. I turned to lanky black Doug, sitting silently beside me, nodding and smiling along with this conversation. 'Have you ever seen Ayer's Rock?' I asked. He smiled. 'No.' He'd never been further than Darwin.

At supper Dorothy and I joined the three lads. In comparison with the noisy conversation at the other table ours was a bit stilted. How nervous they were with us, legs jiggering visibly under the table as Dorothy tried to break the ice by asking, 'So, d'you eat like this every night?' Jason laughed. 'No, it's just the three of us here. We might have a can of beans, something like that.'

The next day we sped across the empty beautiful green plain of the forbidden Aboriginal lands. We identified and tasted the food the Marranunggu, many years ago, would have lived off in the wild. Jason caught us a turtle, Doug wrestled impressively with a five-foot freshwater crocodile. We saw the local dreaming site, the rocky hill where the Sea-Eagle Ancestor had retired to sleep for ever under the earth. We swam together in a crystal clear rockpool. At lunchtime Ned and Margi bonded on the subject of welfare ('I tell you *whad*, if people give you anything you want you don't respect it. But if you *earn* that money . . .') and, more crucially, denims:

'Levi is the only work-pant . . .'

'They *are* a good strong denim . . .'

From welfare it was a short hop to Aboriginal politics.

Margi had no time at all for the state-funded bureaucracies, the Land Councils and ATSIC. 'When we go into Darwin,' she said, laughing, 'we raise hell. Tell them they're feathering their own nests and what about the poor ordinary Aborigines they're supposed to be helping.'

ATSIC was top-heavy with over-privileged Aborigines. The houses, the cars they had! The Chairman of ATSIC in Darwin had a car and a house for when he was in town and a car and a house for when he was out bush. 'And we just have to drive around in our rusty old Toyotas.'

The money was distributed in all the wrong places, she said. If I really wanted to see how badly out of hand things had got I should go to Groote Eylandt, the big island off Arnhemland where the Aborigines had a stake in the mining operations; preferably on the day when the royalties arrived. This friend of hers had seen people there gambling, on royalties day, with $24,000 on the table between them, and someone had come in and chucked petrol all over it and set it alight. The whole lot!

The tragedy was, she went on (sounding not unlike the policemen in Mapangoola), Groote Eylandt had some of the best fishing in Australia. 'There's turtles, there's barra, mobs of them in the river there, and all you see by the roadside is old bully-beef cans. They've lost it. They just live from welfare cheque to welfare cheque.'

In the evening, when we went fishing, I sat beside her on the riverbank.

Her people had only got the title to this land they were on now in 1991, she told me. Before that it had been untenanted Crown land; before that a grazing licence. Ironically, it had been her father, a white man, who'd held the grazing licence, so she was coming home in more ways than one. (She was Marranunggu on her mother's side.)

To get title you had to prove you'd lived on, continued to practise ceremony on, and used the land. They'd now got absolute title to the forty-two square kilometres we were on here, but the larger area where we'd been turtle hunting, Wagait, was still under dispute. 'Some other mob claimed the whole lot. We're still waiting, impending on a committee. They made the other mob traditional owners of the Wagait land in 1983. But our dreaming stories go right across there.'

'So they say they've got dreaming stories?'

'It's all bullshit. Lok-Kungerakin they call themselves – but they don't know anything about the country. They just looked on the map and saw Loch Kungerakin.' She laughed. 'Shows how much they knew.'

The authorities had come out from Darwin and tricked her Uncle Fred and her Auntie Billhook and her Auntie Pam. Made them sign documents that weren't true. She looked at me sadly. 'They came in waving this letter, saying, "We won! We got our country back!" And then we read it and we had to tell them they'd just signed their country away.'

There were only thirty of them actually living on the land they'd fought so hard to claim. The rest of the hundred or so Traditional Owners were in town, victims of the grog. 'Al-co-hol,' Margi mouthed softly. She'd never touched it.

'Where do they stay?' I asked.

She laughed. 'Long grass. You stay long enough in Darwin you'll hear about the long-grassers.'


## Frog Hollow

Back in town, in the little park called Frog Hollow, I found the 'long-grassers', sitting drinking in a circle under a tree. 'Merry Christmas,' they shouted at you as you passed. Then: 'You got a cigarette, mate?' Was one of them a relative of Margi's, a self-exiled Traditional Owner of Wagait? Now at last I felt I had something to discuss with these fringe dwellers. I went off to buy some iced coffee and cigarettes as an introductory offering; but when I returned they'd gone, every last one of them, leaving nothing except a circle of cans and green Moselle boxes. In their place was a frightening-looking whitefella with a shaved head and a big stick, marching up and down muttering to himself.

## Eddie Mabo and the Island of the Octopus God

My Plaza time had run out. I'd moved into Ivan's (one of the numerous Backpackers' on Mitchell Street) which was, like Sun 'n' Surf in Surfers Paradise, a hastily converted motel. Still, a word from my NT Tourist Board friends and Ivan provided me Free of Charge with a four-bunk dorm all to myself. Where I lay naked fifteen inches under a slowly-revolving wooden fan trying to get to grips with the complexities of Australian Land Law, Native Title, and, most particularly, Mabo.

I'd heard about this ground-breaking legal case endlessly. It was one of the key constituents of The Story. 'And now, since Mabo,' people would say; but when I asked what exactly Mabo was, they were generally rather confused. Ah look, they said, it was a fantastically longwinded and complex judgment. It had meant that Aboriginals could now lay claim to untenanted Crown land; defunct leases; Bennelong Point; the whole of Australia if we weren't bloody careful, mate. 'You need to read and understand about Mabo,' they told me with furrowed brow. 'It's terribly important.'

Now I discovered that all the fuss centred on a volcanic island called Mer, so small it wasn't even named on my 207-page Road Atlas of Australia. It was well over halfway across the Torres Strait to Papua New Guinea, peopled by the Meriams, eight small clans who had been originally unified, in their religious legend, by the god Malo, who'd arrived on the island in the form of an octopus (one tentacle for each clan).

In 1879, Mer had been formally annexed, along with the other Torres Strait islands, by Queensland (a single shot from a gunboat had done the trick). Almost a century later, in 1981, representatives of a Land Rights conference in Townsville had decided to use Mer as a test-case and launch a claim for individual title to the island. Eddie Mabo was the chief of five plaintiffs.

It took ten years of legal shenanigans before judgment on *Mabo and Others v. State of Queensland (No. 2)* was formally handed down by the High Court in Canberra. (In the interim Eddie Mabo had died.) It filled over two hundred mind-numbing pages but the crucial point was that the doctrine of *terra nullius* – that Australia had belonged to no one at the time of settlement – was found to be wrong. It was this that had sent such a shock wave across Australia. What were those lefty judges thinking of? If they told the bloody Abos that, yes indeed, they'd actually, legally, been here for all those forty thousand years, who knew where it would end?

## Flesh-Eating Flower

My early scoffing about Darwin not being as hot as a sauna had given way to the realisation that I'd arrived on a comparatively cool day. Now it was so sultry and humid that even walking thirty yards drenched your shirt in sweat. Going into town any time after about 8 a.m. involved a series of air-con pitstops just to keep going. Besides the sprinkling of little cafés there was the Post Office, the Public Library, the Smith Mall Food Hall and the Arts Centre.

The big hit there was a play called *Dragged Screaming To Paradise*. Written by a Melbourne woman whose husband had been posted to Darwin on a three-year public service contract, it told the compelling story of a Melbourne woman whose husband had been posted to Darwin on a three-year public service contract. The title gave away the plot. She hadn't wanted to come North at all; but after a year she'd been seduced by the lush and tropical otherness of the place:

SHE: In the morning the pool is covered in a carpet of leaves and sticks, patches of orange and red, Tulip flowers and Poinciana petals, waterlogged dragon-flies, dark beetles, pale caterpillars as thick as your finger and indigo blue and brilliant orange feathers from the Kingfishers and Lorikeets who dart and swoop down to drink from it.

The sky is blue and the sun shining. The perfect Frangipani tree looks even more washed and gleaming green, the white blooms hanging in waxy posies. A pair of butterflies with patches of *Swan Ink* blue on their wings spiral past in a pas-de-deux, and dragon-flies with jewelled bodies and shimmering wings hover and buzz in the still, warm air.*

Ah yes, Darwin was getting to me too. Late in the afternoon I would go and lie on the grassy, palm-tree covered slopes of the Esplanade. One evening a man and a woman appeared with four little white posts each topped with a great blossom of white flowers. I thought I was in for a Sydney-style Japanese photoshoot, but it turned out to be a real wedding, timed to coincide with sunset over the sea. The celebrant was a dapper woman in blue. A ghetto-blaster gave us Elvis Presley's 'Love Me Tender, Love Me True' as the couple kissed and the horseshoe crowd applauded.

Most evenings I found myself at the sailing club. It was just one of those places where you always seemed to end up – with either a lawyer, a public servant, or a lawyer in public service. I wasn't complaining. There was a wide, open terrace, and beyond, through the long row of gently shifting palms, the sun set, huge and crimson, in a cadmium yellow haze.

On Saturdays there was Parap Market, a gorgeous feast of colour. Exotic flowers and fruits under dazzlingly toplit red, blue, green and white awnings. Grinning Asian faces selling Thai Noodle Soups, Laksa, Stuffed Chicken Wings, Blended Tropical Fruit Drinks . . .

* Suzanne Spunner, *Dragged Screaming To Paradise* (Little Gem Publications, Darwin, 1994) – p. 39.

Down by the harbour was a 'deckchair cinema' which was showing *Cinema Paradiso*, in which a film in an outdoor cinema is stopped by a storm; just as this scene was over, a real storm broke over us, and the showing was suspended. Virtual reality or what! I dashed along the quay to revamped Stokes Hill Wharf and sat in an empty piano bar as the flat sea whipped to a froth, the rain swept in, the huge cyclorama of starry sky became a magnificent electric-light show.

'There were only two classes in Darwin,' wrote the intrepid female Australian travel writer Ernestine Hill, 'those paid to stay here and those with no money to go.' And then: 'Darwin is like one of those sinister South American flesh-eating flowers that closes over one. Nearly all the old pioneers I met there had come for three weeks, and missed the boat, and stayed sixty years.'

'Go south before you go troppo,' said one of my lawyer friends, only half-joking.

'Darwin is deserted at Christmas,' said another. 'Everyone goes home.'

# 12

# Hard Questions of Love in the Bungle-Bungles

On the Greyhound bus west there was the usual micro-phone-happy driver and chuckling mate combo, over-explaining the rules and facilities to a bored audience of backpackers, Aboriginals and schoolchildren going home for Christmas. 'Why it's called a restroom has got me beat, and it'll get you beat too if you go in there, as it's not a restful place.'

In the jeans and chewing-gum ads a Greyhound is a hot, fly-blown, half-empty vehicle with a silent driver and a beautiful blonde girl sitting alone half-reading a book as she half-gazes out at the desolate landscape and half-looks at you, so conveniently located as you are just across the aisle . . .

Dream on. These modern buses were trying so hard to be aeroplanes it was a wonder they didn't take off. Certainly they'd left far behind any rough and ready romance of the road. First, you had to book in advance. Second, the air-con was turned up so high you were forced to wear a jersey. Third, and most heinous of all, the overhead video was on *at all times*.

For a while I tried to ignore *Bushfire Moon* and look beyond the lurid purple curtains at the sunny infinity of eucalypts that once again comprised the landscape. Then I made a bold attempt to read. In the end I gave in and, absurdly, found myself in tears over a costume drama about a hard-hearted Victorian station-owner who got taught to be kind just in time for Christmas dinner.

At Timber Creek everyone piled out into the heat to stretch their legs, buy cold drinks and ice-cream, and sneak surreptitious looks at each other. There was the Aboriginal family from the back; the beautiful, raven-haired girl in the maroon T-shirt and her floppy blond drip of a boyfriend; the guy with the long grey hair, pressed blue denims, big stockman's hat and smart black briefcase; the chatterbox schoolgirl going home for Christmas; and a pretty, late-twenties-looking woman in a blue skirt with whom I exchanged the briefest of smiles.

At the next stop we were treated to a perfect bush vign-ette. Against the darkening blue-grey sky a group of white-trunked albaes stood by a white four-bar gate. In their branches a flock of white birds. On the horizon white light-ning forked down. To one side, a white ute with wiry Dad, plump Mum and gap-toothed little boy were waiting. Our white T-shirted schoolgirl ran across to her mother's arms, Dad smiling, waiting, shaking his head behind. 'Merry Christmas everybody!' shouted the girl, as she retrieved her bag. 'Merry Christmas everybody!' echoed her falsetto brother. 'Come along now,' said the driver. Leaning against the wall of the bus the young woman who'd smiled at me in Timber Creek was videoing the scene.

I'd booked to Kununurra, and planned to spend the night in a motel, but right by the steps down from the bus was a bearded man with a clipboard and a quietly persuasive manner. Before I knew it I and the young woman in blue – Sonja was her name – were side by side in the Backpackers' minibus. 'D'you want to see the sunset?' asked the beard. 'We're going to get a great sunset tonight because there's a gap in the clouds.' There was a peculiar insistence in his tone, as if sunset were the key thing about Kununurra – once missed, for ever regretted. Stopping at the pair of bungalows that was the Backpackers' he ran off and returned with two German girls, a white-haired English-woman and a young Japanese couple.

The vantage point was the local mountain, a steep, almost triangular projection strewn with big orange rocks, known, rather charmingly, as Kerry's Knob. The road stopped halfway up. 'Ignore the NO ENTRY signs,' said our provoca-teur (his name was Neil), 'mostly people like to go right to the top.'

A gaggle of strangers, we climbed round the two fierce-looking security gates and paced on up to stand by the big dishes and alarming aerials of – what was it? – a tracking station? And each on our rock we sat, the ever-keen-for-experience backpackers, and in silence watched the big yellow sun go down over the chubby little rounded hills of the Kimberley.

Directly below us was the Aboriginal community, a ragged square of tin huts and dirt tracks, from which, on the still evening air, floated up the sound of singing. All along I'd been trying to avoid making comparisons with South Africa, but this little place could so easily have been in the Transvaal or the Orange Free State, the comfortable white bungalows on one side of the *kopje*, the dusty shacks, the litter and the song on the other.

Walking back to the Backpackers' in the gloaming I got talking to Sonja. She was Swiss, on a six-week holiday from her job as a travelling toy saleswoman (Christmas being her slackest time), meandering solo towards Perth. She'd done the East two years before, now she wanted to see this – the wilder side, she hoped. And me? 'Oh,' she smiled, 'both of us. Zere's another English boy coming here,' she added, after a few moments. 'I met him in Katherine. He's from Kent.'

It turned out that Nigel and I were sharing a dorm. As I wrapped my towel round my waist and headed for the shower I heard him greet Sonja enthusiastically in the hallway. 'Hello *stranger*, well how are *you*?' When I returned they were arranging to go out for a drink together. 'I'll just freshen up,' he grinned. It was clear from his expression that a friendly fellow Englishman would not be welcome.

In the morning I was relieved to see Nigel asleep in his bunk alone. I jogged up to Kerry's Knob and found the triangle of scrub below it littered with VB cans and broken glass. Three little black kids were walking down the road in the early sunlight. I waved but they didn't wave back. 'Money!' they shouted in unison. 'No money, sorry,' I replied. 'Let us know if you want to run up there,' said the tallest, sternly, nodding towards the community. He was all of nine.

Back at the Backpackers' Sonja was emerging, pink as a prawn, from the shower. She and Nigel had been out and got a Chinese takeaway. They'd eaten it on a bench then been to see some live music. Then they'd gone on to a nightclub. And all the I's of the previous night had suddenly become we's.

I sat under a parasol by the swimming pool reading and snoozing. Sonja and Nigel returned from the market, conversing loudly in r-less Estuarine and th-less Swiss. In the pool they romped merrily, arms round shoulders, head in legs, laughing extravagantly at the slightest thing.

We were a jolly party, the following morning, rattling south towards the Bungle-Bungles in the dawn. Two white-haired adventuring widows, one plump and East Anglian, the other stick-thin and Australian; a fifty-something lone female from Sydney with dyed black hair; a Germanic-looking couple, early thirties; Katrina, a squat, crop-haired, English bleached-blonde; Jerome, a wiry, eager-to-please Californian student; Sonja, and me. Nigel couldn't afford to come. Ha ha. I, having shown my journo credentials to Neil, had got the trip F.O.C.

As we left town Neil pointed out the sights. On the left, the Celebrity Tree Park, where visiting identities were invited to plant a tree. Rolf Harris and Princess Anne were already represented. On the right, Australia's largest uncontrolled airport. ('There's no tower. You just look to the left and to the right and take off.')

The Bungle-Bungles, where we were headed, was billed as 'one of the finest of Australia's natural wonders'. It was a huge escarpment eroded over the millenniums into a fantasy city of beehive-like rock domes, striped dramatically, laterally, sienna-pink to alizarin mauve, not unlike those sands in glass tubes people bring back from the Isle of Wight.

It had only been opened up to tourism since 1982. A TV programme called *The Wonderful World of Western Australia* had shown an aerial view. The ABC switchboards had immediately been jammed with people wanting to visit. Now Helen from *Neighbours* took painting holidays there and the demand had really taken off.

It was a six-hour drive, two on tar, four on dirt through the pretty green Kimberley hills. Side by side Sonja and I snoozed, played cards, ended with a long Emotional-CV swap. She was thirty-six, though she looked younger. Four years before she'd ended a long marriage-style relationship and decided that she'd never be tied down in that way again. Every year she would travel. 'I couldn't have done zat before,' she confided. 'I could – but I couldn't.'

Eventually, around lunchtime, the scene we'd all bought copies of already hove into sight across the gum-sprinkled, blonde-grass plain. The group woke up, became chattery and excited. It wasn't perhaps quite as astonishing as the aerial view on the postcard, but we were *here*. We pitched camp, trooped off up a narrow gorge where the orange rock towered two hundred feet above us to a crack of bright blue sky. Tiny palm trees perched precariously on invisible ledges: here, a luminous green; there, an inky silhouette crowning a dark sweep of shadow. 'It may sound silly,' said Neil, 'but don't forget to look around you as you walk up the gorge.'

With the sun low in the sky our guide became mildly twitchy. Of course! It was sunset and Neil knew the perfect

viewpoint. Soon we were scrambling up a heap of lime-
stone rocks to stand with our backs to the sun, cameras
cocked at the Ayer's-Rock-style crimson glow on the orange
surface of the long escarpment.

Stuck for metaphors, I enlisted Sonja's help. 'How would
you describe this?' I asked.

'Ze Bunkle-Bunkles lying down like a bikk fat hamp-
burker between trees and clouts. Ze clouts and trees are ze
bread, ze tomato sauce is ze small rocks here in front. Only
ze ekk is missing.'

Just after we'd retired to our tents there was a noisy
storm. The lightning flashed, the thunder crashed; and
Sonja, unseen by anybody, stood naked at the centre of the
camp, letting the rain course over her tingling flesh. ('It
wass great,' she told me the next day.)

In the morning we were woken before dawn. Driven for
an hour to see a bunch of rocks on the far side that were
even more beehive-shaped and weird, then up another
gorge to a huge domed cave with a perfect echo. Despite
the extraordinary splendour of her surroundings, Sonja was
in an agony of indecision. Should she get off the bus at
Derby, so she could go and see the Windjana Gorge? Or
should she go straight on to Broome and meet up with
Nigel? She liked Nigel, but . . .

'You must do what you want to do, Sonja,' I said.

'Yes. But I don't know what I want to do.' She laughed.
'Oh, I'm crace-ey. I must enjoy zese Bunkles . . .'

At eleven there was the optional helicopter flight, where
for $120 you could experience for yourself the aerial view
that had made the rock formations famous. Truly, they
were a post-modern phenomenon. The clambering around
gorges was all very well, but it was like trying to appreciate
the Mona Lisa on your knees with an eyepatch over one
eye. To get the full, breathtaking bizarreness of them you
had to be twenty-five feet above them, as I was now – then
soaring over a precipitous cliff, revealing a dizzy drop to a
gorge-bottom far below – then diving down into the shade

of a chasm – then up into the sunshine over row upon row of bulbous domes – this isn't *reality*, I kept telling myself, clutching the handle above the tiny diving bubble's door.

Back in the minibus Sonja leant towards me. 'Now I've decided,' she said. 'If Nigel is on the bus tonight I will go to Broome. If he isn't I will go to Derby.' She smiled, relieved at her decision. 'I'm sinking, if he's on the bus, he cares about me a little.'

'Yes.'

'But I don't sink he'll be on the bus.'

'No?'

'No.' She shook her head and smiled. 'I don't sink so.'

At Turkey Creek the afternoon passed slowly. The place was just a garage, a store and a sprinkle of bungalows down the road from an Aboriginal community. Every hour or so a huge road train would draw in to refuel. Then a bunch of Aboriginals would appear in a Landcruiser to load up with ice-cream and sweeties. 'No,' said Sonja, 'I don't sink he will come. But I'll go to Broome anyway, because I'm too tired. I need to rest before I see another gorge.'

Standing outside by our suitcases she suddenly turned and gave me a long, emotional hug.

At 8.10 precisely the bus arrived, a horseshoe of orange lights down the dark empty road. And who should be there, clean-cut and cheerful, but Nigel. Throwing a twisted little smile at me she fell into his proprietorial embrace.

# 13

# Boat People

A mile up the creek, past the foreshore camps of a curving
beach, where Malay sail-makers bend to the big white canvases, and the caulking-mallets of ships' carpenters ring from
morning till midnight, is the Japanese quarter – Sheba Lane.
There you may see sleek little Yum-Yums and Suzukis that,
having come in before the passing of the Aliens' Restrictions
Act, are elderly now, but with their high-piled hair still raven,
and a solemn, smiling politeness, always charming. Here are
the Chinese stores that provide biting curries, tumeric and
blachan for the Malay crews; Chinese tailors bending above
their sewing-machines, innocent as Smee the pirate in *Peter
Pan*; the Tokyo Club and the Jap boarding houses, head-
quarters of the divers ashore; the shell-packing shed and the
old Roebuck Hotel, that looks out on Buccanneer Rocks,
where Dampier beached his crazy sloop two hundred and
fifty years ago, and just missed the big news of a new continent. Still she comes, they say, when the south-easter sings
in the shrouds before the season of mists, the ghostly *Roebuck*
into Roebuck Bay, a mysterious frigate of other days, with
sails milky-vague as the moonlight, and that should she pass
you close enough you may even see upon her poop deck,
cloaked and high-hatted, the shade of Black Bill Dampier,
who feared neither the devil nor the deep sea, buccanneer
and cut-throat, figure-head of a new world.*

So wrote Ernestine Hill in 1935. Now 'Chinatown' was two

* Ernestine Hill, *The Great Australian Loneliness* (Jarrolds, London, 1937)
– p. 57.

placid little streets of white, iron-roofed buildings refurbished as tourist shops and galleries with names like Kimberley Kreations. The phone boxes and bus-stops were done up with kitsch little pagoda-style helmets. The Roebuck Hotel was a Motel-cum-Backpackers'. Even the old jail had been turned into The Original Broome Lock-Up and Coffee Shop. (Only Sun Pictures, the open-air 'picture-garden' with its original 1916 interior, retained – some of – the romance I'd hoped for.)

I'd imagined a compact, bustling little port. But beyond the big, central green where a clutch of Aboriginals staggered in familiar caricature poses the rest of the bungalowed town was so spread out that a bicycle was recommended as the best way to get around.

I pedalled off west, pessimistically seeking adventure. By the Seaview Shopping centre (more bogus chinoiserie) I found the little Broome Museum, presided over by a grumpy Yorkshireman reading the *Weekly Telegraph*. Holiday-making couples were losing themselves for a few minutes in the black and white records of that vanished world of Japanese pearl-divers and Jewish gem-buyers, of fortunes gained and lives lost, of fathoms, furled sails, moonlight and corroborees... before returning with a bump to the banal, cappuccino-guzzling present.

A little further down the track I came to Mangrove Point and, looking out along the sandy curve of Roebuck Bay towards the distant harbour and jetty, began to understand how you might, after all, grow fond of Broome. It was the sea–sand combination that did it: the loveliest, milkiest aquamarine set against the deepest red-gold. In the beach-side Stairway Café they were talking about dolphins; I'd just missed three.

I turned left, swigging at my waterbottle as I pedalled down shimmeringly hot tarmac through the Broome Industrial Estate. Here romance took a back seat again as Paint, Blinds and Power Tools gave way to Lambs Vacation Village, the Broome Golf Club and the Pearl Coast Pet

Motel. Seeing a roughly scrawled sign saying ART EXHIBI-
TION I stopped on a whim. What did I expect? Gaudy oils
or splish-splosh watercolours of local scenes – certainly not
an installation about boat people by a blow-in.

Peter Cosgrave (a.k.a. Phedair MacOscair) was a serious-
eyed, curly-haired Irishman of almost exactly my age. He'd
found one of the Cambodian Boat People's boats,
impounded by Customs, left to rot and be eaten by white
ants in the dunes, and turned it into furniture. It was such
beautiful rainforest wood, he enthused, running his fingers
down the deep grain of a tabletop. 'What I'm trying to do
is show people that this wood is useful. The other boats
are just crunched up and buried. But the wood is a commodity. I think to let it rot – that's wrong.'

In among the tables and chairs were sculptures made
from other 'found objects': pearl shells, fishing line, one
involving a prosthetic leg he'd picked up on Cable Beach.
Another was a driftwood model of the kind of house Pol
Pot had locked his enemies in, which Peter had filled,
poignantly, with objects he'd found on the abandoned boat:
tiny old-fashioned aspirin bottles, a needle, a battered
brooch. By the entrance was a display of newspaper cut-
tings: the group of one hundred and eighteen refugees had
been one of the biggest to enter Australian waters since the
late Seventies.

He was a lost Damien Hirst, was Peter. For *Black and
White 1984* he'd built a table in the shape of Africa which
he'd chopped up with a chainsaw. Meanwhile a black guy
who'd started off sitting on the table drumming was banished to a corner of the performance space. The action had
ended with the black guy trying to put the pieces of the
table back together again and failing. *WASP*, about the
world created by White Anglo-Saxon Protestants, had presented a giant (twenty-foot) wasp that had slowly, then
with increasing speed and frenzy, stung itself to death.
Another piece about modern and primitive man had featured a guy sawing up a sheep while Peter dived out of an

Ionic Greek column and was attacked by a hunchback. (This one, I confess, I didn't quite follow.)

When he saw I was cycling Peter insisted I borrow his car. It was a battered white Holden with a big lamp mounted centrally at the front. The roo bar had an enormous ostrich feather tied to its centre. There was no back window and no ignition key, just a little makeshift knob that fired the engine.

This was more like it! In my bizarre new transport I sped comfortably down the long straight road to the port; paced purposefully out along the narrow pier, chatted to a lounging Indian crewman on board the moored *Geo Pacific, Panama* (they were 'looking for oil'). By the empty dirt road at Gantheaume Point there was nothing but the wind and red-ochre rocks petering into the azure. On the far side of the promontory, Cable Beach was a magnificent clean sweep of white sand and surf down to a Forbidden City of mock-Chinese at the Cable Beach Club; where, by a reception desk manned by eager chaps with floppy blond hair, a sour-faced, exquisitely dressed young woman flicked in bored fashion through *Australian Vogue*.

Peter's home was the lower half of a cream clapboard house with a long veranda right next to a huge mango tree. The ripe orange fruit, half-squashed most of it, littered the driveway and lush long grass of the lawn. Narelle, his Aboriginal wife, was away in Perth and there was rather a lot of wine left over from the exhibition's opening. With the candle flickering on the table under the slowly revolving fan we talked about Peter's preoccupation with the nuclear threat, which was, he thought, 'far from past'. He was more than happy to be away from Europe, which was basically, now, 'just an ex-warfield industrialised to the hilt'. Quite apart from the acid rain and the p.h. balances in Swedish lakes the fish stocks in the North Sea were annihilated. Not a herring left. The Irish Sea was the most radioactive sea in the world. If you had a trawler in Dublin, well, you had to go a hundred and fifty miles either way before you could start fishing. Did I know the fish that came into Dublin off the Welsh Coast were all run through a geiger counter to check whether they were radioactive—

We were interrupted in this line of argument by a plump, blond-bearded, red-faced fellow called Bruce who worked in a Rehab Centre for Aboriginal alcoholics on the edge of town. He certainly knew his subject, swilling back claret as if it were Ribena. He was an ex-journo, had been the editor of the *Broome News* at one time. He was writing a book too, he told me. Well, he was going to write a book. He had all the documentation. He just had to pull it together.

His subject was Lord McAlpine, Mrs Thatcher's chum, ex-Treasurer of the British Conservative party, who had, famously, 'fallen in love with Broome' and been responsible for much of its 1980s renovation and development. Bruce shook his head and gurgled into his wine. 'Lord McAlpine of West Green, the Saviour of Broome. Pig's bum was he the saviour of Broome, mate.'

The English lord, Bruce said, putting a surprisingly antagonistic spin on 'lord', had first come to WA in 1974. His father had sent him over to do deals in Perth. He'd returned in 1980, around the time the Labour Party in WA were beginning to change their face. New people were coming in, the young up-and-coming lawyer set from the universities. Men like Brian Burke and David Parker, who were to become Premier and Deputy Premier respectively. McAlpine had got to know them.

On a holiday, he'd come north to Broome. He'd liked the place. Bought an old house and the Sun Pictures cinema. Then he'd gone away.

A year or so later, Labour won the election. 'And it all started to happen for Broome.' McAlpine went into partnership with the Government's newly launched business and development arm – WA Inc. – and built the Cable Beach Club. Nobody knew what it had cost, but $70m was a fair estimate.

Then McAlpine had started his famous zoo. Then he and

his partner had decided to branch out. South of Broome they'd bought a hotel in Exmouth and plans were drawn up to develop that little resort too, again in partnership with WA Inc. who were going to build a marina.

In the North, meanwhile, McAlpine had bought a huge area of land called Woolcott Inlet. In 1978 this had been recommended for a National Park. Now the National Park was forgotten and McAlpine had acquired the newly created pastoral lease for $20,000 dollars. 'It was 250,000 hectares of land, so they got it off the Government for around 80 cents a hectare. It's a beautiful place,' Bruce added. 'Very difficult to get into. You can really only get there by sea. It's also very important to Aboriginal people. There wasn't much consultation with them either.'

The *Broome News* had written about McAlpine's activities at Woolcott Inlet and they'd got sued. For $5m dollars. 'And we won,' said Bruce, a triumphant smile crossing his rubicund features. 'I won. The *Broome News* won.'

Shortly after that the Royal Commission into WA Inc. had been set up. The zoo was closed down, it was announced that McAlpine was facing financial difficulties, then he'd left Broome and Australia, apparently for good. As a result of the Royal Commission's findings both the Labour Premier, Burke, and Parker, his Deputy, had been sent to jail, where they still languished, along with a number of other leading WA politicos and millionaires.

Those were the facts. The allegations were wilder. They ranged from quite plausible suggestions that McAlpine had helped Burke to raise political funds using the same techniques he'd developed for Margaret Thatcher in Britain; through wilder accusations that secret deals had been done with developers – if they contributed they'd be awarded with contracts after the election; to outrageous charges that he'd been a dealer in stolen Aboriginal artefacts and endangered species. ('I saw them with my own eyes,' Bruce told me, after he'd described going to McAlpine's house for a party, opening a freezer by mistake to find row upon row of champagne bottles, and nestling among them, two incredibly rare frill-necked lizards.) None of it was true, surely, but it made for a good story, as the claret went down and the crickets sang in the darkness.

## Another Immigrant

Whom should I find on the Greyhound bus south but Sonja and Nigel, flushed and happy after their three days in a motel near Cable Beach. Nigel grinned and shook my hand and Sonja came down to my seat to show me her snaps of the Bungle-Bungles. Her thing with Nigel was more than just a holiday fling. They got on so well. She felt so relaxed with him. 'You know. When you know it feels right. You know what I mean. You *know*. That's how it is with Nigel.'

Six hundred kilometres down the track, across an endless blasted heath of spinifex and mulga, Port Hedland loomed into view. Huge conical piles of white salt dazzled in the afternoon sun. Behind, the gantries and pipes and chimneys of the iron works rose from a rust-red landscape: everything in the place was covered with a finger-smudgeable coating of iron dust. (The town had no cashpoints; they had yet to invent a machine that didn't get clogged.)

By the sea-channel where a huge container ship was being loaded up with iron ore, I found the Pier Hotel. The courtyard bar was full of well-developed men with tattoos and goatee beards, direct eye contact with whom it was probably best to avoid. There was a terrible din of heavy rock. Up on a central wooden stage in the sunshine two leggy young blondes in g-strings gyrated lewdly.

Out at Cooke Point, having fibbed my way into the leaf-strewn visitor's yard at the Detention Centre, I found the man I'd come to see, Fok Kheng, who'd been locked up for four and a half years since arriving from Cambodia in a boat exactly like the one Peter had recycled into tables.

He was in his early twenties, in his neat blue tracksuit

as clean-cut, well mannered and potentially productive a young man as the most xenophobic Australian housewife could hope to meet. Just now, though, he was suffering from dreadful headaches and was unable to sleep. There'd been hunger strikes among the detainees, then a spate of suicides – seven, he thought. 'Such things happen make me think a lot and worry a lot about myself.'

Most of all, though, he worried about being sent home. 'Some night they going to grab us back to Cambodia, that's the main thing I think about, because this been happen to the Chinese. That's the main thing that make me think a lot and make me headache and also just frustrated to get out of here.'

Sometimes, Fok said, he felt he hated the Australians because they'd kept him locked up for so long. On the other hand he knew that return to Cambodia meant death. 'They have spies inside the province and if they want to kill us they can kill us.'

If he was released, yes, he'd like to live in Australia, even though the rest of his family was now in the States, where they were free.

Had he known, I asked him, when he'd got on the boat, that he would almost certainly end up interned – Australia's policy being to send a clear signal to the hordes of potential Asian refugees.

'When I got on the boat I thought only three days to come to Australia. I thought that when I arrive in Australia they'd not lock me up, at least that's what I thought in the beginning. Also I did not know it'd end up twenty-eight days to get to Australia. With the very rough seas and big waves and we were very frightened. Especially we had seasick.

'When we got to Darwin, they search us and they check us everything and then they bring us out into the bush and they set up a tent like a soldier tent and they put us there for about five months and after that they bring us into the

town, and we stay there about one year. Then we come
here.'

Back in the Free World there was a fine array of cocktails
to choose from. They included HARD ON, SPERMCOUNT,
QUICK FUCK and SLIPPERY NIPPLE.

'Normally,' said a large, moon-faced woman at the bar,
'I prefer a Slippery Nipple. But tonight I thought I'd try a
Quick Fuck.' I looked hard in the direction of the barmaid
and prayed she wasn't being suggestive.

It wasn't a problem looking hard in the direction of the
barmaid. She was about eighteen, had a near perfect figure,
and was wearing nothing but lacy black knickers and bra.
Having no knowledge of the respectable WA calling of
'skimpy barmaid' I thought she was remarkably poised,
pouring drinks in her underwear in front of twenty of the
toughest-looking sons of guns I'd seen in my life.

When moon-face had tottered off to the loo, I smiled at
a strangely familiar-looking blonde girl sitting two stools
down.

'Where you from?' she asked.

'London.'

She laughed. 'You've got tourist written all over you.'

'The hat?'

'That and the bag.'

'So what d'you do? I asked, in best English fashion.

'Raunchy dancer,' she replied, in the same way she might
have said 'bank clerk' or 'beautician'.

'Ah – right.' Now I recognised her. She was one of the
gyrating-buttocked g-strings of the afternoon, now demure
as a librarian in long skirt and tightly buttoned top.

Twenty-four hours later I was rattling south towards Perth.
On the faster, inland route there were just two passengers:
myself and a part-Aboriginal youth who was glued to the
ever-present video.

Outside the view was spectacular: the loaf-shaped hills

and chocolate-brown rocks of the Chichester and Hammersley Ranges glowed crimson-pink in an Ayer's-Rock-style sunset; to the right the sky was a fabulously layered chiaroscuro of orange and blue-grey, the tiny trees etched in glimmering silhouette along the ridge. Even the reflection of *Hot Shots 2* in the window couldn't spoil it.

I slept badly through the stops and shuffling embarkations; woke to a bleak yellow dawn. Then the sun was up on huge undulating honey-coloured wheatfields, broken by copses of taller, grander eucalypts, more like those at Belltrees than anything else I'd yet seen; the silhouettes slumped in their shade were sheep, not Aboriginals. The farmsteads were neat little places, with stone gateposts and formal driveways. The dry gullies were no longer 'creeks'; they were 'brooks'. Stepping down for breakfast there was an unfamiliar chill in the air.

The coach-driver was humming now, wittering flatulently over the mike to his little captive audience of fifteen. 'Doo-dee-doo-dee-doo . . . No, folks, I can't whistle either.' Then, suddenly, there was Perth, six and a half little skyscrapers across a gently rolling landscape of smallholdings, market gardens, here and there fir trees – an almost French scene.

In twenty-four hours' time I would be sitting in the airport with tears in my eyes as a choir of forty little girls in black and red uniforms sang 'Silent Night' and through the sliding doors from International Arrivals came . . .

A fat Malaysian gentleman in a brown suit.

A beautiful troop of saronged air-hostesses from the Singapore flight.

A middle-aged Italian woman who was immediately surrounded by a huge, weeping family.

At last, an hour late, looking altogether younger, thinner and wispier than I'd remembered, my girlfriend, Leonie.

# 14

## Club Perth

There is of course no class system in Australia but none the less the two lovely beaches on the surfless north-western side of the Cape Naturaliste Peninsula attract a decidedly different sort of punter. Meelup, which is larger, and just a short ride from the caravan parks of Dunsborough, has beefy blokes with short hair, very tight crimson speedos and voluptuous wives in canary-yellow bikinis who threaten to smack their naughty, noisy children. Eagle Bay, smaller, ten kilometres on towards the light-house, an elegant curve of clapboard *residences secondaires*, has languid, pigeon-chested chaps who stroll out of the exquisitely rippling turquoise and say, 'Annette! Haven't seen you in ages. How long are you *down* for?'

Meelup has a hot dog van; on the hill above Eagle Bay is Wise's Winery, where you can sit, growing fonder of the thickly forested green valley beneath with each sip of the vineyard's own Oak-Matured Chardonnay, attended to by pony-tailed young studs who put Claridge's to shame. 'D'you want the *crostini* now?' 'Is your wine still cold enough, sir?' they cosset obligingly, without even a flicker of superciliousness.

Leaving at 3.30 you decide that, stuff it, you're on holiday, and you'll go back to Eagle Bay.

'They're putting pressure on Rory to do something about

it,' say the men you float gently past. 'It's not a thing we should take into the criminal courts, I don't think.'

The women, stringier and scraggier by and large than their Meelup counterparts, admire each others' dogs and wonder what to do with the turkey leftovers. 'Ah've been reading all these rissipies,' says a woman with a Jo'burg accent.

'I'm going to go for a little walk now,' says a pot-bellied greybeard who, though only up to his ankles, is wearing a watch suitable for diving several miles under.

'*His* story is that he's separated from his wife . . .'

I fall into a gentle and exquisite doze.

'She exercises all the time' . . . 'I ree-versed, I thought oh my god' . . . 'Tennis?' . . . 'Better get there before the youthful tribes' . . . 'Took a blinder at short leg, it just went clunk and out it came' . . . 'Were they hee-ah last yee-ah?' . . . 'Oh – how are *yew*?'

We'd laughed at the Christmas decorations against the endless blue sky of central Hay Street. We'd sat on the veranda of the Blue Duck in Cottesloe, watching the surf white under the moon, as Santa, in full beard and robes, had climbed in at the window and boogied with an office party. We'd taken the squeaky-clean, *carpeted* Transperth overground down to trendy Victorian Fremantle, drunk Macchiatoes at Old Papa's, banana smoothies at the market, and been tunelessly serenaded with 'In the Bleak Midwinter' by a sweaty little girl in a gold witch's hat.

We'd hired a big white car and sped south, *Priscilla* as our soundtrack. We'd been disappointed by Busselton and Bunbury, then found the wonderful curve of surf at Yallingup, swum with dolphins at Margaret River, driven on through the spectacular, sunlit-dappled jarrah forests to cold and windy Augusta. Inland, by the darkly reflecting waters of the Blackwood River, we'd been driven crazy by the flies, ended up eating our picnic waist-deep midstream.

On down through Balingup, Bridgetown ('Santa arrives

on a Fire Truck 7.00 p.m.'), Manjimup and Walpole to be
disappointed by our holiday grail of Albany, where the sky
was grey and the landlady of our 'English Guest House'
so gin-stinkingly drunk she could barely climb the stairs.
Turning back, we'd stumbled on the magical lagoon of
Green's Pool, then returned to our favourite Margaret River
only to discover that it was everyone else's favourite too
and there wasn't a bed to be had. Except in the brand-new
Adamson Riverside Apartments where the carpets were
fresh off the roll and Thelma our landlady, who'd been
waiting for this opportunity for fifteen years, thoughtfully
added two quarter bottles of Carrington's sparkling-pink
'Blush' to our Christmas morning 'brekky tray'. Contrary to
my lifelong fantasy the beach at lunchtime was not
shoulder to shoulder with bronzed Aussies having turkey
and plum pudding in the sun; indeed we, with our elaborate picnic, were the only people on it.

In the evenings we'd caught up with such delights as the
year-before-last's Christmas Special of *Birds of a Feather*.
Back in Perth we'd cheered in the New Year with the Northbridge crowds, waving sparklers and pink plastic trumpets
in the air. We'd had a wonderful holiday and I'd been
reassured of the truth of Jonathan Raban's dictum that, for
best results, travel writers should go alone.

But now I *was* alone, gazing at a man with a face roughly
stained with rouge chomping on his dripping fried egg.
Another guest, with veins on his nose and a wobbly mouth,
shook visibly as he attacked the off-pink sausage that
resembled a flayed penis. The 'orange juice' was not orange
juice at all, but thin orange *drink*. The fruit salad fizzed; it
had surely been there for days. The heap of processed white
bread by the toast machine curled up like parchment; the
thin brown coffee stewed evilly in the bottom half-inch of
the glass filter pot.

Last night, up in my narrow cell with the sick-green
walls (EDWARDIAN OPULENCE lied the key tag) I'd dined

off the remains of the sushi given to us as a New Year present by the very nice man at our favourite little Japanese restaurant in Hay Street; washed down, tragically, with two tepid stubbies of VB, while I'd watched the *Clive James New Year's Eve Special* all the way from Blighty. It had been good to see Clive's egregious mug again and catch up on the latest jokes about John Major and Boris Yeltsin, but it had also made me dreadfully homesick, made me wonder whether I could perhaps call my book *Everywhere but the South* and be done with it.

In the pillowed comfort of the holiday I'd vowed that I wasn't going back to a Backpackers' again, but pacing along the BO-scented blue corridors after breakfast I passed the open door of a single room three along from mine. It was the same old man as yesterday, skin and bones in a pressed nylon shirt, sitting on his made-up bed watching the TV. At 10 a.m. on a bright, blue, cloudless summer's day. *Oh Christ!*

I made a phone call and delivered myself over the railway to the Northbridge YHA. What a contrast! For a third of the price I had a view down the late-Victorian buildings of William Street to the sleek grey silhouettes of the skyscrapers beyond. Directly opposite, a red-brick campanile looked down on little black tables and chairs in the courtyard of Vulture's Restaurant. A slender eucalypt beside it waved sinuously. The breeze tickled my crimson curtains, bringing with it the comforting melodies of Sade, casting dancing shadows in the square of sunlight on the roughly whitewashed wall.

Perth in January was like London in August. Hot, half-deserted, all the important people away. Phoning my list of contacts I kept on getting answerphones and secretaries. 'We are knee-deep in the turquoise waters of Eagle Bay. Please call back at the start of February.'

I'd read that Perth was 'the remotest city in the world'. Now I felt it. In the East, the Centre, even in Darwin I'd had a surfeit of phone numbers. Not here. My friends in the East who'd been regularly to Europe had never even visited WA.

With no one to talk to I sat in the trendy cafés of Northbridge drinking iced coffee, watching the cool young dudes and sheilas wandering past in their designer shades.

'The man himself! Howyagarn?'

'Good thanks.'

'*Yoo-hoo!* Haircut!'

Back alone to my cell at the YHA. A half-smile exchanged maybe with a fellow backpacker, then to bed with the windows closed tight and wax plugs in my ears. Relaxed and pleasant though it was by day, by night Northbridge became a disco inferno, a blaring no-sleep zone of bands and clubs and pitilessly grooving youth.

## Tiggy Puggenheim in Widji

In Albany, we had visited an extraordinary warehouse-sized gallery called the Extravaganza – a showcase for West Australian art and craft. It was an odd mixture of stuff: classic cars, kites, sheoak furniture, turtles carved from jarrah, cases of Margaret River wine and, all around, walls crowded with art ranging from studiously representational watercolours of familiar WA scenes to ... well, what *was* this? I'd wondered, coming upon a hand-coloured print of a series of sketches, mounted in an elaborate gilt frame. *Gauguin and I saw these cave paintings on tues, when painting in the bush* was scrawled under a pointillist drawing of a pelican. *I must try dots like the aboriginal paintings in my next work in Paris* was the note by a leaping orange and yellow kangaroo. Underneath was printed, on artificially age-mottled paper:

> SEURAT'S WIDJIMORPHUP NOTEBOOK
> INK AND WATERCOLOUR ON FRENCH PAPER
>
> Used by Seurat to describe the Australian

> landscape and Aboriginal dot paintings that
> he later developed into the Pointillist Movement.
> Acquired by Tiggy Puggenheim in 1959.

The artist was Leon Pericles, famous not just in WA but (greatest of compliments over here) 'Australia-wide'; the joke, I discovered, visiting him in his studio in North Perth, was in two elaborately realised stages.

Part One was Widjimorphup, a fictional West Australian outback town he'd first dreamed up while doing post-graduate studies in Birmingham, England. The butt of Monty-Python-style teasing by his fellow students Leon had disarmed them by drawing satirical sketches of his own. 'One of the first ones was a painting of a one-armed violinist playing at the Widjimorphup Sheep Festival. It was just a flippant name I invented very quickly.' (Years later he'd discovered the subliminal source of his inspiration when he'd been contacted by the tradesmen of a real WA outback town called Widgimooltha. Was it too late, they'd asked, for him to change the name of his successful fiction from Widjimorphup to Widgimooltha?)

The town wasn't exactly modelled on Meekatharra, where Leon had grown up and his father had been publican of the local hotel. If anything, he said, it owed more to nearby Cue, once a booming goldmining town, now (pop. 399) 'dying from neglect and lack of finance'. Whatever, 'Widji' had undoubtedly become the centre of Leon's imaginative world. Etchings, screenprints, collagraphs and collages on outback themes had titles like 'The Widji Clock Shop', or 'Widji Starline Drive-In'. 'Down Town Widji' showed the single main street: Greasy Sam's on the corner next to the Family Chemist, Farm Supplies and the Honest Trading Co. Further along was Dodgy Dave's Second Hand Shop and the Stuffed Toucan Night Club.

In 1983, at a one-man show in Perth, Pericles had gone the whole hog. Works on display purported to be by members of the Royal East Widjimorphup Art Society.

There was a souvenir stand of 'Widji' T-shirts, pens, post-cards, emu eggs and 'tasteful mallee-root sculptures'. At the opening, actors took the roles of Shirl, Gayleen and Sybil (the Steering Committee of the Widji Art Society), the Lord Mayor, and members of the Fruit Fly Control Board. Appropriately, distant superstar Dame Edna Everage had consented to be the patron of the society.

Part Two of the joke was now being realised in an exhibition that Pericles was on the point of taking on an Australia-wide tour. 'Tiggy Puggenheim' had been born after a Pericles family visit to Venice in 1980. A wealthy American art-collector who has known all the greatest figures in European twentieth-century art, Tiggy has moved, in her declining years, to Widjimorphup, 'wooed by the unpretentiousness and egalitarianism of Australian country folk' ('the Tiggy Puggenheim story also began to echo the real-life story of Lord McAlpine' said the accompanying lavish hardback) and has brought her magnificent collection with her.

### MATISSE, SUNDAY AFTERNOON WITH TIGGY AND THE GOLDFISH

Tiggy posed for this work on the day she gave Matisse the goldfish which he used in many later works. These sacred national living treasure goldfish were originally a gift to Tiggy from the Japanese Emperor but Matisse in an intense painting session accidentally washed his brushes in the fish bowl. The precious fish died causing a political rift that many believe eventually led to the involvement of Japan in the Second World War. Accessioned to the Tiggy Puggenheim Collection in 1951.

Other works on display included Vincent van Gogh's 'Sunflowers for Tiggy', Salvador Dali's 'Five Seconds after the Egg Germinated at Tiggy's Tea Party', Kandinsky's 'Out Yachting with Tiggy'. All had similar lighthearted provenances.

What was most interesting to me was not Pericles's

affectionate mockery of a rural Oz now rapidly becoming history, nor even his two-fingers-up to patronising Europe and, indeed, the cultural cringe – but how prosperous he was. Even my taxi-driver remarked on the splendour of his house; (the adjoining studio was topped by a folly in the shape of a terracotta bell-tower). 'Yes,' Leon told me, 'Australia has this voracious appetite for its own art. We really are trying to find our culture and we support artists very well here. None of my colleagues from Birmingham are doing very well at all. Yet they're not any less talented or producing less good work. It's just that England has got this incredible history to compete with. European art is all there. Here we're on our own and the patrons really want to support us.'

## A Fair Go

Queuing in an off-licence I'd heard a couple of crisp South African accents fussing over their choice of wine; and remembered that in the bad old days of apartheid, supporters of the pro-reform Progressive Federal Party – the PFP – were mischievously nicknamed 'Packing For Perth'.

Now I called on Robert, a Cape Town barrister who'd made the break three years before and was already a partner in a prosperous Perth firm, with a big desk high up in one of the six and a half skyscrapers and a lovely view down to the white sails bending on the broad blue expanse of the Swan River.

Remembering South Africa he tensed up visibly; moving to describe his new life in Australia you could see the softening of his manner.

'Is there a sense now,' I asked him, 'as you lie in you bed at night, of relief . . .'

'Oh-h,' he replied with a sigh. 'I couldn't explain it to you. Couldn't put monetary terms on it. That absolute sense of relief that you don't have to fear for your personal

safety, for your family. You know, Perth is losing its inno-
cence. It's gradually becoming a city. But we used to boast
when we first got here and wrote home, "You don't have
to lock your windows and doors." '

Sick of the violence in South Africa, fearful of the future,
it had been getting married that had finally galvanised him
into making the move. 'It was that that opened up my eyes
to: Where could I get a peaceful future for any children I
want to bring into the world? Then he'd seen an advert in
the South African *Sunday Times.* 'Do you want to come to
Perth?' it had read. He discovered that he could requalify
as a lawyer in a single year. Having visited England and
seen 'the pathetic excuse of a London sun' and being in
any case a dedicated surfer, he'd decided to take up the
offer. Now he raved about his adopted country.

'The wonderful thing I find about Australians is they're
a very tolerant democratic society, they're very flexible,
it's a very open society. I doubt whether we South Africans
could advance so rapidly in this society to senior positions
if it hadn't been so flexible and tolerant. It's the old cliché.
We will give everyone a fair go. Australians do that. And
I admire them for that. It's a melting pot of all cultures and
they judge you for the quality of your person and your
ability. If you're prepared to work hard and make a go of
it anyone can be a success in Australia.'

He liked the sense of humour, the political freedom, the
fact that politicians could be lampooned in the media. 'They
can't strut like pompous idiots as our politicians did.'

Australia was also a caring society. Even as evidenced in
the little things: the parks in Cottesloe, with their play-
grounds and public barbecues; the cycle path to Fremantle.
'And the childcare facilities,' he smiled, 'I know it sounds
trivial but they're amazing.'

There were, Robert reckoned, over twenty thousand
South African emigres in Perth.

Had anyone gone back?

Yes, there was pressure on quite a lot of the marriages

because the wife had to do all the housework. Robert chuckled. 'There's a joke about this: the Johannesburg housewife would rather be murdered in her bed than have to make it.'

## Between Two Worlds

All around Northbridge there were posters for the Between Two Worlds exhibition at the Perth Museum. It dramatised the story of how, in the earlier years of this century, part-Aboriginal children had been forcibly removed from their mothers and put in homes, where they'd been trained to become domestic servants for whites. 'Assimilation' had been the policy then, and it had evolved from a very different way of thinking to ours. Here is Baldwin Spencer, Chief Protector of Aborigines 1911/12:

> It must be remembered that the half-castes are also a very mixed group. In practically all cases, the mother is a full-blooded aboriginal, the father may be a white man, a Chinese, a Japanese, a Malay, or a Filipino. The mother is of very low intellectual grade, while the father most often belongs to the coarser and more unrefined members of higher races. The consequence of this is that the children of such parents are not likely to be, in most cases, of much greater intellectual calibre than the most intelligent natives, though of course, there are exceptions to this . . .

Forced removals had been thought of, or at least described, as 'rescuing' part-descent children from 'the degradation of the blacks camp'. In institutions such as New Norcia and Moore River the children would be given 'a fair start on the road to a civilised life'.

> . . . we must not forget that these human beings are aborigines with the mind of a child, and are regarded as a distinct and separate race, outcasts in fact, who can never compete or live under the white man's conditions. They are so helpless when thrown upon their own resources, that were it not

for the protection they receive, but do not appreciate, their lot would be hopeless. As these people have to speak the white man's language it is but right that they should be taught to read and write that language. Beyond that it is doubtful whether a school education is of much benefit to them. The most that can be expected of them and for which they seem best adapted is general housework for the girls, and for the boys training to farm and pastoral pursuits . . .

(John Brodie, Superintendent, *Moore River Settlement*, 1926)

Now, in the 1990s, when 'self-determination' was the policy, the whole enterprise was seen as the cruellest of mistakes. Haunting music was set alongside taped testimonies of individual part-Aboriginals, now elderly, who'd never been reunited with their mothers. Pressing a button by their photograph you could hear them break down and weep when asked about this lifelong separation. There were photographs, schedules, descriptions of the atrocious food served up in the 'settlements', even a letter from a policeman who, charged with the grim practicalities of tearing a child from its mother's breast, had protested to his superiors, in deferential and unconfident terms, that surely this couldn't be a correct or humane policy.

At the end was a comments book. These were some of the reactions in the first week of 1995:

It's fantastic to be potentially creating an awareness of the atrocities of the past. We are all responsible to make black and white Australia come together in the future. A moving and thoughtful exhibition.

I am proud to say that these are my people.

As a white who does live among Aborigines I am ashamed more people are not aware of Australia's own APARTHEID system!!

Neglected the Emerald River Mission and the other side of the story – some Aboriginal people say even now they were better off at the missions because they were treated like vermin in their own communities. One sided (as usual).

If I had a choice either to see white or black people at the museum I would see white people as black people can get stuffed.

I am disgusted that things like this happened. But they did and it's over now. Best we all know about it and come to terms with it.

So sad to think my family may have been involved. Well done.

We cannot change the past. It is wrong to judge past events as wrong or right from our perspective.

I enjoy this place very much, but I expected more dinosaurs.


If I thought I had left Aboriginal issues behind with the heat and dust of the North, I was wrong. Though there were few 'full-bloods' in Perth, there was a large community of these 'part-descent' Aboriginals, many of whom had either experienced the policies of 'assimilation' directly, or were the children of those who had.

But if I was going to try and write about all this, I would have to be exceedingly careful, the thoughtful, liberal whites I met in Fremantle told me. What you didn't do, didn't *dare* do, was make any suggestion that someone who was of 'part-descent' was in some way not completely Aboriginal.

There was a famous writer in Perth called Sally Morgan, whose mother, Gladys, had been one of these 'rescued' children. When Sally had been little, Gladys had pretended, to the outside world, that she was white. Only in her teens had Sally discovered different. As an adult she'd written a book about her childhood, *My Place*, which details her gradual awareness of her otherness, before switching gear to tell the stories of her quarter-Aboriginal mother, and half-Aboriginal grandmother and great uncle. The book had become a surprise hit, selling over 420,000 copies Australia-wide; and being subsequently published in the UK, the USA and translated into nine other languages.

Here would be someone to meet, I thought. Perhaps, as

an outsider, I could put that question that made my Fremantle acquaintances throw up their hands in nervous
horror: Why, if you are only an eighth Aboriginal, do you
feel this need to identify so strongly with your 'Aboriginality'? Because of outside prejudice; because there is something about the Aboriginal tradition that you'd rather
identify with, or that you are prouder of than the white
tradition; because you seek, consciously or subconsciously,
to preserve the values of a culture that might otherwise
vanish? Or do these kinds of answers completely miss the
point?

In the back of my head I could hear all those voices from
the earlier part of my journey. 'The full-bloods are okay,
it's the half-bloods who live in the cities, who are neither
one thing or the other, that cause all the trouble . . .' I could
even see myself, sitting by the pool at Murray Hills, scoffing
quietly at the photographs of some of the 'Aboriginal'
artists (Sally Morgan, indeed; she painted as well as wrote)
who were paler than I am. 'All kinds of people are jumping
on the Aboriginal bandwagon,' I'd been told, often enough.

But it turned out that Sally no longer gave interviews.
There was no point in even calling her, said Clive Newman,
her publisher at the Fremantle Arts Press. After the success
of *My Place* she'd become something of a folk hero in
Australia. 'She did a couple of talkback TV shows, and
being a very articulate, very presentable, very attractive
Aboriginal woman the country embraced her. Basically,
because they felt comfortable with her. She wasn't one of
the fringe dwellers, that might have been drinking too
much, or sloppily dressed or whatever.'

Now she'd 'crawled back into her shell'. 'She feels
uncomfortable being the icon for Aboriginal Australia.'

However, Clive did also publish another part-descent
Aboriginal woman who might talk to me. She was May
O'Brien, whose children's books based on local Aboriginal
stories had just this year been taken onto the schools' cur-
riculum in WA. In some ways she might be more interesting

than Sally, as she'd been one of the institutionalised children herself, brought up on the Mt Margaret Mission near Laverton on the edge of the goldfields.

## May's Story

'When I was born, my mother was Aboriginal and my father was an Englishman. I don't know the story. I don't think it's a one-night stand. He was working up there for a while, out in the bush, looking for gold, see. When I was born my mother was too young. Working back from her death certificate she must have been thirteen or fourteen then.

'Both of them had no interest in me. At all. So I went from Aboriginal group to Aboriginal group within my own group family. It's under a kinship structure. You're just about related to everybody, not by blood, but through the extended family.

'So from a toddler I was boss of my own life. That's how kind Aboriginal families are. They'd take you in and look after you as if you were one of their own. I got tired of one lot so I'd go over *there*. In my day mothers were still breast-feeding the babies at five or six years of age. So if someone was feeding their baby I'd go to the other boob and have a feed.

'I ended up staying with this part-Aboriginal couple. But they couldn't look after me because they were trying for their citizenship rights and to get them they had to renounce all their relations and go and live like white people. You had to leave everybody behind when you got your citizenship rights. And you couldn't be seen talking to Aboriginal people because they'd put you in jail.

'So when I was about five I went to the mission at Mt Margaret. The Government never gave me permission to stay there. Even while I was little the policeman from Laverton used to come looking for me. The police were protectors, see. Their role was to take away every part-Aboriginal kid and send them down here to Perth. So when any white people came the mission people would say, "Go run for the bush." So we fair-skinned ones would go and hide.

'I had my name changed that many times I didn't know who I was. I had an identity problem! One minute my name was Margaret, next minute Genevieve, next Lorna . . .

'But the police wouldn't take us from inside the Mission. They were too scared of Mr Schenk, the Superintendant. He was German. Schenk, see. The police would have to argue with him. And we were safe because Mr Schenk would tell everybody about us. He had this network all round the world. He had a lot of people in England. Big strong group of English people used to write letters to the papers and all of this.

'My mother came to the Mission about three times while I was there. Just came and went. She'd only see me in the morning. Gone by the afternoon.

'We liked the Mission. Lots of Aboriginal people and white people they'd say, "Oh but the Missions are no good." But our Mission was *good*. All the United Aborigines Missions were good. What they were trying to do is educate us so that we could take our place in the wider Australian society. And in those early days they kept us from being shot and killed off. A lot of Aboriginal people were killed, you know. People used to just come and shoot at us like a pack of mongrel dogs.

'If the missionaries hadn't been there, our group would have all been dead and gone. And nobody would have given a damn about us. I tell you, we'd walk over glass to defend those white missionaries who came to Mt Margaret.

'I am what I am because of what the missionaries did for me. I wouldn't be in the position I am now. I wouldn't have become Superintendent of Aboriginal Education for the State of Western Australia if it wasn't for the missionaries. We had good teachers, and especially one called Mrs

Bennett. She was a famous lady in those days, a great advocate for Aboriginal people.

'She came from a rich English family, she'd been a lady-in-waiting. Then she'd married this captain of the P and O. When he died she just left England. Left her family. She didn't tell any of her family where she was going.

'She made us more English than the English. Taught us so much. Snap to attention when "God Save the King" was being played. Oh, and we had to speak correctly. She used to say to us, "You're not allowed to speak Aboriginal in the classroom." We had to speak English in the classroom.

'We had another English couple there too. Mr and Mrs Jackson. "Pop" we called him. Pop Jackson. He came from Lancashire, from the cotton mills. He used to play soccer. Oh, he used to do all kind of tricks with the ball, we couldn't get over it. We said, "Pop! Do those tricks with the ball!" He'd been a child labourer in the cotton mills. He didn't have a family either. We all loved Pop.

'It never entered my head about disliking white people till I left the Mission. And saw all the prejudice that's around. The Mission was quite a haven for us, 'cause we were out in the bush.

'I remember I was booked to go on this train. This lady came in and she looked in and I was in the carriage first and I'd got the bottom bunk. I wasn't going up there, I don't like heights. Anyway, she came in and she said, "Of course *I'll* be sleeping here." I said, "No you won't. I was first in. I'm staying here." She walked out and she must have seen the guard because I heard her saying, "I'm not going to sleep with that *native* in my carriage." So I had the whole carriage to myself, which was good!

'I went to church once in Adelaide. With a friend. I won't say the name of the church because I quite like this denomination. We sat in this row and – you know in those olden days when they had the gates to your pew? Anyway, we went in that pew, three Aboriginal ladies, we all went in and sat down. One of the elders came through and tapped us on the shoulder and told us we had to sit at the back. We marched out of that church and never went back!

'There were other things too. Like, "You haven't got any brains" and all of this. They'd make derogatory remarks and, you know, "It's only a *native*", and things like that.

'So I became very bitter about white people. I wondered what on earth God made white people for. Why they came to this country. This is our country. And they came and took over our country, stole it off us. I still believe they stole this country off us, and this is why there should be some sort of reconciliation and some sort of acknowledgement that they did take this country.

'So I used to be very angry. I used to lead protests and all of that. But then I changed when Billy Graham came to Australia in 1961. He talked on forgiveness. And I thought, Oh yes, that's it. It pricked my heart and my conscience.

'I'm proud to be Australian but I'm also proud to be Aboriginal. My Aboriginal past is the most interesting thing about my life. More than my affiliation with the white people. And I'm a better person because I've got both and because I'm between two cultures. Aboriginal culture hasn't died out, it's still going now, stronger than ever, because the kids who are growing up now still want to be proud of their Aboriginality.'


## Irene

Irene Stainton was Director of Link-Up, an Aboriginal agency which worked to try and reunite 'rescued' children with their surviving relatives. Her mother Helen had been one such, removed from her family to New Norcia, one of the institutions for 'fair-skinned' Aboriginals that May had been lucky to escape.

Irene was altogether angrier. Had May been like this before she'd heard Billy Graham? Had Helen had a harder life? Was it just a contrast of personalities? Or was it that the indignation belonged a generation down, to the children of those who had suffered. Like the shock being felt way after the accident; or the concerned, involved observer being strong enough to feel more aggressive about the justice of the case than the victim.

'My mother was removed from her mother and grew up in an institution. And when it was time for her to get married – I've seen her Native Welfare file – it says things like, "It'd be okay for these two *quadroons* to get married, because the likelihood is we're breeding out the colour" – so it was genocide.

'It was couched in terms of, "Yeah, you'll get a better deal, you'll get access to education, you'll get this, you'll get that," but the real thinking was to breed out the race.

'You look at statistics in terms of the number of kids that came out of those sorts of institutions and realistically they were only trained in terms of domestic services. My mother worked for the rich people that lived in Nedlands. That was the reality.

'She lived at Toodjay, which is a country town not far from Perth. She was the second youngest of a family of eight kids. Her father was a farmworker, a white man. All the other kids had an Aboriginal father. On her file it makes reference to the fact that Helen should be removed from those people because she had very fair skin. She would get a better deal if she was removed.

'Now on the file it says stuff like the farmowners wanted to employ her as a domestic for themselves so that she could be paid and in employment and still be close to her family. But the authorities said "no". It would be too detrimental to her future development to stay in that grouping with those people. So mother was removed to New Norcia, a Catholic set-up, a big brick-wall situation, it was almost like a prison, under the name of Christianity.

'So mother went there and I've seen references on her files that talk about her stepfather writing to the Department and trying to get her back. And the response that used to come back to the stepfather was, "Well, you're not her natural father so you don't have any say." So she was forced to be raised away from her family.

'Mother also went through the experience of being brainwashed in those various institutions. About denying Aboriginality. About being Aboriginal wasn't any good. About, "Your family don't want you, you wouldn't be here in this orphanage if your family wanted you." But the reality was that the family had been making all these approaches and of course Mother didn't know.

'Mother's seventy-six now, and it was only about five years ago that we got access to her Native Welfare files. So it's only since then that we've read the files to her and let her know the realities of what actually happened. For years she carried around that stuff of, "My family didn't want me so I'm an outcast." For *years*.

'So for me, as a child of someone who's been removed, there was no connection with cousins and aunts and uncles.

'My dad is an Aboriginal man, dark-skinned and fiercely proud of his Aboriginality. So for me being raised here in Perth it was a case of mixed messages. Like you had Father saying, "It's wonderful to be Aboriginal and you should be proud of it and you can do this for your people." And on the other hand Mother saying, "I don't like it, you shouldn't be, you can't tell people you are." Now Mother's reasons for saying that were: (a) that she'd been brainwashed about the value of being Aboriginal, but (b) she was scared stiff that we were also going to be removed.

'I would have been thirty years old before I actually gained acceptance within the Aboriginal community. Because you're neither one thing or the other. You've not been raised with an Aboriginal community background so you're not accepted. The Aboriginal community see you as thinking you're too good for them, standoffish. They don't look at what your background was or how you were raised. And on the other side, the white community don't want to know you. I mean, shit, you've got black skin! So you walk that tight line right down the middle.

'It's actually interesting, too, because I was married to an English guy and the Aboriginal community saw that as being, "Yeah, well, she thinks she's too good for us, so she's married to this white guy." And then, when the marriage broke down and I went to work for a housing company and I actually worked extensively with the Aboriginal Housing Board – that was like acceptance time for me. It was like, "She doesn't have this white partner, she seems to be okay, she's doing all these things for us."

'Yes, there is mistrust of the white community. The other thing, too, that happens within our community – I think you can trace it back to the European influence in the country – is that there's this, what I would call the tall poppy syndrome. Where you don't even trust your own and someone like myself perhaps that's seen as a bit of a high-flier is not only attacked by the non-Aboriginal community but even more severely by your own community, your own people.

'The people on the ground think you're wonderful. It's the people a little higher up in the community pecking order, who you're starting to surpass, then it's like, "This one's getting a bit big for her boots, let's pull her back." Within the Aboriginal structure prior to colonisation that wasn't the case. Whereas now it's very much the case.'

'An interesting thing for me, Irene,' I said, 'from the outside, is this thing of declaring your Aboriginality. Which is, presumably, a fairly modern development, is it?'

'It is. Before 1967, when the Aboriginals got voting rights, there was a feeling within us, as a people, that you didn't outwardly say, "Hey, I'm Aboriginal." Everyone knew you were. But in lots of circumstances it wasn't advocated. To get social security benefits, for example, you had to disclaim your Aboriginality.'

I gave Irene what I hoped was a tactful *precis* of The

Story; and an outline of what Philip the priest had told me in Alice Springs. 'So people say,' I concluded, ' "I'm prepared to listen to a full-blood, but I don't consider X or Y who's only part-Aboriginal to be speaking for Aboriginal people." '

She wasn't upset, angry, or even defensive. She just nodded and said, 'That's actually an interesting comment. That that's the view of rural people. In the city it's quite different. Here it's like, "Irene Stainton's accepted because she's articulate, she's obviously educated, she can't be one of *those* people, look her skin's quite fair, and look, she dresses immaculately, she's one of us, she's managed to assimilate." City folk would see me as assimilated and okay and why would she want to claim to be Aboriginal and why would she want to acknowledge her Aboriginality?'

The very question I'd been seeking an answer to. So why did she? It would be easy, Irene replied, to turn her back on it. But she felt it – she tapped her chest – in *here*.

'D'you think,' I asked, pushing it further, 'it's because there is this race of people that has survived, against all the odds, and now what you're doing, really, is saying, "I'm part of this race, this race is important, will be part of Australia, I represent the survival of this race – " '

'No, no. To me my stance is very simply: I got brown skin, doesn't look as if I'm ever ever ever going to be accepted totally by the non-Aboriginal community, because of the colour of my skin and because my heart's with the Aboriginal people, and our struggle isn't over, and I've got to be part of it.'

'That's the key thing I'm trying to get at. Why is your heart with the Aboriginal people? Because you will never be . . .'

'I'll never be accepted on the other side.'

'Yes?'

'Not totally, not totally. Ever.'

'And you're fully accepted, say, if you went to the Kimberley?'

'Oh yeah. I'm accepted everywhere. Now. But it's been a long struggle to gain that acceptance.'

## Over the River

Despite my initial enthusiasm for the YHA, I'd soon got fed up with nodding at broad-shouldered Canadians on the stairs, striking up conversations with giggling Japanese girls in the communal kitchen (they were always about to go cycling, alone, around Rottnest Island).

In desperation I phoned a number given to me by one of the women I'd met (for what? all of three hours) in Brisbane. How could I have mistrusted the ever-hospitable Brisbanites? Cassie was *expecting* me.

I swept on the freeway over the choppy, blue-grey expanse of the Swan and came to the southern suburbs. Here was another Perth. Street upon street of sprinkler-green grass, lush flowers and trees, charming detached bungalows with backyard pools.

Cassie and David were both lawyers. He, bald, cordial, softly spoken, was in his mid-forties, a partner in his own firm; she, blonde, attractive, vivacious, in her early thirties, had been with the same firm but now worked from home, doing adjudications on family court matters from the glass-topped table in the middle of their living room. They shared a huge *Saint* Ber-*nard*, Imran, who spent most of the day on his back in the corner of the lounge, snoring loudly.

She was Catholic; he was Jewish. She was from the East; he was from the West. WA was different, she said. For a start there were different names for everything. They called a party 'a show'; they called the pavement 'the verge'. ' "Don't park on the verge." In Brisbane they wouldn't park on the pavement anyway,' she laughed. 'They don't need to be told!'

Oh, Cassie missed Brisbane. She missed the gossip, the warmth. They were so much friendlier over there, weren't

they? Ridiculous, said David, still smiling as he disagreed.
That was because her friends were from Brisbane, there
was no way you could say a *place* was *friendlier*. Oh but
you could, said Cassie. I understood, didn't I? Brisbane
was just – much – friendlier.

This was a silly argument, said David, but yes, Western
Australia *was* different; they were so remote. Perth was the
remotest city in the world, said Cassie. Yes, David agreed,
Perth was the remotest city in the world.

Over the next few days, Cassie took delight in making
sure I got the most from Perth. 'I love doing this sort of
thing,' she told me. 'Organising people.'

So I became Suburban Man, riding into Perth on the little
green bus that stopped once an hour right outside their
house; but that neither of them had ever used, having a
car apiece. I made appointments and went to meetings.
'Obviously in Perth the beaches are a big thing,' said one
man. 'We've been through a bad patch with entrepreneurs,'
said another. 'It's not a bad lifestyle,' said another, 'if only
we had a bit more water. We've already got a sprinkler ban
between 8 a.m. and 8 p.m.' 'This is the most isolated city
in the world,' said another, 'and there's a tendency for
isolation to produce a burning desire to be the best. In
Perth, anything from the Eastern States is to be defeated. If
one of our players doesn't get picked in the Ashes team
it's only because they're Western Australian and the Eastern
Australians are trying to keep them out. It's a tremendous
incentive, but it's also a millstone round your neck because
everyone turns round and says, "We're being discriminated
against." ' There was still quite a feeling, said another, that
WA should secede altogether from the rest of Australia. In
1930 there'd actually been an attempt to do this and eighty-
two per cent of the people in WA had wanted to become
a different country. But it couldn't be done because the
constitution decreed that you had to have a majority of
people in a majority of states.

Back over the water Cassie would have cleaned the house

twice and be sitting in front of the word-processor working her way through another pile of child-support claims. 'I tell you what,' she'd say, hurling a file to the floor, 'these two should never have got divorced. They *deserve* each other.'

## Prix d'Amour

'Sand and millionaries and boring, boring, boring,' had been one East Coaster's summary of Perth; but though I'd seen plenty of sand I'd yet to meet a millionaire. The most prestigious, obviously, would be Alan Bond. But I was getting no reply from his lawyers; he wasn't to be found at the Blue Duck where he habitually had breakfast; and then – *bang!* – he was suddenly all over the headlines. BOND FACES $1B CHARGE read the *West Australian*. He was to be arrested and charged over a deal which was 'one of the most controversial of the WA Inc. period'. By the next day it was MASSIVE CRIMINALITY: BOND TO FIGHT $1B CHARGES, the journos were camped outside his Cottesloe mansion and I could kiss *that* interview goodbye.

Juanita Walsh had been Perth's premier gossip-writer during the high old days of the 1980s when the Labour Government was in power and Bondy was buying Van Goghs and McAlpine was in Broome and WA Inc. was a thrusting initiative and not the label attached to yet another jail term.

'It *was* incredible,' she told me. 'You just drank French champagne all the time, it was nothing but the best. I mean people would spend $5000 on a lunch and give champagne to everyone and have limousines waiting for you after-wards. Just over-the-top waste of money. It was bizarre. Because it became so real. I remember saying, and I genu-inely meant it, "Oh, not more Moët. Do I really have to drink Moët *again*? Oh not crayfish! Oh no!" ' In the sober daylight of the 1990s she half-raised a skilfully plucked eyebrow. 'It's a very bad way to be.' Now her newspaper days were over and, coolly elegant in mauve, she was organising functions for the Albion Hotel, Cottesloe.

'Anything now is very low-key, and is kept very quiet. People don't want it in the newspapers. So social columns have just died.'

What about the politicians and millionaires who were now in jail? Had she known them? Yes, of course. 'Because Perth's so small, it's not that many people, everybody that was sort of social knew them as a friend or knew of them. And now everybody that got hurt is angry, it's like, "Your friends robbed me," or, "Your friends are in prison." I've been in some awful arguments about it, but I say, "Hang on a minute." Because a lot of those people were very good to me, they didn't do anything to me, I didn't invest my money with them. They gave me money hand over fist for charity. And,' she met my eye and smiled, 'they were great *stories*.'

One millionaire who still survived to live in style, however, was Rose Hancock. She was the widow of Lang 'Raging Bull' Hancock, the man who had discovered the iron ore in the Kimberley and had subsequently become, they said, Australia's Richest Man. Rose, they went on, had been a penniless Filipino barmaid. Or worse. Whatever the truth, Lang had been in his seventies, Rose in her early thirties when they'd married; and it was under her supervision that their splendiferous white mansion, Prix d'Amour, had been built, on top of one of Perth's most exclusive Swan-side hills. Then there had been a long and public feud between Rose and Hancock's daughter, Georgina Rope-Rheinhardt, (followed by another quarrel between Rose and her own daughter, Johanna Lacson; both had been covered in frenetic detail by the glossy magazines Australia-wide).

Now it turned out that Juanita knew Rose, was in fact her great friend, would suggest to Rose that she might see me. Cassie was thrilled. 'Can I come too?' she asked, when the appointment was confirmed. 'I could always be the photographer or something.' 'Look, if it goes well,' she said, as she drove me across town on the Saturday afternoon, 'and you want me to come and pick you up I'll be at home. I'd do anything to get a stickybeak inside.'

I could see why. Prix d'Amour was quite a mansion. Gleaming white in a setting of formal French-style gardens (all gravel and topiary) it was on the itinerary of the Perth guided tours, and when Cassie and I drew up there were no less than three other sightseeing cars parked outside.

Pressing the entryphone at the tall, wrought-iron gates I got the distant voice of an Asian-accented maid. There was no record of my 2.30 appointment. 'They've gone to see a movie,' she said, 'phone later.'

'That's so rude,' said Cassie, as we drove home. 'I'm fuming, on your behalf.' Phoning later I got a sister who sounded exactly like the maid. No, Rose hadn't been to a movie; she'd had a relapse with her neck and had had to go into hospital for an X-ray. Could I try tomorrow please?

In the morning it seemed that I'd reached Rose herself. She sounded like a sleepy version of the sister and the maid. She was so sorry about the cancelled appointment, she never cancelled appointments, but just this morning she'd been taking sedatives for her neck, she was very tired, could I possibly try later, at 3.30 maybe. This time it was a smooth-sounding Transatlantic voice. No, Rose could not see me today. Maybe tomorrow.

Cassie was incensed. 'I can't believe it,' she said. 'She's just got no class. I mean you could understand it if she just said 'no'. I reckon you've been speaking to the same person all along. She's crazy.'

But in the morning Rose sounded immensely cheerful. 'Oh hall-*oh*,' she cried, 'I'm in a *very* good mood this morning. I'm prepared to talk to you about all kinds of things. You can come over at three this afternoon. Or if you don't mind just seeing me as I am, in jeans and T-shirt, you can come now.'

I didn't dare risk it. What mood might she (not to mention her maid and her sister) be in by this afternoon?

There is a buzz and the tall gates swing open. Then I'm up past the topiary and the gravel at the big front door of the mansion. And here she is, Rose Hancock herself, her hair pulled back tight from her head with a little crimson velvet band. She wears white T-shirt, blue denims and white sneakers.

She smiles a little flash-smile of welcome. I'm not intending to write nasty, tabloidy stuff about her like all the others, but I must report that her eyes are rather glazed, and as she leads me into her hall (magnificent chandelier, super-long dining table, gilt-framed Impressionist-style landscapes) and up her grand marble staircase she totters slightly.

I follow her politely into her little 'morning room', sit myself down on the crimson sofa. A tiny old Filipino house-keeper brings us tea on a silver tray.

So, swaying ever so slightly, Rose tells me her story. About her convent-school education and wealthy back-ground. How she'd worked for the family firm, 'one of the top five corporations in the Philippines', and then had a row with her brother and, 'impulsive me, with very little money, I said, "I'm getting out of here." ' She'd run to Perth with a girlfriend and answered an ad for a housekeeper, 'and of course the story is, as you know, a couple of months later the widower mining magnate Lang Hancock was in love with me'.

She's never been forgiven by Australian society, she says, for marrying Lang. They think she's just a mail-order bride, like all the other mail-order brides that came to Australia. 'They don't want to know the truth. They want there to be a saucy story where here comes a girl from a bar in the Philippines with no education, marries an old man, uses sex to connive and get everything and get to the top as she is now.'

Even though she pays one of the biggest income taxes in Perth and is an Australian citizen and does a lot of charity work for the good of Australia she's still, she complains, always called by the press 'Filipino wife'.

'D'you think it's mostly envy,' I ask. 'They see your big house on the hill?'

'Oh yes, sure. Here comes this nobody from Woop Woop. Comes in here and steals one of the most eligible, one of the richest men in the country, Langley George Hancock – he was a living legend, you know.'

'Can I show you something?' she says, and leads me off into a small room full of photo albums and bulging files. 'Aside from this,' she says, 'I've got another filing room. Since my life with Langley George up to the present day, this is all the fan mail, begging letters, things like that. And photo albums, as you see, chronologically arranged. They're all filled up with the same thing. My life with Lang and my life now as Rose Porteous. These are all my interviews, pictures, things like that that have gone out on television.'

'So d'you like appearing on television?'

'No! I had to appear on television before for my husband's business. And then, I have to consistently show the public that I am not what they think I am. I speak fluent English. I went to a good school. Because if I kept quiet I would have been identified as the typical Filipino mail-order bride. And also my husband wanted to expose me in the sense that he was dealing with millions and billions of dollars overseas and people were always saying, "Oh you're going to die." '

She smiles a fleeting smile. 'It always helped create a scene when Lang would say "My wife is coming." When they had boardroom meetings, I never appeared with my husband. But I would come about fifteen minutes later, so he would enjoy the faces of the people really gloating or gawking at me when he says, "This is my wife." They expect an eighty-year-old woman with a cane, and here I come, I'm young, thirty-four, thirty-six when I married him, and being Asian I looked very young, I looked like a small kid, you know, plucked out of the kindergarten, he was forty years my senior . . .'

'How did you feel about that? He was obviously a very attractive man.'

'He was what you call a very Richard Burton man. You know, where the sex appeal is there, the animal instinct in the man is there. Very sensual person. Behind that gruff look.'

'Personal questions I perhaps shouldn't ask: Was it a real love match?'

'It was a real love marriage, yes. I felt committed to him. And wherever he went I used to look after him. I was everything: a nursemaid, a housekeeper, a nanny, a cook to him, because he was so set in his ways that you couldn't just hire a housekeeper and say, "Look after Mr Hancock." If I hadn't married him, Mark, he would have died years ago and that is public knowledge. They always say, "Whatever you say about Rose Hancock, she made the old man happy." He lived another ten years.'

'But from your side? Was he a genuinely attractive fellow?'

'Of course, it's very natural, being courted by an old man over candlelight at Maxim's in Paris is better than going to a hamburger joint with a man your own age.'

I laugh. 'I mean,' says Rose, laughing too, 'let's be frank about it!'

So she would prepare dinner for the old man and his friends, 'and after dinner he would say, "And now my dear go in and show off the worldly wares that you bought from Paris." And I had to put on a fashion show. For dessert time! He loved Scarlett O'Hara type clothes. He loved me in plunging necklines. He loved seeing me all spruced up, because deep inside he loved Fred Astaire and Ginger Rogers, that kind of Hollywood line. He was very soft inside. What you call a very gentle giant.'

Now the gentle giant has moved on, to a world where money can no longer take him to Paris with a bride with plunging necklines. But Port Hedland is still covered in red-ochre dust and Rose always wears Chanel. She goes twice or three times a year to Europe. Her best friend in Paris is Pierre Cardin, and her home in Paris is Pierre's hotel in the Avenue Gabrielle. 'It's called Maxim's.' She has a flat in London, too. 'Amazingly it's ten minutes from London by tube, although I never take the tube. It overlooks Common Ealing.'

Back in Perth, she is married to Lang's old business associate, a handsome Canadian who is younger than her, William Porteous. The rumour I've heard from Cassie and everyone else is that he's gay, it's purely a business arrangement, etc. etc. But when we talk about him Rose melts visibly. 'For the first time in my life . . .' she begins; then, 'I've been married four times and this is probably the best turning point in my life, that I married William. And I'm very happy with him. The marriage is based more on companionship and friendship.

'Of course,' she goes on, 'we live a very strange life and he has to watch what he says in public. I still have to guard myself. I cannot have a full-time housekeeper. I have to kick them out by five o'clock, because my private life has to be cushioned.'

'You wouldn't even trust a housekeeper?' I say, wondering why a housekeeper would be upset by a marriage based on companionship and friendship.

Rose smiles. 'No. Friends today, press tomorrow. I belong to the media now. I am public property. The press would like to know what my domestic life is.'

'Is that frightening? Them being so intrusive?'

Rose thinks for a while. 'Becoming public property is fun. Then you realise you have to pay the price. You can't just go back and say, "Erase me from everything, you know." '

'Are there times when you wish you hadn't been on this trip?'

A long pause, then: 'Yes, there are.'

So I see round her Prix d'Amour. Every room has the same magnificent view. The garden running down the hill. Below, the lovely blue sweep of the Swan.

I see her bedroom with its axeproof, bulletproof sliding door. There is, for the record, just one (huge) double bed in there. Off to one side her dressing room is filled with Chanel suits, gowns, gold belts, rack upon rack of shoes. 'This is like Imelda Marcos,' I joke. 'The difference is,' Rose replies, 'she took it from the people.'

'This used to be all mine,' she shrugs. 'Now my husband has taken over.' There is a rail of Valentino suits, a Gatsbyesque collection of beautiful shirts, a rack with two hundred ties.

Along the corridor is her daughter's room. Earlier, Rose has told me how she won't have Johanna at home in Perth because she gets into the wrong crowd. Now, as she fingers the turquoise walls, she says, 'I can't understand why she doesn't like to live here. As soon as this house was built she says it's like a prison to her.' Rose has even thoughtfully provided a sumptuously decorated guest room for her daughter. In case she returns and wants a friend to stay.

We walk back down the sweeping marble stairs, past numerous pictures of her by the same artist, René Gruau, 'who's a contemporary of Coco Chanel, still lives in the South of France'. We admire the chandelier, 'featured on the front cover of the *Waterford Crystal Magazine*'. We stroll into the room where there is a Steinway piano and a rose-wood table sealed up, 'the way they do with a Rolls-Royce – it's a Rolls-Royce finish'. There's a cabinet here with gifts from Nicolae Ceausescu and the Korean Goverment and Gorbachov and various Royal Families in Europe, (all of whose countries, presumably, had a need for iron ore).

Down in the cellar there is a vanishing perspective of Dom Pérignon bottles.

'To be honest with you,' says Rose, 'I am not a social butterfly. This is why I've been able to maintain this sort of enigma because very few people know me. Outside I've put on a big façade and it's just like Princess Di shaking hands with people, you know – but inside, my natural life, I always shield it.'

Before she married Lang, there were two other husbands?

'Yes. After I finished college I met this young persistent man, a polo player and grandson of a magnate in the Philippines, very spoilt. And of course I married him. That lasted for about a year and a half. And then we busted up. I was left alone with a child. In a Catholic country where divorce is not allowed. So . . .'

'People turned their noses up at you?'

'Yes, yes, oh yes. I was a family outcast. I was the black sheep. Because separation was unthinkable. I mean people preferred to . . . incestuous relationships, you know, but behind closed doors. It was just obscene that a twenty-two-year-old girl now suddenly has a baby and the father has left her behind and the marriage has bust up. Who would go for me? I mean, a young man, even if he's twenty-eight years old, from a good family background, will say, "I'm not going to marry her – she's *perdida.*" It's a Spanish term for, "She's lost, she's lost her virginity." Those were the Sixties, you know, where virginity was very important to the husband.'

'Even though he abandoned you?'

'Yes.'

'You fell out with your family at that point, did you?'

'Yes.'

That night, though I didn't realise it at first, I found myself surrounded by millionaires. David and Cassie had taken me along to a wedding anniversary in a swanky Italian restaurant patronised by the wealthy cognoscenti of the southern suburbs. It was a gang of David's old schoolmates and of the four men there David was, he laughed, by far the poorest. The man I was sitting next to was a millionaire. The man at the head of the table was a millionaire. Behind me, at the next table, was another bunch of millionaires. And Tony Barlow, they reckoned, the guy in the orange shirt, (founder of Tony Barlow Menswear), was a multi-millionaire. Juanita was right. Perth, which had been so ostentatiously wealthy, had learnt the lesson of old money. Discretion was the watchword now, though within the walls of the Campo del Fiori we were still allowed a loud and private laugh.

# 15

# Gold

It was quite a sight. A big room packed to the back window with wizened, handsome, ugly, clean-shaven, moustachioed, bearded, lean, plump, male faces, most with the tans and the screwed-up-against-the-sun eye wrinkles of the ockers in the lager ads. And then, running back and forth getting the drinks behind the bar in the middle, the skimpies, looking to my stunned eyes like three pornographic angels dropped into a masculine hell. The Sunsilk-pretty blonde wore nothing but cream-coloured bra and panties; the tall, thin one with the helmet of mahoghany hair had fishnet shorts tight over a leopardskin bikini; the fey-looking seraph with the tumbling brown curls wore a magenta silk nightie.

I edged gently through the braying pack and up to the bar, pushed in alongside a huge bearded bloke with shaved head, peaked cap and glasses, talking to, or rather yelling at, a lean, fit-looking fellow in a maroon rugby shirt. Before I knew it he'd shaken my hand and was buying me a drink. Then: 'We've got a bloody *Pom* here!' he was bellowing, half-turned in his seat, towards the gallery of mates behind. To the skimpies: 'Mark's a *Pom*. The Pom wants to see your tits, Donna – I didn't say that, the *Pom* said it. Ha ha ha!'

Nor was this just cheery, non-PC badinage; in Kalgoorlie it was a business proposition. You tossed a little gold $2 coin and if you won, Donna, Casey or Serena pulled down her satin or leopardskin bra and showed you her breasts. More – she took her nipples gently between fingers and thumb and waggled them six inches from your face. If you lost, of course, she kept the money.

'Oh my go-o-o-od!' Pete was moaning theatrically, having finally won his bet and tantalised himself with Donna's milky white teenage mammaries for a good ten seconds. 'Donna really wants to marry me,' he sang, as she fetched the next three stubbies. 'She doesn't know it yet – but she does.' 'Where d'you live?' he asked her as she returned. She gave him a patient smile. 'Burdekin.' 'That's in Queensland.' 'Yeh.' 'Are you single?' 'Nye.' 'Disre*gard* that last comment. Are you *not* single? Ha ha ha! Anyway, where's your old man?' 'In Perth.' 'You said you were from Queensland.' 'So. I'm based in Perth now.' Donna stuck her tongue out at him like a six-year-old. Geoff shook his head. 'Now there's a tongue Mark'd marry, I tell you. Ha ha ha!'

With half an ice-cold stubby of the amber nectar gurgling down his throat he was back to singing, drumming his knuckles in time on the bar. *'Walks like a man, talks like a man, walks like a man, my son. Far as I've heard, from every single . . .'*

'Shut *UP!*' shouted Rob. Next to this burble we'd been having a serious, technical conversation about how the old shaft mines had been replaced almost entirely by open pits. Rob was manager of a mine site; Geoff was unemployed. They'd met two hours before, here at the bar, and Geoff was now, only half-jokingly, trying to get a job from him; had indeed produced his CV from his bag and was now calling Rob 'boss'.

*'They asked me how I knew, my true love was true-ue . . .'*

'Don't give up the day job,' chirped Donna, hurrying past with a fistful of stubbies.

'I haven't got a day job. I was going to become a skimpy but Mum says I'm too in-tell-i-gent. Whoah!' Geoff crowed. Ah look, he said suddenly, there's more to see in Kalgoorlie than the Fed. So two proposals of marriage later we're in

Rob's car riding on a jovial tide of expletives down the road to Boulder. 'Don't go to the Exchange, mate,' Geoff tells me, 'it's a blackfellas' pub.' 'It used to be really good,' said Rob, 'but it's all fucken niggers in there now.' 'Fucken blackfellas. Not a good pub.' 'Very hard not to be racist in this town,' says Rob, sensing my unease through the darkness. 'They're cunts,' says Geoff. Rob's a Kiwi, as it turns out, has a lot of time for the Maoris, so isn't a racist, 'but you come over here and see the fucken Abos, it *makes* you a fucken racist'.

The issue is left – thank god – at the door of the Foundry, which makes the Fed look like a feminists-only wine bar. The skimpies, to match the tattooed and leathered clientele, are much rougher. They don't just show here, they take your beer bottle and rub its neck on their nipples, dribble the lager down their altogether larger, firmer, maturer breasts. For three dollars they bend over and wiggle their g-stringed bum, or run their hands suggestively over their crotch. For five, this one, Gemma, has got right up on the bar and slid Geoff's glasses up her fanny. He's touchingly nervous about this. 'They're very expensive glasses,' he moans, as Rob hoots with laughter. But now he's leaning forward manfully and pulling them out with his teeth. They emerge, smeared. He wipes them on his sleeve and puts them on.

'I would love to stick my dick between those tits,' he tells me. 'Show us yer strobes!' he yells. 'D'you want to come home and have some safe, serious, good-fun sex?' he proposes.

'What would my boyfriend say?' says green-glitter bikini flirtatiously.

'He's in Perth.'

'No thank you.'

'You don't have to have sex. You can lie back and I'll have it for you. Ha ha ha!'

In the dunny I stand beside a man who is living proof

of the theory of evolution. 'Ah that's great,' he sighs as he pees. 'Sometimes, mate, it's even better than a root.'

In the dazzling oven-heat of daytime, Kalgoorlie was my fantasy of Alice Springs realised. A magnificent broad main street of intact, turn-of-the-century Australian architecture. Even if the ground-floor shops were KEVRON 1 HOUR PHOTOS, TARA SHEEPSKINS and CHARIOT AUTOTORQUE, above them were elegant stucco façades, painted up in white, pale blue and sienna. Every fifty yards or so was a splendid example of Outback Hotel c. 1900, with ornamented cast-iron pillars holding up elegant latticed-wood or wrought-iron verandas. The Exchange had a little tower on one corner; the York, where I was staying, two splendid silver domes and a central gold cupola embellishing its roof.

Despite its established feel, Kalgoorlie lived on the edge, its only reason for existence being gold. All around in the desert were ghost towns, deserted by their populations once the mines were finished. 'Kal', I was told, was undergoing a boom because it had recently been discovered that the enormous 'Superpit' on the edge of town was going to be good for another twenty years. 'In Kalgoorlie,' said Peter Jeanes, editor of the *Kalgoorlie Miner*, 'that's a long time. They've never had twenty years before. Twenty good years without any major problems. People can build on that.'

I drove out in the dawn to Kanowna Belle, which Peter had told me was the most modern mine around. Here, at the wealth-creating cutting edge, the scene was as sober and orderly as the Fed and Foundry had been the opposite. David Miller, Manager, Mining, was competence and reasonableness personified. His 'single-status' workforce moved briskly and cheerfully around the bright, air-conditioned offices, shirts ironed, fingernails clean. There was no trouble with unions. 'If there *is* a problem,' David told me, 'it's sorted out by the individual coming to chat about it.'

Out in the huge 'open-cut' pit, fifty per cent of the 140-tonne-truck drivers were women. (I rode to the boulder-strewn bottom with Sharon, an exuberant granny from Port Hedland who 'loved her job'; at $12.60 an hour it was a lot better than the farming work she'd done before.) Environmental issues were taken 'extremely seriously' by the company. In twenty years' time, when production was completed according to schedule, the only thing left would be the pit, which would be flooded to become Lake Kanowna. Meanwhile, the dumped rock surrounding would be landscaped, rippled, topsoiled and seeded. And as for that most vexed of bar-room issues, Mabo: 'We believe,' said David quietly, 'it's only a matter of time before one of the claims is accepted.' The biggest problem was the uncertainty. But they were already 'looking at strategies to deal with scenarios that could arise'. 'It might even become as important as the cricket,' he chuckled, as he sped me back to town.

Not everyone went to the Fed or the Foundry. In Claude de Bernales, the nearest thing Kalgoorlie had to a yuppy hangout, you could sit and observe, up at the horseshoe bar, fifteen clean-cut young men sitting goggle-eyed watching *Models Inc.*, the absurd *Baywatch*-style American series set in a model agency. How many of them knew, I wondered, that one of the six drawling Californian babes – Kylie Travis – originated from Kalgoorlie?

Can you judge a place by its books, I wondered, pausing at the window of the main bookshop to see:

BREEDING ROTTWEILERS
STAFFORDSHIRE BULL TERRIER
YOUR HORSE'S HEALTH
AUSTRALIAN CATTLE DOGS
SNAKES OF WESTERN AUSTRALIA

It was a very hardworking town, I was told, where people had no truck with pretension. In Perth, a millionaire would park his Merc in the front drive of his mansion; in Kal, he'd be more likely to drive a battered ute, and the house would be unostentatious. In Perth, accountants and lawyers did deals over long lunches; in Kal, someone would come out to the site, make a proposal, and if it was worthwhile it would get done.

They didn't have much truck with bureaucracy in Kal, either. A couple of years ago it had been generally agreed that a bypass road around the south-west of the town was needed. The Government found all sorts of delays and obstacles: a rifle range here, a problematic lease there. In the end a group of local contractors got together one Friday night with over a hundred pieces of machinery and just bulldozed a road through in a weekend. Now it had become *the* road.

## Hit and Run

A couple of days before I'd arrived in Kalgoorlie there'd been a hit-and-run accident. A twenty-three-year-old woman, daughter of one of the wealthiest mining magnates in the town, had been at a party and had drunk too much. Stumbling, in the dark, off Skinny Park, the narrow strip of grass and trees that runs down the middle of central Brookman Street, she'd been knocked down by an Aboriginal driving a Landcruiser (possibly drunk himself) and killed.

'I can understand that the driver possibly panicked and did not stop, but not to report the accident is pretty bad,' First Class Constable Becker said. 'We just want the driver to come forward and help us with the inquiry so that we can put this thing to rest.' He said it was possible the driver would be charged with failing to report an accident. It would most likely be the only charge preferred.

Something strike you as a bit odd about that report from the *Kalgoorlie Miner*? Police reaction rather laid-back in the circumstances? The report is verbatim; but the story was of course the other way round. The dead female was a twenty-three-year-old Aboriginal; the driver of the Toyota Land-cruiser a whitefella not known to the blacks at the scene. The reaction among many of the people I spoke to (in every other way the decentest, most generous, what-can-I-get-you-mate? fellows you could hope to meet) was almost that the woman had asked for it.

*Well she did ask for it! You Pommy liberal!* I can hear them cry, even from here. *Those Abos they sit drinking in Skinny Park, they get so pissed they can't even see, they crawl into the middle of the road, night after night, we don't ask for them to be there, it's illegal to drink in public in this state, they're a fucken liability to themselves and everyone else mate . . .*

## The Man to See

That's the girl I buried yesterday,' said Don Green, leaning forward over his desk and running a white, plump hand up his bushy grey sideburns through his thick, black, rather Mod-style hair. The truth of the matter was that yes, Peggy Porter had crawled, drunk, into the middle of the road. After hitting her, the driver had stopped and got out to help – but he'd driven off when a group of angry Aboriginals had run at him.

Now Don had been asked by the community of desert Aboriginals from which Peggy came to get these 'fringe dwellers' off Skinny Park. 'We don't want people dying like this,' he told me. 'As far as I'm concerned we don't even want people drinking in the street. So I've now moved a motion in council that the police get off their butts and do their job.'

He was an unusual fellow, Don Green, among the whites of Kalgoorlie. DON GREEN: (said his oversized green-and-white business card) THE MAN TO SEE. Then, underneath: DRIVING SCHOOL, ABORIGINAL ART, CONCRETING, TREE-LOPPING. He was also an ordained pastor, a local councillor, a would-be Federal MP (he'd stood for the Liberals against the incumbent Labour MP in the last election) and – this was the controversial bit – an unofficial helper of Aboriginal people.

'Somebody said to me, "You'd go a long way in this town if only you'd leave the Aborigines alone. You'd be Mayor tomorrow." ' He shook his head and smiled. 'If only they realised I'm trying to help them.'

Of all the whites who'd told me they 'knew the Aborigines' Don was the most convincing I'd yet met. The son of one of the missionaries at Mt Margaret, he'd grown up alongside May O'Brien and the other Mission children. He'd learnt to speak Pitjantjatjara fluently. And he was now devoting a lot of his time and energy to unpaid direct action on behalf of the Aboriginal population of the Western Desert.

Peggy Porter's had been one of two funerals he'd flown out to the desert to officiate at just in the previous week. And on his desk in his cluttered little office he had copies of faxes he'd sent off to the white adviser of this or that community, asking for money for individual Aboriginals, currently stranded in town. They came to see him. He got their money sent down for them. If they needed to go home he tried to help them get home.

He had (it seemed to me) a clear, unsentimental understanding of what it was like for a desert Aboriginal to be stuck in Kalgoorlie without funds. 'The white people say the Aborigines get a lot of money. And a lot of money goes through the system, yes. But when you only get $65 a week it's not a lot of money, and if it's kept by the advisers in the community – it's nothing. So how do you survive down here – other than bludge on others?

'A lot of white people think they spend all their money on alcohol. Well, yes. A lot of money is spent on alcohol.

But if you're hungry you're going to get drunk the next morning with a teaspoon. So you're paralytic for the next day, and you can't eat anything because you've got no money to eat and so you scrounge and so forth; then again you've got nothing.'

Don didn't get paid a cent for his work. He had nothing to do with either the Government or ATSIC; indeed, perhaps predictably, he was highly critical of this much defamed organisation. 'It's all out of kilter. Millions and millions of dollars are going into ATSIC. This money should go to the communities, but it's not getting there, it's being caught up in offices, in cars, in people.' More Aboriginal people came into his wife's shop and sought assistance than went down to ATSIC.

And when ATSIC people went out to the bush, the only people they spoke to were the white advisers. 'Maybe one or two of the Aboriginal leaders. But as for general, run-of-the-mill Aborigines – they wouldn't know what they're talking about. I speak the Aboriginal language fluently. And they tell me I'm the only person that walks around the camp when I'm visiting. If you have no communication with the grass roots you'll never ever learn.'

If he was in charge, he'd abolish ATSIC altogether. Redirect the money directly per head of the community. 'And I could do so *much*. With just a little, you know.'

Don was, by his own admission, very forthright. Not only was he happy to blow his own trumpet, but he had no truck with, and little understanding of, the PC terminology of Perth. It wasn't just 'Aborigines' for 'Aboriginals'. He bluntly described the desert blackfellas as 'Stone Age people'.

'Chap came to me the other day complaining about Aborigines camping outside his place and making a mess. Fair enough. He has every right to complain. But he doesn't understand – they're Stone Age people. They came from the spinifex. Forty years ago they were nomads. And now, all of a sudden, you're trying to fit them into something they've grown up without for thousands of years. Give them another thousand years and they'll be as clean and tidy as we are. But it's a gradual process.'

Nor did he mince his words when it came to the issue of 'part-descent' Aboriginals. As well as being 'ostracised by whites' he was, he told me, 'ostracised by coloured people who don't understand where I'm coming from. Because they see me helping Aboriginal people and they're jealous. I get it from the half-castes, the quarter-castes, the people that think they're blackfellas but they're not.'

I interrupted him here, pointed out that the 'part-descent' Aboriginals I'd met in Perth loathed descriptions like 'half-caste'. May O'Brien, for example, whom he'd grown up alongside. (I could hear her voice now, 'We *hate* those terms.') 'Well she is,' Don replied bluntly. 'And the black people I talk to say, "The half-caste people are the ones causing us a lot of trouble." "It's not us," they say, "it's them, wanting to come and take us over." They've sat here in this office and said it.' He threw out his arms, gave me his warm, inclusive, difficult-to-argue-with smile. It was quite simple. May O'Brien was brought up at Mt Margaret. She wasn't an Aborigine, living on the land. *Mt Margaret* was her culture. Likewise the coloured people they put in ATSIC, they were all very well educated, had grown up in our society, our culture, 'not Stone Age culture'. Generally, they had *no understanding* of what it was like, being an Aborigine in the bush. 'Although, of course, stereotype Aborigines are very important to them.'

He could understand why people wanted to be Aboriginal. There were a lot of benefits at the moment being thrown at Aborigines.

I didn't think it was that simple, I said. I told him Irene's story; her final words about never being accepted in white society.

'I think that's totally wrong,' Don replied. 'That's a thing they ride along, like riding a horse. You *can't* ride on the past, you've got to ride on the present. They're wanting sympathy, they're wanting a shoulder to cry on. You've got Indians here now, you've got Filipinos, you've got all cultures. As long as you're clean and getting on with the job no one will recognise you. They'll accept you as an Australian.'

That was the key thing, about which he was passionate. 'We've got to be Australians first, and whatever else we are second. I feel that's the way we've got to go.'


## Ground Floor, Starlight Hotel

As Don had been telling me about the Aboriginals of the desert, showing me the photos, the scrawled faxes, I'd thought: I should cancel my train ticket, phone home, raise some more money, hire a four-wheel-drive and *get out there*. Drive back to Alice through the desert by way of Warburton and Giles; even though I don't speak any of the languages, try and talk to some of these 'Stone Age people' . . .

'You could do that,' Don said. 'You'd need to wait for a permit. Some of the roads are pretty impassable at the moment. Or you could just take the bus down to Boulder Reserve, have a yarn with some of the fringe-dwellers there. They come from all over the desert. You'll probably get as good an idea there as anywhere.

'Now there's a way of doing this,' he explained. 'Don't march up to them and ask questions. Just go in there, you know, sit down under a tree, read the paper, write your notes, do what you do – let them see you. Then, after twenty minutes or so, you can go over, say, "D'you know Don Green? He's a friend of mine. He said there was a funeral yesterday and everything went good." Okay?'

So I took the bus down to Boulder and found the Reserve, which was a dirty little park behind iron railings at one end of the tattered main street of Kalgoorlie's poor relation. Sure enough, there was a largish group of Aboriginals there, sitting under a tree in the morning sunshine, drinking, shouting, laughing.

I sat down on the littered brown grass. I was quietly excited. I'd been wanting to do this since Musgrave Park in Brisbane. By the Todd River, in Frog Hollow, even finally, in Weld Square in Perth, I'd watched these groups of 'long-grassers' from a distance, grown irritated with my inability to go over and talk to them. Now, at last, it seemed, Don had given me a key.

The group had noticed me now, discussed me, gone back to their badinage. I was just wondering how much longer I should sit, incongruous whitefella reading his *West Australian* ('DPP WON'T GIVE UP BOND SECRETS') when a guy with frazzled hair and beard walked over, circled me, then announced that his name was Willy Young. I told him mine and he leant forward to shake my hand.

'You writing something?' he asked.

'Writing something?'

'About Aboriginal people drinking?'

'No, no. *No*.'

'What you doin' here then?'

'Just travelling, looking around.' I smiled and gestured feebly at the burnt grass and scattered stubbies. 'Sitting in the park.'

He nodded. 'You got a cigarette?'

I gave him one from the packet I'd bought way back in Darwin, for this very purpose. 'If you want to have a yarn,' he said, when he'd lit up, 'come over. Now . . . later.' He stood five yards off and watched me. 'You wanna come now?'

So I went over. To the yabbering circle sitting on quilts under the big tree, at first glance a mixture of wizened greybeards and plump women short on teeth. The noise lowered as I approached and was formally introduced around the circle. This was Arthur, Willy's brother; Annie, his little sister . . . then on round to an old man who'd met the Queen. No really, Willy's eyes gleamed. He'd been *over there*. To London. To the palace. Over that Maralinga. 'Yeah,' the old man confirmed, 'over that Maralinga.'

But we didn't talk about the issues arising from Britain's nuclear test at Maralinga, we talked about Prince Charles. It was a pity, they all agreed, that he'd split up with Diana. 'Them two – split – shame,' said a man to the old man's right, who was in that state of drunkenness where he was making more sense to himself than anyone else. 'So Charles,' he went on, 'she'll give him that crown. He – think – good.' I nodded and smiled; his returning nods and smiles were full of deep, unrealised significance.

'So where d'you all live?' I asked.

'Here,' said Annie with a grin, pointing at the ground.

'This place, that place,' said Willy. 'We move around.'

'We sleep under the stars,' said Annie. 'Ground Floor, Starlight Hotel.'

A large woman to my left was trying to tell me a story about a preacher who'd been followed by two angels across the desert. 'Excuse *me*,' she began, whenever there was a lull in the chatter. Which wasn't often as Annie was now insisting that Arthur had gone all round the world with Billy Graham. 'Shut up,' said Arthur. 'It's true!' Annie was shouting. 'He did. He went with Billy Graham . . .'

Willy pointed out a bright-eyed, bearded young black-fella who'd just driven up in a Landcruiser. 'See that guy there. He was the last one out of the bush. Four years ago, he was living in the bush . . .'

'On what, bush tucker?'

'Yeah, bush tucker, honey-ant . . . and camels. He eats camels,' he laughed. 'He does,' laughed Annie. 'Camels.' 'And look now,' said Willy, 'he's got a Toyota. He's smart, very smart. Four years ago in the bush – now he's got a Toyota.'

People came and went. The Moselle was passed round. Squirted into the plastic waterbottle from the silver wine-box bags under the quilt. All around little squabbles blew up, followed by elaborate reconciliations. 'You should have been here yesterday,' said Willy. 'Big fight. There were bottles everywhere.'

Now Annie had got to the tearful and angry stage. 'You fucken did go with Billy Graham,' she screamed at her brother. 'Shsh,' went Arthur. 'You fucken did. He fucken did.' She reeled off into an hysterical stream of abuse.

Willy wanted to get ten dollars off me for a drink. Arthur waved a stern finger at him. 'No, Willy. Don't be a bludger.' But when I gave him the money it mysteriously ended up, not with Willy, but with one of the South Australians on the other side of the tree. They cleared off and didn't return.

We'd got to that happy point when they'd started to teach me their language ('Nuyntu – *you*', 'Baiya – *good*' etc.) when I looked up and saw a white guy standing over us. He wore jeans tucked into knee-high leather boots; atop his long yellow hair was a leather hat; his arms were thick with tattoos. They called him Cowboy and he was married to the woman with enormous breasts wearing the T-shirt that read ABORIGINAL ART.

'Where you from?' asked Cowboy.

'England.'

'Whereabouts?'

'London.'

'You a Londoner?' He did a terrible imitation of a Cockney accent, 'All right, moite?' I laughed, weakly. 'I used to work with a Scouser.' Cowboy slipped into a cod Yorkshire accent. When he'd been in Perth, he said, he'd been taken for an Englishman. Really? I replied. But he was, in fact, from Kalgoorlie. 'There's some new policeman here, trying to arrest me for being disorderly. Told me to get out of town. I told *him* to get out of town. I was born here.'

'So what d'you do for work?' I asked after a while.

'Work!' Cowboy laughed scornfully. 'I don't work.' He lived in Boulder; drank in the Reserve; went home and slept.

He was rather amazed that I was sitting down with these blackfellas. 'They don't like whites,' he told me. 'You're lucky,' he repeated, a couple of times; though I'd been invited over, and before he'd arrived I'd had nothing but warmth and courtesy from them.

## Hay Street

It's a wide, dark backstreet, the most famous street in Kalgoorlie. Tonight the wind tugs at the little trees that line the pavement, that run past the little front gardens of town-centre bungalows. There are three brothels. The first, Questra Casa, is painted bright pink. A door stands open. Through it, you get a glimpse of pink-lit bedrooms beyond. But where are the girls, the 'crackers' as they call them in the Fed? Where is the welcome, the sales pitch? I pace on.

You can't miss what's on offer at the second. They sit out on stools under the streetlight, so you can get a thoroughly good look at what you're about to have. Behind, their little booth-bedrooms wait for action, doors open, music pumping. Two are shut as I pass. Of the four young women waiting, three aren't for me, too haggard, even in yellow neon. The fourth, though, is sluttishly desirable, with shoulder-length ginger hair, jiggering up and down in a black catsuit at the gate to her little stall. She doesn't catch my eye as I pass, or wink, or even give me a coquettish smile; she just keeps tapping her restless foot and looking over the road.

The third lust-stop is altogether easier to get drawn into. There are six or seven girls on stools outside the front door, chatting, laughing, smoking. 'Where are you going, mate?' asks one as my pace slows.

'Just looking.'

'What are you – a tourist?' asks another who is dolled up in a tight red miniskirt and black jacket.

'Sort of thing.'

'Want to have a look inside?'

'Okay.'

'It's rather like a raunchy YHA inside, with double beds

instead of singles in the little cells. Outside, under lush foliage, there's a spa, 'where you can relax afterwards for as long as you like with a complimentary beer'. A muscly young miner is doing just that; he has a little blonde with him, running her finger ever-so-slowly down his back.

Above the bar is a menu: $60 for ten minutes, $80 for fifteen, $100 for twenty.

'So are you interested in any of our services?' asks crimson miniskirt, in as natural, unwhorish a way as a hotel receptionist.

'No really,' I say, 'just looking.'

'No worries.'

Two girls in pale-blue nighties appear; they are students up from Perth, no more than nineteen, cute enough for even the handsomest college bigshot. They've just had a little argument with the madam, my companion tells me. It's their last night and they want to go out, but she won't let them. Either one, or both, is available now.

'So we can't tempt you?'

'I'm fine, really.'

'You'll be back,' she says, as I leave. As I wander in mature fashion past the little stool-party, 'See yer *lay*-der!' they call. Further up, the three ugly sisters are still idle and ginger-nut is dismissing a young, skinny, tousle-haired client. Freshly sexed-up she gives me a look that would be corny if it wasn't in the right-here-and-now.

I walk resolutely on, then pause. Then I turn, stand for a long minute watching her tapping her foot to the rock music that blares from her little box. The Trans-Pacific leaves Kalgoorlie at 11.05 p.m. My luggage is packed and my seat is booked. Across the Nullarbor to Adelaide; two nights and a day, 'one of the great train journeys of the world'. It's one thing to be unfaithful, I tell myself as I pace past Woolworth's at a clip, another to pay to be unfaithful.

At the empty, polished bar of the York I reward myself with a farewell stubby of Emu. Four young studs come in

and order Tequila slammers. 'Nice to see someone enjoying their work,' says the one ordering to the grumpy bar-girl.
   'You're pissed, remember,' she replies curtly.

# 16

## Grey Marble
## and Pink Shorts

Could this really be Adelaide at last? Outside tall eucalypts and taller skyscrapers made green-black silhouettes against the livid yellow dawn.

I was exhausted. All night I'd been kept awake by fifteen-year-old Katherine making friends with sixteen-year-old Steven. 'If you could go to one place in the world, where would it be?' Gems like that, on and on into the small hours. 'Stop talking now, Katherine,' her father had commanded, shortly after midnight, when the carriage was dark and next to me the surfer from Philip Island was snoring lightly, his Walkman silent at last. But sweet Katherine took not a shred of notice. 'Are you ready to slape?' she asked Steven eventually.

'No.'

'Good, because I'm going to stay up.'

'Katherine,' her father grunted, 'stop *talk*ing.'

'Nye,' she replied, kneeling up on her seat to regale Steven with an anecdote about how she'd made this teacher who'd been rude to her apologise in front of *the whole class*.

It was our second night on the train. All the long day in between the Nullarbor Plain had rattled featurelessly by, hour upon hour (upon hour) of red earth thinly covered with metallic-green scrub; here and there a tiny bush, a scattering of white rocks.

Out there, only fifty clicks or so to the north, was 'Ground

Zero', that very Maralinga that had delivered the old Aboriginal man I'd met in Boulder Reserve to Buckingham Palace. In 1957 Robert Menzies, Liberal Prime Minister and craven admirer of Empire, had allowed the British Government to test a nuclear bomb without even consulting his own Cabinet, let alone his country. Thirty years later, raw plutonium lay scattered on the ground 'like talcum powder', in the words of John Pilger, who'd visited the site in the late 1980s. (Plutonium, he points out, is so dangerous that even a third of a milligram gives a fifty per cent chance of cancer.)

During the tests there were thirteen Aboriginal settlements within three hundred kilometres of Ground Zero. Pilger quotes Patrick Connolly, who served in the RAF at Maralinga and was threatened with prosecution after he revealed that 'during the two and a half years I was there I would have seen 400 to 500 Aborigines in contaminated areas. Occasionally, we would bring them in for decontamination. Other times we just shooed them off like rabbits.'*

Now a sign warning of the RADIATION HAZARD stands on the rim of the bomb crater. It is translated into Italian, Greek, French, Spanish and Arabic – just in case any confused oil sheik should stray into the area. There is, however, no translation into Pitjantjatjara; and in 1987, when tests were finally carried out on the local population, plutonium was indeed found in the camp where the three hundred or so displaced people of Maralinga now live.

Just along the track, at Ooldea, the eccentric 'genteel Irishwoman' Daisy Bates had lived, for years alongside the blackfellas in a white tent. Kabbarli, they called her – the Grandmother. She wrote a famous book called *The Passing of the Aborigines* which records her adventures with the people she found so much easier than her own, though she could never abandon the values of her own, and wore,

* John Pilger, *A Secret Country* (Jonathan Cape, London, 1989) – pp. 170–74.

even to the end, and in the fiercest heat, the shirt blouse, high collar and long skirt of her Victorian youth.

Now I fell from the train into the arms of an Irish back-packer tout called Patrick, who was offering a bed in Glenelg. A *bed*. Who cared where it was? But when the backpacker-crammed minibus finally arrived at the tatty old house by the sea, it turned out that, oh dear, Patrick had miscalculated. There wasn't actually a *bed* as such till checkout time at eleven.

Too tired to argue I crashed out on the beach, in the inky shadow of a Norfolk Pine, nose down on the fine white sand. Waking an hour or two later to discover that Glenelg was enjoying a 'Summer Sunday Sponsored by Coca-Cola'. The early morning joggers had given way to elegant, tight-lipped old couples promenading in straw hats along the front. Then, as I yawned and rolled over, and the sunshine grew hotter and stronger, burly men arrived with trampo-lines, sound systems and tents, and soon the grassy strip above the beach was full of people picnicking while a rock band played cover versions of all our old favourites. Here were two women flat out in the Massage and Reflexology tent; there, a lanky fourteen-year-old did crazy things on a ramp with a mountain bike. In the street by the Town Hall were stalls selling beads and hand-painted scarves and pottery Buddhas.

There's a tram from Glenelg to central Adelaide and what a delightful transport it is! Two cars with deep crimson seats, polished chrome railings, varnished wood walls, leather hanging straps. *Bzz-bzz* – we're off! Up the very centre of Glenelg High Street, past Bayside Recollec-tions, Love at First Bite and Geoffrey Cock, Pharmacy. *Clang! Clang!* go the bells as we cross the Brighton Road. Up through the glorious homes of the suburbs, sunlight flashing through the eucalypts. Here's a nice one. No. 70. White pillars on its corner porch; outside four privet bushes are topiarised into neat upside-down bells. *Bzz-Bzz!* Now we're through a park and into the city. SOUTH TERRACE. The buildings are three or four storeys, ugly and modern as anywhere. But now here's a wide boulevard, King William Street, with sunlit plane trees and La Trattoria restaurant. Then eight- and ten-storey buildings grouped around flat green lawns. *Clang!* We're at the end of the line, right under the statue of Queen Victoria, who is not amused to be still stuck here, shat upon by kookaburras, in the farthest corner of her dominions.

She is not the only one subject to such indignities. Along North Terrace, where the sandstone State Library, South Australian Museum and Art Gallery are set back behind shady green lawns, there's a whole row of ex-achievers: from EDWARD VII, KING AND EMPEROR to SIR SAMUEL PATRICK WAY, BARONET, P.C, LIEUTENANT GOVERNOR, CHIEF JUSTICE AND CHANCELLOR OF THE UNIVERSITY.

Behind Parliament House on the corner (Kapunda marble and West Island granite) there's a startling change of tone. A decidedly groovy Open Space, filled with red, yellow, and black geometric shapes and a weird array of primary-coloured pillars (is 'pillars' what they are?) leads over to the funky white curves of the Festival Centre. It is, as I'm to discover, a deeply symbolic transition.

## Cheers, Dears and Queers

Paul was in his late thirties. Almost entirely bald, with a smile that flashed on and off like a cartoon character, he lived in a pretty little house in Eastwood, a twenty-minute walk through the ring of parks that completely surrounds Adelaide's oblong central grid.

Out back was a terrace with a vine, and running down the garden fence were seven magnificent marijuana bushes. I'd never seen such plants, five foot high at least. And all entirely legal. In South Australia cannabis had for over a decade been decriminalised; you were allowed up to eight plants for personal use.

It was this liberalisation that had brought Paul to Adelaide. He'd lived in Japan for a long while, then tried Sydney and Cairns. But Adelaide, he reckoned, had everything. It was a manageable size, you could get up into the hills in twenty minutes, the climate was Mediterranean.

After a while the doorbell rang and Tim appeared. Until this point Paul's sexuality had not been mentioned. But now, with the arrival of this crop-haired, triangular-faced blond who was clearly Gay-with-a-capital-G, things were all slightly more out in the open.

Paul offered us some cake to go with our beers. Tim declined, but when it turned out to be *dope* cake he rapidly changed his mind. Not being a great marijuana man I picked gingerly at mine, enjoying the sensation of the drug tingling up the back of my head, making me feel that this is really a very different sort of Adelaide from the one I was expecting, which was a 'City of Churches', of 'wowsers' (puritans), or at least, in the words of one Sydneysider, a city that's trying so hard to be genteel but in fact has the highest murder rate in Australia . . .

But all that's way out of date now. I see Adelaide to be a city of glowing vines and glowing jug ears (backlit by the sun, Tim's shine crimson) and with the mellowest, most laid-back conversation where tedious issues of sexuality DO NOT ENTER . . .

Now Tim is explaining how he came originally from a farming family in Victoria whom he still doesn't speak to and his four brothers won't accept that he's gay, only one of them, and how it was the *gay community* that taught him all the values he has – he slams his hand hard on the wooden slats of the table, nearly upsetting our beers – Respect and Honesty and Love, 'they taught me all I knew', and I'm repeating RHL, RHL because I want to remember this, it's *important* what he's saying, Respect and Honesty and Love, which he never learnt at home and when he was seventeen his brother came at him with a loaded gun but funnily enough that's the brother he gets on best with today, the one he *can* talk to . . .

But I know I won't remember this because I've eaten not one but two slices of cake now and Paul has told us how putting chocolate in gives the cake flavour and colour which it otherwise wouldn't have, it would otherwise be BRIGHT GREEN because the butter is BRIGHT GREEN and for a moment now all the thoughts in my head are BRIGHT GREEN like the lovely backlit vine except of course Tim's ears which are BRIGHT PINK . . .

Tim is a thoroughly nice and decent person. He works at the Daughters of Charity in Hutt Street once a week. I should go there. Every Thursday they serve up a meal to the homeless and it's a really good meal for sixty cents the best stew he's ever had and he was sitting next to this Aboriginal woman last week and that's really why he goes for moments like that . . .

Now Paul's boyfriend Jonathon has returned home. He's rather pretty and sulky-looking with short black hair bobbed around his ears and big sensual lips and he came over to Australia when he was four and Paul thinks of him as British and he's rather gentle and polite but a bit *floppy* as if in some way life is an awfully wearisome *bother* and oh *god* do I *really* have to sit at home with these people *now* . . .

For some reason Tim has assumed I'm gay so I've dropped in a little girlfriend mention and now Tim is covering his mouth with his big pink hand and saying, 'I'm so sorry, I assumed you were gay.' It's no big deal but he seems very worried about the fact that he's just *assumed* . . .

Now Paul's vanished and we've been joined by a swarthy-looking man and another with a huge bushy black moustache, fifty if he's a day, who's a Merchant Seaman of some kind. Carlo is Australian but of Italian background; he's forty but hasn't yet told his parents he's gay. Tim is sure they know but he's been mothered a bit too much so he just can't come out with it (all this I discover while he's in the loo) . . .

Then there's a thin, twittering queen whose hair is pressed flat on his head and whose lips are a long, thin line curving down suddenly at each end, whose mannerisms are the mannerisms of a bad actress impersonating an old-fashioned woman from the North Country – I mean is he feminine or what? He's called George and he wears a bodyhugging roll-necked black T-shirt . . .

Now here's Tim's brand-new lover who's a wealthy tour-operator from England who smells even from here of cologne and fag ash and in his ironed shirt and silk tie and crisp, slightly shiny grey trousers looks like a London estate agent who's just had a hard day flogging waterside residences in Docklands . . .

He and Tim are full of each other. They hold hands and laugh at each other's jokes and Tim claps and he's moving to England for ever in July . . .

I'm thinking it's time to go but Paul insists I stay and all of a sudden an elaborate meal is before us they've actually been making stuffed Japanese dumplings in the kitchen and having cooked the rice they haven't just dumped it on the plate but smoothed it into the shape of half a rugger ball for Christ's sake around which is delicately arranged the sumptuous colour-coordinated stir-fry . . .

We're all men together and now Carlo raises his glass and looks around conspiratorially and says, 'Cheers, dears and queers!' And I get a glimpse of how it might be being gay but at that moment Andrew is pointing out to Carlo that I'm not and it's apology time all over again and I'm making self-deprecating jokes about English heterosexuals . . .

Eventually, pleading tiredness, I retire. There's a futon in the front room and Paul unwraps me one of his supply of fresh toothbrushes and gives me a Japanese cotton robe and takes all my clothes and pops them into the washer for the night they'll be dry by morning and I wake in the small hours to hear the bang bang bang of the door in the wind and see the little square of streetlight between the

curtains and hear the loud *miaow* of Paul's small grey cat
who has sneaked in here to hide from Alex the rottweiler
puppy (some puppy!) who has very sharp teeth when he
nips you and what on earth

> am I doing here
> in Australia
> in Adelaide
> lying on a strange gay man's futon in the cold grey
> dawn?

There are eucalypts galore in the famous Barossa Valley,
but to me it feels, with its vine-covered hillsides, and
poplars, and narrow lanes, and little villages, like Europe
in late summer. Outside the wineries the coaches are
drawing up, disgorging their dayglo gaggles of tourists
and backpackers. At the wine-tasting counters the elegantly
turned out ladies are superbly upbeat, frank and unpreten-
tious about their products. 'This one reminds me of old
raisins and Christmas puddings,' says one, 'that's if your
Christmasses are anything like mine.' 'Lime marmalade,'
says another, 'nice and sweet but fresh in the mouth.' At
Yalumba (which looks just like the picture on the label, an
Australian French château) we try the Best Muscat in the
World for Under $20. 'It's a bit hard to backtrack after that
one, isn't it?' says our saleswoman sweetly. 'Unless you get
yourself a nice cheese platter and fruit and nuts and choc-
cies and try a port.'

The punters are equally forthright. 'Mm. That's an
unusual taste, mate. What is it?'

'It's late picked, which means it stays sweeter?'

'Ah right.'

Sweeping down the freeway from the hills you see
Adelaide in a new light, flat on its little plain by the sea.
'What d'you think those are for?' Paul asks, pointing out
the strips of plastic mesh hung over the concrete central
reservation. 'I can't guess.' 'Koalas.' He smiles. 'It's to help

them cross the road. Otherwise they get as far as the middle and panic.'

## Home and Hosed

Deborah was plump and pretty with a mane of ginger hair and a wild infectious laugh. Her conversation was a stream of great Aussie expressions: 'It's a real shithouse of a day', 'you're home and hosed', 'I wouldn't go there in a pink fit', 'my heart pumps piss for you, mate'. Inadequate men were 'dropkicks' or 'wusses'.

She was thirty-six, had come back home to Adelaide from Sydney because her father was unwell; now she was wondering why she was here. In the evening sunlight she took me through elaborate plans for the garden of the little house she'd just bought in Northwood (the old Italian district, now being colonised by yuppies like her). The Hills Hoist was going to be moved over there, scrapped maybe; that bessa-brick wall was going to be re-rendered in Italian sienna, there was going to be a hanging vine here, little areas behind bushes where you could sit and read. But the very next morning she giggled and said, 'D'you want to buy a house in Adelaide, Mark? I might just sell it. I've been offered this job in France earning double what I'm earning now.'

None the less she's looking for another lodger. There's already one, Amanda, who has jet-black hair and jet-black eyes outlined with thick black kohl. Her face, contrasting, is pan-white and she wears bright crimson lippy. She's never even heard of Mabo. 'Of *Melbourne*?' Debs shrieks, incredulously. 'No, of Mabo.' 'Oh, Mabo . . . yes, what *is* Mabo exactly?'

The phone rings. 'He's a policeman,' says Amanda, hand cupped over the receiver. 'Do we want a policeman?' laughs Debs. 'Nye. Tell him it's taken.' Then there's a jeweller, who actually gets invited round. 'I've got rid of the jeweller,' says Debs, as I lie on the glorious new crimson couch leafing through a copy of *Cleo* ('Australia's 50 most ELIGIBLE BACHELORS'). 'Why didn't you want him?' 'Not my type. A sissy.'

In Debs's company, Adelaide suddenly becomes a fun and easy place to be. We go to an old English-style pub called the Rising Sun and drink schooners of Cooper's Draught, which is the South Australian beer, better than VB, far better than Foster's, but with a mean sting in its tail in the heavy little headache you get in the morning. We go to a pretty little arthouse called The Chelsea and watch the new movie from New Zealand that everyone's talking about – *Heavenly Creatures*. We head down to Rundle Street and drink sunny South Australian Chardonnay at a table outside one of the numerous restaurants and people wander past and say hello and 'Who's he?' I ask of a fortyish cool dude with shoulder-length hair. 'Oh, just a man about town,' says Debs. He looks like an artist but is in fact a stockbroker.

How many happening young trendies does a population of one million throw up? I think. Everyone knows everyone else. And Debs knows everyone else.

So I want to talk to someone about the wine industry? Who better than Debs's friend Michael Hill-Smith who owns the Universal Restaurant on – guess where? – Rundle Street. The Hill-Smiths are one of South Australia's Old Families; they've been making wine up at Yalumba for six generations, since Samuel Smith came over from Wareham in Dorset in 1847. His grandson Percival Sidney Smith (nicknamed 'Tiger') was a celebrated big-game hunter and a household name in India. Tiger's nephew Wyndham Hill-Smith was one of the big figures in Australian racing in the 1950s. Now Michael, *his* great-nephew, who has a shaved head and 'a bit of a problem with the whole concept of dynasties at the best of times', has sold his share in Yalumba to his brother and 'now has maximum freedom to do the wine and food thing. Rather,' he laughs, 'than just sitting

there and saying, "How many cases of Angas Brut Sparkling Rose are we going to sell this week?" Which is just not
my scene.' After three years' study in the UK he's become
Australia's first ever Master of Wine.

We talk about the Great Australian Food Revolution.
Michael can still remember, as a kid, going out for dinner.
There were oysters, natural, Kilpatrick, Mornay; there was
lobster, Mornay, Thermidor; there was carpet-bag steak, T-
bone steak, with or without mushroom sauce, 'in very racy
places there was a schnitzel or two, and that was it!'

Now there's Woodside Goat Curd with Eggplant Salsa
and Olives, Yearling Rump with Tomato and Chili Jam, and
Braised Roo Tail with Potato Gnocchi. And that's just in
the Universal. Today. Venture down the street and you can
eat almost any animal on a bed of couscous, or stir-fried in
a filo pastry case, or marinated in madeira, or lovingly
lowered onto a mound of sweet-potato fritters. And Australia now has the largest *per capita* consumption of wine
of any English-speaking country in the world.

'What I like about the Australian approach to wine and
food,' says Michael, 'versus say the American approach, is
that good wine and food in America is very elitist, it's the
domain of the wealthy, the upwardly mobile, it's wine
clubs, it's smart dinners, it's all that sort of stuff. We have
that also, but wine-drinking and the recent improvement
in the food goes down to a base level. Even if you went to
the most working-class barbecue on a Sunday there would
be people drinking wine there. They'd also,' he grins, 'be
drinking a fuck of a lot of beer.'

## Don's Place

Don Dunstan remembered the old Adelaide too:

During the First World War the dissenting churches and the
Women's Christian Temperance Union had worked success-
fully to establish early closing of all outlets for the supply of

liquor – so hotels had to close their dining facilities at six p.m. By 1950 licensed restaurants could serve liquor till nine, but at that time your glass was whisked from the table whether you had finished your meal or not. In any event, it was well-nigh impossible to find an eating place open in Adelaide after seven p.m., other than street carts selling meat pies and pea soup. There were some establishments where one could go to dance – such daring innovations as the samba and the gypsy tap – but drinking liquor was forbidden within three hundred yards of such gaiety. One could not get a licence for a members club, nor a retail liquor shop, nor a hotel, without a poll in the locality as to whether there should be an increase in licences ... Dress was carefully prescribed. Men and boys were required to wear suits and collars and ties. Students at Adelaide secondary schools and clerks in the Public Service must wear collars, ties and jackets done up in the streets on days when the temperature exceeded 40 C. On the beaches, it is true, councils had ceased to prosecute men wearing topless bathing costumes. However, no respectable clothier in Adelaide would sell a pair of men's bathing trunks without a frontal skirt being attached to conceal their unthinkable and unmentionable bulge in the crotch.*

So it had been in 1950, when he'd started in politics. Now, in 1990, the ex-Premier received me in the neat lounge of his home in Northwood wearing nothing over his compact, well-tanned torso but white shorts and a string vest. Times had changed, and he, the great radical leader of the 1970s, a figure as significant to South Australia as Margaret Thatcher was to Britain, would have to take a good part of the credit for changing them.

At the end of the Sixties, after a brief first spell in Government, he'd set out a blueprint for reforming the Wowser State. Elected again in 1970, he'd put his programme into practice, bringing in, among other measures, consumer protection laws, anti-discrimination legislation (race and sex), expanded social services, votes for eighteen-year-olds,

* *Felicia: The Political Memoirs of Don Dunstan* (Macmillan, Melbourne and London 1981) – pp. 22–34.

beach nudity, an easing in censorship, reformed licensing hours, increased subsidies for the arts, and land rights for Aboriginals. A menu of policies, in short, designed to make a member of the Adelaide Establishment go pink with rage. (Pink as the shorts that Dunstan had famously worn one day to Parliament. Though, as he explained to me now, like most things people are famous for in the twentieth century, they were a media fiction. It had been white shorts he'd worn to work that hot summer's day; but with a radical, openly gay Premier, it was the pink-shorts story that travelled best along the wires; to make news not just Australia-wide, but internationally.)

The irony, of course, was that Dunstan was no outsider. His aunt, with whom he'd lived as a child, had been Mayoress of Adelaide; her father had been the Lord Mayor. He himself had attended St Peter's College ('Saints') then as now the premier private school in the state. 'I don't suppose we were considered one of the great families at all, but yes, I grew up among the Establishment. And came to loathe both the humbug and the cynical manipulation that was going on.'

'Did it make you a more effective battler, being an insider?' I asked.

'Yes, to a certain extent, yes.'

'Because you knew where they were coming from, had grown up with them around the place?'

'Yes.'

By the end of the 1970s, the power of the Establishment and the old, interlocking families and company directorates had been broken to a very large extent. 'And yes, of course they blame me. So they don't like me.'

'Not even socially?'

'There are a number of members of the Establishment who regard me with considerable personal distaste.'

We discussed the details of his period in office. He agreed that South Australia being relatively small had facilitated the speedy transformation he'd achieved. 'In terms of experiment, yes, it was manageable.' He felt that he'd made the right appointments, although there had been some bad mistakes, particularly among those who'd subsequently attacked him in public. Nor did he feel that, like Mrs Thatcher, he'd fallen into the trap of listening only to his own cabal of advisers. Not only had he worked very closely with his cabinet, he'd appointed an officer in the Premier's department with a special brief to keep backbenchers informed of all forward moves in all departments. He'd held weekly meetings with trade union and business leaders, and everyone was 'made to feel they had complete access to me'.

In short, 'overall, I think, it went pretty well'. Though, because of his sudden illness in 1979, he'd only achieved about half of what he'd really wanted to do. He'd had ambitions to do something about, for example, the nineteenth-century style with which Australian management and unions insisted on persisting; the corporation laws that had institutionalised, 'the kind of piracy that still attracts jail terms in the United States . . .'

It was not to be. His more moderate successors hadn't had it in them to continue. 'It was all thrown in the wastebasket.' And not just the agenda, but the way Dunstan would have achieved the agenda. 'You can't do it just by legislation. It has to be a whole, lengthy process of administration, experiment, pressure and the like.' Now, most galling of all, 'I've had academics who are coming in and saying, "If we'd gone ahead with your programme . . ." ' Don shrugged and gave me a philosophical smile. 'I say, "Yes, well, we'd be in a rather different situation." '

But if there was something of the inevitable regret that he'd not been able to rule for ever, there was no sentimental harking back, no desire to be at the centre of things. 'People these days say, "But don't you miss the cut and thrust of politics," and I say, "Not one bit." '

'And you mean that?'

'I had to be in politics a fairly aggressive character. We

were under such attack – because we trod on toes in order to achieve the changes – that I had to be aggressive in defence. And I was regarded as a fairly effective sort of political bruiser, but actually, personally, I'm a very peaceable bloke.' Don laughed. 'I don't like to get involved in rows at all.' He paused and looked across the room, lost somewhere for a moment; then, 'Afterwards, while I was working in Victoria, I had to go up to the Victorian Houses of Parliament to see the minister who was responsible for my commission over there and I'd hear this stuff going on in the House and say, "Thank *god* I don't have to be involved in *that* any more." '

What had I expected of the man who'd worn shorts – albeit white – to Parliament? More flamboyance, anecdote, reminiscence, outrage even. Not this gentle looking back, this careful barrister's prudence.

*How d'you feel when you look at Adelaide and see the transformation you've been responsible for? What was it like, being up there, actually putting your ideals into practice, watching the place literally transform under your adventurous, skilfully managed programme of legislation?*

That was the question I was trying to ask. I told him about Paul's eight marijuana plants, the dope cake I'd legally been offered by a man who'd come to the state specifically attracted by its liberality. (He and how many others?)

'Is that so?' Don replied, with a smile.

'I mean,' I fumbled, 'these are things that you . . . I'm not saying the marijuana particularly, but . . . D'you at times feel responsible, in the sense that you look at Adelaide and think . . .'

'Yes, yes, yes!' Don interrupted. 'Of course I feel responsible. I glow with achievement. It was not just enormous *fun* but thrilling, changing the state into what I wanted it to be . . .'

*Of course not.*

'Well I was certainly,' Don interrupted, 'to a considerable

extent responsible for the changes both in law and in attitude. And certainly the Royal Commission into the use and abuse of drugs was about the most extensive enquiry that's ever been held. I instituted it and provided educational services for people to start to understand what it was all about because our laws have really been formulated by people who were completely misinformed . . .'

How else could he respond? It was this very care and cogency that had got the thing achieved. The Festival Centre, the multicoloured pillars, the funky late-night café society of Rundle Street. A man who'd really worn pink shorts would never have had the follow-through.

If this were England, I thought, as I left him, Don Dunstan would now be in the House of Lords, his accumulated wisdom and experience being frittered away on amendments and twilight tut-tutting on the terrace. Being Adelaide, though, he'd joined in his own revolution and opened a restaurant – Don's Place. (He ran it, so they told me, in a pretty hands-on way.)

# 17

# Wizard Man

*In the Dreamtime, the Murray River was just a small stream. Ancestor Ngurunderi travelled down it in a bark canoe, in search of his two wives, who had run away from him.*

*A giant cod fish, Ponde, swam ahead of Ngurunderi, widening the stream with curving sweeps of its tail so that it became the twisting Murray. Ngurunderi chased the fish, trying to spear it from his canoe. Near Murray Bridge his spear missed and was changed into Long Island (or Lenteilin as the Ngarrindjeri people call it). A little further down, at Tailem Bend, he threw another; the giant fish surged ahead and created the long straight stretch of the river.*

*At last, with the help of Nepele, brother of one of Ngurunderi's errant wives, Ponde was speared; by now it had left the Murray and swum into Lake Alexandrina. Ngurunderi divided the fish with his stone knife and created a new species of fish from each piece.*

*Meanwhile, Ngurunderi's two wives had made camp. On their campfire they were cooking bony bream. Ngurunderi smelt the fish and knew his wives were close. He abandoned his camp and came after them. His huts became two hills.*

*Hearing Ngurunderi coming, his wives just had time to build a raft of reeds and grass-trees and to escape across Lake Albert. On the other side their raft turned back into the reeds and grass-trees. The women hurried south across the huge, salt-white flats of the Coorong.*

*Ngurunderi followed his wives as far south as the point where Kingston now stands. Here he met a great sorcerer, Parampari, who challenged him. The two men fought, using weapons and magic powers, until eventually Ngurunderi won. He burnt Parampari's body in a fire. The remains are the granite boulders you can see today. Then he turned north, pacing along the endless Coorong beach. Here he camped several times, digging soaks in the sand for fresh water, fishing in the Coorong lagoon.*

*Ngurunderi made his way across the Murray Mouth and along past Hindmarsh Island and Encounter Bay towards Victor Harbour. At Middleton, he threw a big tree into the sea and made the seaweed bed. Then he hunted and killed a seal; its dying gasps can still be heard among the rocks. At Port Elliot he camped and fished again, still without seeing any sign of his wives. He became angry and frustrated, hurled all his spears into the sea at Victor Harbour; they became the islands there.*

*Exhausted, Ngurunderi rested in the giant granite shade-shelter on Granite Island (Kaike). Now he heard his wives laughing and playing in the water near King's Beach. He hurled his club to the ground, creating Longkuwar (the Bluff), and strode after them.*

*His wives fled along the beach until they came to Cape Jervis. At this time Kangaroo Island was still connected to the mainland and the two women began to hurry across to it. Ngurunderi had arrived at Cape Jervis, though, and seeing his wives still fleeing from him, he called out in a voice of thunder for the waters to rise. The women were swept from their path by huge waves and soon drowned. They became the rocky Pages Islands.*

*Ngurunderi knew that it was time for him to re-enter the spirit world. He crossed to Kangaroo Island and travelled to its western end. After throwing his spears into the sea, he dived in, before rising to become a star in the Milky Way.**

---

* Based on *Ngurunderi, An Aboriginal Dreaming* by Hemming, Jones and Clark (South Australian Museum, 1989). See also R.M. Berndt, 'Some aspects of Jaralde Culture, South Australia' in *Oceania* 11 (2), pp. 164–85.

## Race Relations

Philip was a Government planner for the Murray-Darling River System. He was driving down with Ian Greenwood, friend of, and adviser to, the Ngarrindjeri people, to meet some of the elders and get their input on his forthcoming plans for the Murray. He outlined his respect, as a scientist, for Aboriginal Dreamtime stories. The Murray-Darling had twenty-six catchments; it needed to be dealt with in an holistic way; the Aboriginals had always understood this. 'If you look at that story about Ngurunderi,' he told me, 'the giant cod fish, Ponde, is a symbol of all life in the river and an explanation of how the river should be treated. If you regulate the river and raise the banks you get rid of the billabongs and the river will die. Fishstocks will go down and the whole ecosystem will destroy itself.'

Yes, Ian agreed, but it wasn't just that. The Dreamtime stories – the songs – taken in conjunction with the songlines which they detailed, held an awesome amount of natural knowledge. 'The geology of that mountain . . .' he began, gesturing out of the window at a biscuit-brown hill. 'It's the southernmost outcrop of the Flinders Ranges sandstone. There's a songline that goes all the way up from there to the Flinders Ranges.'

Besides geology, he went on, the songlines reflected boundaries of a whole host of animal and bird species. This very same mountain, for example, was the regional limit for the yellow robin.

'What you're saying,' said Philip, 'is that Aboriginal people were keen observers of Nature and interpreted it in a religious way.'

'Manipulated it actually,' Ian replied, before going off into a long explication that became increasingly hard to follow. Fantails came together here, bandicoots and yellow robins there. There was a sacred ratio. 'Within their land management,' he concluded, 'Aboriginals manipulated species on a national scale.'

'What you're saying,' said Philip, 'is that man influenced the landscape.'

'No, it goes further than that,' said Ian.

He wasn't just a friend to the Ngarrindjeri. He was also a senior elder with the Banggala and the all-but-extinct Mirning People of the Nullarbor. 'I'm the first white man to be taken to this level,' he told me proudly, holding up his Aboriginal elder's stick, carved from a single piece of acacia. 'You could say it was a wizard-wand.'

As far as the Banggala people were concerned, he'd literally inherited tribal responsibility. Ever since his family had arrived in South Australia in the 1850s they'd been different from the other whites in that they'd taken the local Aboriginal people under their wing and actually adopted them as a second family. When his grandfather, 'Smiler' Greenwood, went into town from the station, he'd come back with two identical saddlebags of supplies. One was for the white family and the other for the Aboriginals. Smiler would say to Les, the senior elder, 'Here, take your pick. They're the same.' As a result of this, the Banggala people had given them this significant place in their tribal structure. So now, elders from all over Australia would walk up to Ian and say, 'Eh you, you special fella. I can tell *you* this' . . .

Whether Ian was more of an authentic tribal member than all those other whites I'd met who'd boasted of their adoption into local Aboriginal structures, I didn't know. But besides the stick, he certainly had plenty of stories to substantiate his claim. He'd been to a desert community once to meet some elders. The white coordinator had been hoping just to get together a few Aboriginals, but when Ian appeared, suddenly there was this huge crowd. And this one elder stood up and spoke, eyes blazing, and later the coordinator had said, 'What I didn't understand, Ian, was that that fellow was directing what he was saying at *you*.'

But Ian had understood.

We came off the rolling Adelaide hills, over the Murray

at Murraybridge, down past the Tailem Bend where Ngurunderi had thrown his spear, along past Lake Alexandrina to the Coorong. It was a spectacular landscape: low sandy hills, shimmering mirage-like across the vast flat plain; beyond, the gleaming white sheet of the salt-encrusted mudflats; all this, under an overarching sky that made Lincolnshire look like Dorset.

Until 1966, Ian explained, the Ngarrindjeri people had lived out here in bush camps. 'Until Australia's apartheid ended and they were allowed to live in the towns.'

Robert Trevorrow, one of the Ngarrindjeri elders, who spoke with an almost West Country lilt and accent, elaborated: 'Just in camps we lived, in shacks made out of bark or tin or whatever you could pick up. We were given ration tickets every week by the Government, collected from the police station, otherwise it was bush tucker. Fish, ducks. Things like that, the wildlife. That's the way we had to survive, until things began to change.

'In the Forties and Fifties the Welfare people used to come out and check the camps. All we had in those days for mattresses were the boughs and that that we'd break off the trees. Put a bag over them and that was your bed. The Welfare would check them and say, "Well, you don't have proper beds, you don't have sheets, so we'll have to take your children." They wouldn't give you any blankets or any beds or any houses; but they expected you to have 'em. And if you didn't have 'em they'd take the light-skinned children away. To the Welfare Homes.'

'So you were dark enough to stay?'

'Stay here, yeah.'

'Did you have brothers?'

'I had three brothers and a sister taken away to the Welfare and it took me years to find that family. My eldest brother was fifty before I found him.'

Now, years later, with assistance from a more sympathetic Government, they'd set up Camp Coorong, which Robert and George, his somewhat paler cousin, described as an Education Centre. It was the fulfilment of a vision, they said, a dream they'd had a long time ago to set something in place, 'where we could teach the white people about the real history of our people and what's truly happened. Because we think the Government education system has really let people down over the years.'

'You could do Australian history,' said George, 'right up till recently and the kids in year twelve would not have heard *one word* about an Aboriginal person.'

We were three thousand kilometres from Perth but it was the same old story: white indifference, black hurt.

Part of it was that George and Robert still wanted to air the grievances of the past, the injustices that still irked in the angry edge to their otherwise gentle and reasonable voices; not just the indignities of the camps and passes and stolen children, but the idiotic inconsistencies. That prior to '67 they'd been classified as 'flora and fauna', yet Robert's father had been taken from the camp for possessing wine. 'They put him in a witness box and made him swear on oath with the bible in his hand – and I've never seen a flower or an animal do that yet.' The evasion of responsibility, too: 'The funny thing is,' said George, 'when I get into a debate on a lot of these issues they always blame the Pommies. They say, "That's them people did that." The buggers are always pointing the finger and saying, "Oh don't blame us, that's the bloody British." So I think the British should start kicking their heels up a bit and saying, "Hey, come on, it's a long time since we've been gone. You people have had plenty of years to change things. Stop avoiding the flak, you know." '

On a more positive note they also wanted to get across key aspects of Aboriginal culture: the relationship of the traditional beliefs to the land, the significance of the land, a proper understanding of what a sacred site was.

'People just throw that term around so very loosely,' said George. 'But there's a whole range of different layers of what we can call sacred sites. And without a lot of them, the survival of Aboriginal people – it's not there. We must retain some of them to be able to carry on.

'See we don't look at things the same way, I guess. We're looking at the Universe, the galaxy, everything's linked. And if you gonna take away one important link-up, just because you want to dig it up or something, you're destroying all these links we have, that's running all over. It's like taking away a part of you. When we're driving along the Coorong, any of us, it's not like you would, saying, "Look at that and this and that." We're relating stories to our children, every couple of hundred yards sometimes. These happenings have taken place at these spots. It's like a big book, as we drive through this country. We're opening pages and teaching our children as we're going. But over the years you lot have been tearing out those pages. And so we're going to slip and miss a few every now and then. And sometimes whole chapters have been moved and so you're jumping, you know. So you're not building your children's lives.'

'Let's look at it a different way,' Robert interjected. 'Compare it with the European way. When you say, Why should we have so many sacred sites? Well, why should you have so many church blocks? Why should you have so many football ovals? Because they have special meaning to you. And if you look at it you might have twice as many sacred sites in the European way as the Aboriginal people got. You've got reserves, you've got theatres to go to, you've got council chambers. They're all for a certain purpose. And so are Aboriginal people with the land. It's all for a certain purpose. There's initiation areas, there's burial grounds, it's the same thing.'

If the white children could grow up, they said, knowing something about these things then they'd be in a position to do something about it, 'because the kids that come through here, they're going to be doctors, they're going to be lawyers, they're going to be politicians and we're hoping that they'll remember what's been taught to them and they'll begin to change the system – because the dollar's not doing it'.

Their aspiration was that Camp Coorong would be the model for race-relations centres, Australia-wide. 'See,' George continued, 'when we started learning this white man's culture and education we got flogged and whipped and rations stopped and children taken away, all that. Because we had to learn his way. But now there's a move, all across Australia, we're inviting white people to come and sit with us and talk with us and try and understand what *we're* saying. People who don't even know what they're doing it for are doing it, because they're seeing what's happening to this country. It's being ripped apart. They call these people Greenies. All sorts of names they got for them now. But they're just people that care for the land, for the environment. Because that's what's killing us, this continual bashing of the environment.'

## An Ancestor Returned

It would have been good, nay authentic, to have gone to see the sacred sites of the Coorong with a Ngarrindjeri, but George was feeling unwell and Robert had to have his meeting about the Murray-Darling with Philip. So Ian the Wizard Man and I took the Landcruiser down the coast to a point where a low crumbling cliff overlooked mudflats glinting with dried salt and a channel running along to a shallow, sky-reflecting lagoon. Just over the narrow stretch of water was an endless line of tall dunes, beyond which was the 130-kilometre-long beach of the Younghusband peninsula.

Where we sat was a sacred site, Ian explained. An inter-section of songlines, a natural fish farm and a symmetry place. At high-water levels, seasonally, the channel filled up and fish moved from the sea to the lagoon. 'All you've got to do is dip your net into the channel and you've got a feed.' This was another of the key aspects of the songlines; they accessed the natural resources. So if you knew your songline you could go from resource to resource methodically. But if you were an alien, and this wasn't your territory, and you didn't know the song, you couldn't pillage another group's resources.

'Can you see that area of vegetation there?' he asked, pointing over the channel to a clump of thick green bushes on top of the dunes. 'Well, that's a marker. Directly below that is a permanent freshwater spring. And just next to it the patch of sand is an access route through to the ocean. The songline goes straight through there, that's where it's carved its way through the dune system.'

*Carved its way through*? But Ian would hear of no scepticism: a songline could and would directly affect the landscape. Now, getting increasingly excited, he showed me how, if you took his wizard wand, you could see how the symmetry-place aspect worked; you could divide the landscape around us into significant features separated by an identical distance. So: from the gap in the dunes to the end of the channel; from the end of the channel . . . and so on, in a radial fashion: hill, dip with lagoon in it; hill, dip with lagoon . . . *None of this was accidental.*

'As an Aboriginal person walks through the landscape,' Ian continued, 'his relation to the landscape is such that as he walks over a site that's significant or sacred he will actually experience a physical, tangible sensation. That all Aboriginals present will sense in some way. And if they're particularly connected to that site, or are the custodian of that site, they may be so overwhelmed by the feeling that goes with the place that they may have to sit down and meditate to get their act together.'

Over all the years that he'd been working with Aboriginals he'd become increasingly aware of these feelings. 'It's a really interesting exercise walking around with them. Whereby I'll say, "Hey, we've arrived somewhere, I feel it."

And they'll say, "Yeah, you're right as to why you're feeling the way you're feeling." '

Later, Ian told Philip and I more about his extraordinary engagement with this Aboriginal world. He was deeply involved with the lawmen; he was on intimate terms with the National Custodian of the Moon Dreaming; more sinister, because of his unique position with the Mirning people, he was currently being 'sung' by enemy sorcerers, who were trying to destroy him so that they could lay claim to Mirning traditional lands.

Ian had recently, in fact, become very ill and had had to be operated on by traditional Aboriginal doctors. Which *was* amazing. 'One moment I was in agony, minutes later I was fine.'

They'd removed a green stone from the area of his liver, without cutting his flesh. There was no scar. But had he seen it, we asked. No, but it had existed. The Aboriginal doctors were going to send it to him. In any case, his girlfriend Linda, who was a nurse, had seen the green spot on his stomach.

He'd also had a six-inch-long sorcerer's spear removed. And that, had he seen that? No, but he'd felt it slide out, every millimetre of the way. Again it had left no mark.

'Did the sorcerer physically give you the spear?' Philip asked tactfully. 'Or perhaps it's symbolic?'

No, it hadn't been symbolic, it had been real. He had been in agony, lying on his carpet at home; and he could sense this music in the background, like flutes, didgeridoos, almost like a whale's song. 'When I told George he said, "Ian, you're in trouble, mate, you're being sung." '

Why, we asked, if the Aboriginals really did have these astonishing powers, had they not used them on the white settlers, two hundred years ago. Such sorcery, Ian replied, didn't work on the whites, because the whites weren't as sensitive to the forces that surround us.

The other point was that the Aboriginals had always believed that their ancestors would return as white people.

At this point Ian turned to me and said, 'That's me, mate. I am an ancestor returned.' Seeing my astonished face he said, 'I'm not that bothered whether people believe this or not. I've got enough trouble dealing with it myself. I've got enough trouble staying alive.'

## Plastic Cactus on the Great Ocean Road

Coming into Victoria I imagine the landscape has changed. The verges seem greener, quainter, like a 1930s England, thick with wildflowers. I speed past the empty fir forests and dayglo cyclists of a couple of National Parks. DROWSY DRIVERS DIE says a stern sign, so I stop for lunch in 'historic Port Fairy' and eat tandoori chicken quiche and strawberries beside a noisy foursome of pale-faced Melburnians who've just arrived for a weekend away.

The Great Ocean Road is one of Australia's most famously picturesque stretches of landscape, so naturally, on this sun-blindingly lovely Saturday afternoon, it's swarming with Japanese. Against the gorgeous honey-coloured rock formations of the Bay of Islands, by the Scenic Lookout of the crumbling Twelve Apostles they pose, grinning as politely and light-heartedly as they do outside the British Museum, the Coliseum, the Acropolis. (What makes them so cheerful, you wonder, as always: their culture, escaping their culture, or a soul-sustaining combination of the two?)

At six, exhausted, I arrive at Apollo Bay. White horses fleck the cold cobalt blue of the Southern Ocean. This is not where I'm supposed to be *at all*. Misjudging the distance, I've arranged to meet Alan (an architect I met in Perth) in the Dogs Bar in St Kilda at seven. Now I phone and get his disembodied-sounding answerphone. 'G'day. After a long day on the road of life, you have reached the Palace of Dreams. Please leave your fantasy.'

Mine right now is a stubby of VB in the Dogs Bar, so I

press on, winding along an exquisite, cliff-hugging road peppered with signs saying ACCIDENT ZONE. It's no good. I'm so tired I can barely see, let alone appreciate the beauty of the place, let alone drive into Melbourne tonight. But the clifftop Rookery-Nook Motel is full. And arriving in the dusky, crowded streets of Lorne there are glimmering NO VACANCIES signs everywhere.

I crawl on, as slow as a drunk, hugging the twisting white line in the dark. Eventually, on the hill out of Airey's Inlet, I see the shining beacon of a pink VACANCIES. It's a motel run by Greeks and the only room they have, says the lisping teenage beauty in the white bikini top, is a $140-a-night luck-thurry double thpa. Better than a coffin, I think, as I lie in the heart-shaped bath, massaged by shuddering jets, magnificently alone. Over the road, the decidedly unmatey barman has stopped serving food. So I find myself ... ah well ... in the Airey's Inlet Mexican. In the weird clarity of my exhaustion it seems preposterous that I am here, staring at this plastic cactus in its kitsch pile of yellow stones wondering whether to eat enchiladas or tacos while all around the hilarious Melbourne weekenders booze and shriek and *this* (I think, understanding in a cosmic flash all the doctrines of existentialism) is what travel, Australia, Christ – life is all about, this kind of mad *moment*, not the great objective overview you'd like it to be. 'A book about Australia' – *ridiculous*.

In the small hours I wake, with slowly dawning panic, to realise I am at the bottom of a mineshaft. In Kalgoorlie. I have checked into a *mine*. Then I see the lace. Oh, thank god for that! It's the top of the four poster and I'm in a luxury thpa unit in Airey's Inlet.

'Melbourne weather,' says Cleopatra, making a very English face as she flicks her lovely dark eyes towards the grey swathes of rain outside. Then with Mozart's Clarinet Concerto on a new radio station I'm skimming through a pair of nondescript Tidy Towns (HELP US WIN IT – BIN IT). Scruffy smallholdings give way to BUY ONE PIZZA, GET

ONE FREE. Mature cedars stand stranded by a small airport (SCENIC FLIGHTS – $20). There's a tall church spire black against the sky. VOX MEGASTORE, GELATI, HOME APPLIANCES, a freeway on a bleak, dark plain, distant silhouettes of skyscrapers, a horrible mess of pylons, then I'm swooping way, way up onto a suspension bridge, the orange cranes and gantries of Melbourne docks far below.

# 18

# No Vurrey

There were no Aboriginals on the lush green grass beneath the dripping plane trees of Queen Victoria Gardens. They were over the road in the Arts Centre, in full corroboree-warpaint, blowing into didgeridoos, publicising the National Aboriginal Art Award, whose accompanying exhibition had just opened.

The pale-faced, smartly dressed Melburnians smiled obliquely as they wandered past them into the gallery, to stand nodding and smiling and scratching their heads and saying, 'Ah yes, this one's much more accessible' to each other.

Outside it was raining again, so I followed the gleaming brass handrail along the plush, crimson-carpeted corridor, pushed through smoked-glass doors and found myself in the Treble Clef Café, where the waitresses had tight black skirts and starched white shirts and the 'French Breakfast' had a *Guardian*-style typeface and I was offered not just eggs, but *The* Eggs, and having scoffed those, *The* Pizzas, *The* Cheese, *Side* Orders and – mm! – *Sweet* Tooth.

*The* View, though, was the best thing. Across the narrow Yarra River to the wonderfully jumbled skyline of central Melbourne, which looked as if a child had been let loose with a box of 1930s coloured bricks.

Being a new state there were new newspapers to read. The *Sunday Age*, a beefy, multi-sectioned wodge which put the flimsy tabloids of Adelaide, Perth, Darwin and Brisbane to shame. There was a new go-ahead right-wing Premier, Jeff Kennett (currently on a world tour), and new issues: a proposed extension to the freeway that threatened either the grounds of prestigious Scotch College or the courts of an upmarket tennis club. The *Age* had a feature identifying leading 'Establishment old boys' who would support one route or the other.

Albert Park, meanwhile, was having a Grand Prix track built all over it. The pros were thrilled at pinching the race and the business from Adelaide; the antis were chaining themselves to bulldozers and talking about green lungs of sanity. Several respectable old folk had got themselves arrested and were now, in their dotage, suddenly 'radicalised'. 'Pamela Morison used to be "Miss". Now the 72-year-old former executive prefers the honorific "Ms." ' 'Yes, I'll go to jail rather than pay a fine,' she says. 'Who would have thought retired Carnegie librarian, Mr John Lowe, would chain himself to a truck?' 'I just had to do it: I feel very strongly,' he explains.

Five kilometres down the road on one of Melbourne's numerous green trams (only St Petersburg has more) was St Kilda, the most central of a string of seaside suburbs running south along Port Philip Bay. Once grand, then run-down and red-light, the place was now wholeheartedly groovy, full of pale-faced trendies hanging out in coffee bars, rollerbladers swooping over the tramlines to the tatty stucco frontage of the Esplanade. In the supermarket one evening I was to count twelve ponytails, seven of which were grey.

The Palace of Dreams was in a modern block a couple of streets back from the beach, a one-bedroomed flat with big picture windows overlooking a central courtyard, highly polished floorboards and not a lot of furniture. Alan had recently split up with his live-in fiancée and she'd gone off with most of their stuff: the kitchen table, the chairs, lots of the crocks, even the guest futon and duvet. He was terribly sorry but the only thing there was for me to sleep on was a narrow inflatable mattress – what we Poms call a lilo. ('I'll try and get something more comfortable sorted out,' he said every morning, as I smiled up at him from my squidgy pallet, watching him iron his shirt in front of the TV before he raced off to work.)

I got on the phone. Now here's an interesting thing. Almost all my contacts in Melbourne were couples. And without fail they all said, 'We must organise something for later in the week. I'll talk to my partner and we'll call you back.' Nobody said, as they had in Brisbane, Perth, Adelaide and Sydney, 'Mate! What are you doing *tonight*!'

With time to kill I called on William, the art dealer I'd met buying Emilys in the desert.

His gallery in Flinders Lane was bare except for a huge crate. A new show had just opened, and the artist, Spook (a.k.a Gary James) had challenged the space by taking all his paintings off the wall and hanging them, squashed up against each other, inside the crate; on its floor were a series of dog bowls featuring a monochrome mugshot of the new Premier; EAT OFF JEFF, they said, provocatively.

Meeting William again, I felt rather bad that I'd ever thought of him as Mr Bean. He didn't look like Mr Bean really, at all; he was thoroughly welcoming and obliging; and when I asked him whom I should talk to in Melbourne, he touchingly suggested his mother; (the very mother he'd talked about so fondly to Emily while she was painting). She was definitely a Melbourne identity: a well-known painter, a survivor of the Holocaust, and, in the Fifties, a famous restaurateur. William's father, indeed, had been in possession of Certificate No. 1, the first wine licence in Melbourne. And what had there been before that, I asked. Nothing; William smiled. Not restaurants where you could drink, anyway. It had been the same as Don Dunstan's Adelaide, pubs which closed at six. 'You've heard about the swill?' he said.

The front door of Mirka's little redbricked house in St
Kilda was nondescript enough, but inside was a *lair*. You
could barely get through the door for all the clutter. The
corridor was lined on both sides, floor to ceiling, with
books. The front room was stacked solid with stuff: more
books, wicker baskets, dried flowers, a doll, a buried piano.
Mirka worked in the room at the back, surrounded by
yet more books, a selection of favourite old paintings, her
brushes, a bowl of apples.

She was in her sixties, small and round, with the same
big, dark eyes as the doll-like figures in her paintings.
Instantly you felt welcome. More than that, she gave off a
tangible upbeat energy. I arrived worn out and weary;
when I left, two hours later, I felt recharged. Melbourne
was surely, as Mirka had said in her thick, all-but-caricature
French accent, 'very rare, very sophisticated, not as it
seems'.

It was the place where, after the extraordinary escapes
and dangers of wartime France, she had had an *idée fixe* to
come, because she'd read a beautiful Victorian novelle, *La
Vie de Boheme*, by Henri Merget, 'and in it was a charming
man, who always kept going, back and forwards, to Melbourne, which was so far away in those days, can you
imagine travelling like zat? ... I was smitten when I read
zis beautiful book and I was very intrigued ...'

Now it was the place where, in the Fifties, when the city
was 'a *dessert*' and the Establishment was 'pure Philistine',
she and her much older French husband ('a great friend of
Marcel Marceau') had entertained, in their studio on Collins
Street, a *coterie* of painters, writers, politicians. 'Ar-tur Boyd,
Black-man, Per-ci-val, lots of wonderful composers, Dr
Evatt would come, everybody would come ... in the
morning I would 'ave twenty people for breakfast, it was
a very fabulous time.'

The bohemian breakfasts had led to a little café. 'All ze
great stars came because we were now in Exhibition Street,
where all ze seatres were. I remember Katherine Hepburn

coming, with Robert Helpmann, begging for a sandwich because in zose days people didn't know what good cooking was.'

But still nobody had money to pay for the food, and Mirka had no time to paint, so her husband had formalised things and opened the Balzac Restaurant, 'which was a very proper restaurant, wizz a chef . . . but you had to take ze glass away at ten o'clock and ze Chief of Police would always drink *aff*-ter ze time and his men were outside. It was really a riot, really a comic strip.'

Then at last she could work; and as time went on, she became well known, then 'very famous' when she was expecting a child. 'Every personage I did, I did wiss four toes. Everybody used to tease me, you know, critics and painters. Zey used to say, "Come on Mirka, he's got five toes." And I said, "No, zat's not how I feel, I have to follow my hand, my *image*." And ze child was born exactly like ze drawings, one foot wiss five toes and one foot wiss four toes. So everybody painted angels and zeir personages wiss four toes. Ar-tur Boyd did four toes . . .'

Now, many years later, she had pictures in the National Gallery and just beyond Princes Bridge, on the left, was a big mosaic, 'where all ze lovers from around ze world get zeir photos in front of it. I'm always moved when I see zat.'

Now her only wish was to be immortal. 'I'm very cross,' she told me, 'zat we 'ave to die.'

'Oh come on, you wouldn't want to live for ever.'

'I would. It's okay when you're young, but ze closer you come to death . . . it's not funny.'

Immortal in Melbourne? Oh *yes*. 'It's a town of artists, writers and painters *galore*.'

The only pity was that all the most brilliant people, like Barry Humphries, Sydney Nolan, went overseas. 'And I sink zat was very sad for Melbourne. But zey had to. Zey had to try zeir wings.'

*

'The great thing about Melbourne,' said Barry Humphries, 'is that it's only twenty-four hours from almost anywhere in Europe.'

Off he went to overturn the cultural cringe and turn a Melbourne housewife into an·international superstar while thousands upon thousands of Europeans made the reverse journey. Melbourne is, famously, the largest Greek city outside Athens. There are numerous Italians (more from the North than, as in Brisbane, the warmer South). Mirka Mora was just one of a large Jewish community, many of whose founders had been refugees from the Nazis. There were Turks and a substantial Balkan population, not to mention, of course, the recent waves of Asians.

The assimilation had been rapid, particularly, it seemed, among the Greeks. Distinguished Italians were the Valmorbidas who'd started with a fruit shop and now had the San Remo grocery chain; or the Grollos who were building the Casino and threatening to erect the tallest skyscraper in the world. Among prominent Jews were the hugely wealthy Smorgens, who'd started out with a butcher's shop on Lygon Street which they'd just bought back as a mascot. But Greeks. 'Who are the prominent Greeks?' went my new friends (and their partners) scratching their heads. 'You could phone *Nios Cosmos*, the Greek newspaper,' said one. Another called up a Greek friend ('although I really wouldn't think of him as Greek'). 'This guy reckons the Greeks have all been assimilated. But you could talk to Chris Hatsis, who does the breakfast show with Triple R.'

'People always talk to me about culture,' said Chris, over a post-performance bacon, eggs 'n' cappuccino, 'and what it is to be an Australian and all that sort of stuff. Even Greeks ask me, "What does it mean to be Greek in Australia?" You know, you're supposed to have this great dichotomy, this dilemma of two cultures burning your shoulders, and having to make a decision.

'There were times when I was at school when I thought, "Well why aren't I more Australian?" But it wasn't a problem. The question of fitting in. Of assimilating. A lot of people find that a problem. Trying too hard to begin with. Then reneging on it and being wrong about it. And then going back to their original heritage and trying super-hard to become Greek to the point where you change your name to a classical Greek name that your ancestors had – which I simply won't do. I mean my name's Chris. I'm not going to change it to Christos or anything like that because I've always been known as Chris . . .'

'What were the things you felt you had to do to fit in?'

'Speak the way Australians do was probably the most important. Not have an accent. Speak English properly. Understand everything. And I guess, in terms of the life-style, playing football, knowing how to play it and understanding the culture behind it and all the other things the Australian kids did, like for example – well, I don't know because I didn't get involved.'

'What d'you mean?'

'I never became the Australian I probably wanted to be.'

Vitali Vitaliev (of *Saturday Night Clive* fame) was an unusual example of both sides of the migrant equation. Emigrating to Australia from Russia he'd loved Melbourne, been 'ecstatic' for about a year and a half. 'But, first impressions, you know. It was not so much ecstatic about the country. It was more about freedom and being in a free place, a plentiful place . . .'

It was at this point that he'd written encomia for the *Age* with titles like *Hail to the best cabs in the world* and *Beer and beauty in a world of hats, women and horses*. 'I fell in love with Melbourne,' he'd said then, 'after my first evening walk in the centre. Street performers, musicians and bands were everywhere, the yellow leaves were tumbling from the trees, the people were watching and smiling and trams were passing nonchalantly to and fro. It was a moveable feast, the feast of freedom.'

Now his views had changed. He was tired of the city,

and of Australia. He hankered for – no, not for his Motherland, but England, London in particular. 'Just the joy of living in this hubbub of the world and having this wonderful choice of newspapers and of media and of theatres and being able to go to Paris for the weekend.'

He was sorry to say it, but he now saw Australia as a teenager; with all the complexes and pros and cons of a teenager: the self-imposed inferiority complex, the 'not being entirely sure how to behave in the company of adults'; one moment highly critical, the next, cravenly admiring of their superiority.

The mentality was: 'If this guy's really so successful what's he doing here, you know?' At the *Age* his colleagues had said, 'Why did you buy this house in Melbourne, you won't stay in this country, we're so far away, so parochial.' 'Honestly,' Vitali said, 'I was quite amazed. These people who love their country and were very Australian.' And when he'd appeared, doing readings or public speaking, 'there would always, necessarily, be the question: "Why have you come to Australia?" '

'My point is,' he concluded, surveying his dusty backyard with a jaundiced eye, 'you can fall in love with a teenager, that's what happened with me, but if you're a mature person, you're very soon bound to get bored with her . . .'

I put this point of view to an Australian you could in no way call parochial: Leo Scofield, debonair fifty-something Sydneysider, famous ex-food-critic of the *Herald*, currently Artistic Director of the Melbourne Festival ('It would be immodest of me,' he purred, 'to say it was being revolutionised'). Leo had gone to London on the same boat as his old friend Clive James, when 'going overseas' was 'an automatic sort of Pavlovian response. You simply went to London and anyone who hadn't or didn't was a clown. But that's all over now. I mean young people of my children's generation are not interested. They think Australia's magic, they just want to celebrate it and enjoy it and they don't want to go anywhere. They think England's exsanguinated and has nothing to say to them. They're more interested in what the Aborigines have to say to them – and going and discovering the bush.'

As for Australia being a teenager, well, he shrugged, it was a reasonable point. 'I think Australia is young. Compared to cultures like Russia. It's two hundred years old, white civilisation in this country.'

'When Vitali goes on to say,' I asked, 'it demonstrates the sort of teenage qualities of, you know, alternatively rude to the mother country and culture and then fiercely proud of itself, is there anything in that?'

'Absolutely. But it's hard to say what the mother culture is any more. I mean, there is a partial mother culture. But there are a lot of people who drive taxis in Melbourne or who own small goods shops to whom the mother culture is Italy or Greece or Turkey. So there's bound to be this process that we're going through now which is a melt-down process as cultural influences are absorbed, masticated, and regurgitated in other forms.'

Randal Marsh, 'one of Australia's leading young architects', drove me out to the smart suburb of Caulfield to show me the Gottlieb House, commissioned by a Jewish millionaire who'd made his fortune from sun-block cream.

There were no windows onto the leafy suburban street, just a curve of raw, off-form concrete broken by a stainless steel opaque glass box. It looked extraordinary, like a grey spaceship crash-landed among the prosperous, conventionally idiosyncratic homes around it.

Inside it was stranger. Randal and his partner had designed absolutely everything. Not just the shape of the rooms but the contents: not just the rough concrete and slate partitions and the smooth terrazzo floors but the grey carpets and gold sofas, the glass tables. They'd even suggested the bold Bill Hensen abstracts on the walls.

In the kitchen–dining area a bowl of lemons stood out

startlingly yellow against this controlled monochrome background. Upstairs in the children's bedrooms the bright basketball posters, bluetacked to the concrete walls, looked almost intrusive.

Randal, short and beautifully dressed, his hair a light fuzz on a bald dome, had a flickering smile that – well, how ironic was it? It was hard to tell. 'We put ourselves in a position to do everything,' he told me. 'It's what they wanted.' And all the furniture they'd had before? 'Chucked it all out.' He raised a fractional eyebrow.

It had been a wonderful commission, with a seemingly unending budget. 'This is Melbourne Jewish money saying, "We don't care what it costs." There are very few places in the world where, in your mid-thirties, you can not only design but build. This is what the architects coming back from Europe say.'

Mr Gottlieb absolutely loved it. 'To us,' he said, 'it's a tremendously liveable house.'

Outside I took Randal's photo. He held up a hand towards his creation. 'The Australian Dream!' he said, with a repeat of that quizzical smile.

Graham, the walrus-moustached sales director I'd met in Sydney ('Melbourne is the place where people are serious but they can be frivolous at the same time') took me out for a boozy lunch on one of the restaurant terraces of South Bank. 'It's not the harbour,' he joked, gesturing at the muddy Yarra; then told me I couldn't possibly understand Melbourne until I'd seen an Aussie Rules match. Sadly, the season hadn't yet begun, but there was a practice match, way out over the suspension bridge, among the hoardings and detached residences of the Western suburbs.

It was a different Melbourne crowd out here, that was for sure. Blue singlets, tattoos, torsos that certainly hadn't been developed just picking up the telephone in Collins Street. A T-shirt in front of me read:

```
        MOB
   RIGHT IN YER
   DEAD IN YER
  MAKE YER BLEED
```

'Goodonyer!' 'Kill 'im, Chris!' 'Out on the fall!' they yelled. Just behind us a frail Dame Edna figure in a broad straw hat screamed, 'Get in there Frankie! What are you – a *gu-url*?'

Graham and his friend Richard ('my best friend and I have been mates for thirty *yee-ars*') were both white-collar professionals, but their interest in 'the Roys' seemed every bit as passionate as that of the singlets and thick, glistening necks around them. 'Cranky Pisotto!' 'Oh, he's marked it!' they yelled. Richard's twelve-year-old-son was dressed from head to toe in Fitzroy gear.

At quarter-time, half-time and three-quarter-time the oval pitch was invaded by copy-cat kids and for ten minutes the sky was a blur of orange balls. Little boys who could barely toddle were having a go, trying to kick balls that came up almost to their waists. Those who weren't emulating their heroes gathered round the team and coach, nodding silently at the pep talk. 'You can work, Commo.' 'Your attack on the ball's been bloody good, Douggy.' 'That player's called wow,' said Graham, as we walked off, 'they reckon he's got a W on each buttock.'

'Oh well done yer dip!' 'COME ON ROYS!' 'That is a *shithouse* kick!'

Next to them was a white-hatted solicitor, hardly able to drink his Fanta he was so engrossed. 'He's pissed all week,' Graham murmured to me, 'but he *never* drinks during a game.'

The 'cool change' (as Alan calls it) has passed over; now it's as hot and blue-skied as Alice Springs. Violin music drifts across the narrow courtyard where the breeze tickles the eucalypts and on the balcony opposite Susannah the out-of-work actress is putting out her laundry.

I should be out seeing 'Melbourne'. Meeting all the Establishment 'identities' people keep recommending: Geoffrey Blainey, right-wing historian and Chancellor of the University; Sir James Gobbo, leading light of the Italian community, QC, Rhodes scholar, Oxford rowing blue; John Gough, Chairman of Civic Dunlop and the ANZ Bank . . . But I don't know, I don't know. How can you even start to make generalisations about a city like this? It's 3.02 million different things to 3.02 million people. Yesterday on the tram into town the little Chinese conductor wore the broadest grin I'd yet seen as he went about his immensely tedious work of punching tickets. 'No vurrey' he said, to the backside of a large female in yellow who'd just knocked him to one side.

In her lime-green drawing room overlooking Fitzroy Gardens Lady Potter – widow of millionaire Sir Ian, mother of Primrose (famously deserted at the altar in Venice by a gay Italian count) – poured me tea in a bone-china cup and explained how cruelly the press had behaved over that whole affair. But 'least said, soonest mended' was her philosophy. 'We've just had so much,' she told me with a stoic smile.

'Look mate,' said radical Aboriginal activist Gary Foley, 'you're not going to see fucken Melbourne from a fucken tram.' He cycled everywhere, and reckoned that it never rained in Melbourne for more than ten minutes at a time. There was a fucken unbelievable ride along the Yarra, recently reforested by Kooris (the local Aboriginal 'mob'). 'You should see what happens when the native vegetation is replanted. The first thing that returns of course is the native wildlife. There's such a fucken unbelievable number of fucken birds down there now, you wouldn't believe. Then you've got wombats, bandicoots, ockers.' He laughed, loudly.

'Tis a pity I have so few intelligent female friends,' said

a slender Castilian prince in a production at a fringe venue in Carlton where the sound of rock music, clattering glasses and laughter was clearly audible from the pub next door. 'So what did you *think*?' asked Paul the designer, as we sat in Lygon Street afterwards, eating pasta, drinking Frascati, watching the crowds of dolled-up Italian youth promenading by, for all the world as if we were in Siena or Milan.

'I'm not scared of dying,' said legendary socialite, big-game hunter, racing driver, fixer, 'Captain' Peter Jansen after our fifth (or was it our seventh?) large whisky in the five-storey mid-town mansion where he slept with a coffin by his bed. 'In fact these days I welcome it, because I've done everything, better than anyone. I've laughed better than anybody else, I've cried better than anybody else.' He paused and met my eye. 'But don't ever maim me again. The pain of it, the psychological . . .' He shook his handsome bearded head and tailed off into a long silence.

Outside a cake shop in Acland Street I watched three burly security guards sitting in the sunlight simultaneously eating three huge rumballs. One looked at the other midmouthful. 'Mate,' he said, 'isn't this the best feeling in the world.'

# 19

# The Edge of
# the World

There's a white goat on the grassy verge. An orchard with ripening apples. Soft, temperate clouds in the sky. Up ahead a mountain, a proper one, with its rocky tip vanishing into clouds, not those big dry hills they call mountains on the Mainland.

Suddenly homesick for Europe I drive towards it, through winding lanes awash with yellow flowers, till I see a sign to NOWHERE ELSE; which leads me steeply down through fir forests to a blue-rippled lake where I find a deserted jetty and take a swim in this cool, clear water that reminds me so strongly of Windermere in the Lake District where we went for summer holidays long ago as children.

A dog yaps on the far shore. Otherwise silence.

I lie in the gentle sunshine skimming stones out over the water. All those Melbourne voices, opinions, attitudes, jingle-jangling in my brain, seem utterly absurd here . . .

'How d'you castrate a Tasmanian?' – 'Punch his sister's chin.'

'What's the definition of a Tasmanian virgin?' – 'A girl who can run faster than her brothers.'

They're all so rude about Tasmania on the Mainland. It's an Ireland for them, a butt of all those comforting jokes about stupidity and provinciality and incest and inbreeding. 'They all have two heads down there,' someone said, 'so they'll take twice as long to interview.'

It certainly wasn't regarded as essential that I visit the tiny seventh state. (It's less than one per cent of the total area of Australia, though at 68,331 square kilometres roughly the same size as Ireland.) Many of my Melbourne friends had never been there. Only disgruntled Vitali Vitaliev was wholeheartedly enthusiastic, describing it as 'glorious', 'gothic', his 'home away from home'.

I left the wonderful silence of the lake and drove on, my car having decided to take me down the wild west side of the island rather than across to the more populous Tamar Valley and Launceston. The road wound ever upwards, lined on both sides by tall, jarrah-like eucalypts. In the middle of nowhere I stopped at a little Alpine chalet. It was a Tea House and oh dear, though Mein Host and his wife didn't have two heads apiece, well, her eyes were alarmingly close together and he had an elfin beard, hooded eyelids and a kind of 'bang me over the head with a dustbin lid and I'll still be smiling' look.

Up on the heathland around the Cradle Mountain National Park were armies of half-dead eucalypts, shining white and leafless in the low, bright sun. Broken branches littered the ground like bones. Away to the left, the mighty silhouette of the mountain kept pace. I didn't have my ropes and crampons with me, so I sped on, across house-less, pylonless, magnificent emptiness.

Rosebery was a straggle of bungalows beneath a moun-tainside zinc mine. As the setting sun bathed the forest in a gorgeous pink, three plump teenage girls trailed home up the track, giggling and kicking stones. In the Returned Servicemen's League there was nobody but Sue the Kiwi barlady playing cards with two men she called possum. 'Could you be upstanding please for the nine o'clock service,' she suddenly announced. The lights flicked on and off and a taped voice intoned, 'At the going down of the sun and in the evening we shall remember them ... lest we forget.' Then we all sat back down again and the hand was resumed.

In the morning drizzle I came upon the notorious bald mountains of Queenstown. There's nothing natural about this wonder. They chopped down the trees to feed the smelters of the local copper mine; said smelters belched out sulphur fumes which murdered the regrowth and, absorbed into soil and tree stumps, encouraged regular and terrible bush fires. Rain swept away what was left of the topsoil, leaving just chalk and sandstone. Result: a landscape that looks as if an alien giant has pissed on the moon.

Needless to say it's a tourist attraction, and as you wind up the steep, twisting road out of the blighted valley, marvelling at the folly of Man and reminding yourself to join Greenpeace at the next possible opportunity, you narrowly miss tourist coaches full of sedately gawping grannies, visibly wondering whether they will pass on before the world does.

Then you're over the (no) treeline and back into paradise. Huge, shimmering lakes and (ah!) tree-covered mountains. Roadside verges thick with wildflowers. A row of abandoned pylons announces the World Heritage Area of the Franklin Lower-Gordon Wild Rivers National Park.

In 1976, the future leader of the Greens, the now legendary Dr Bob Brown, was persuaded by a friend to take a yellow rubber raft down the Franklin River, 'bobbing and spinning through the wild rapids, paddling slowly through the peat-brown silence of the smooth stretches; alone, lost in a silver-splashed green dream that twisted and unwound as magically as the river . . . there was no detergent in its waters, no heavy metals or sewage; there were no beer cans or broken bottles or old iron in its bed; there were no blackberries on its banks, no ragwort or willows; there were no sparrows or rabbits, no bridges or culverts or boat ramps . . . it had become the last wild river.' But then: 'Around a sudden bend . . . man. A survey team belonging to the Hydro-Electric Commission.'

Dr Brown returned immediately to Launceston, where he had just started work as a locum, and set up the Tasmanian Wilderness Society. In 1978 he gave up his practice to work for the emerging Green movement full time; in 1983, after the huge Green blockade of the HEC building site and access road, and assisted by Bob Hawke's newly elected federal Labour Party (the Tasmanian Labour Party, like the Tasmanian Liberal Party, had been aggressively pro-dam) the Franklin River was saved by a four–three vote in the Australian High Court.

Now, in the mid-1990s, the only sign of this heroic battle was a charming riverside Nature Walk, just off the main highway, complete with little display boards featuring pro-Green poems written by children of Queenstown Secondary School.

Then mile upon mile of pristine emptiness unrolled on each side of the single-track tarmac racetrack. Here, clumps of eucalypts on a wide green plain; here, bold silhouette of craggy peaks; here, branches of dead tree stark white in sunburst against dark forest behind.

At the Derwent Bridge Hotel the barn-like bar was full of red-cheeked hikers rubbing their hands in front of the big open fire. 'So that's garlic bread for thirteen!' said bald Ken, getting a round of titters from his largely female table.

In the beautiful blue-green morning I drove on into the other side of the argument – hydro-electric country. Lakes, dams, and at the bottom of steep, shady valleys, generating stations. At Tarraleah, a sign said VISITORS WELCOME, so I pushed through a tall wooden door and found myself on a balcony overlooking a hall with floor-to-ceiling windows and three enormous, old-fashioned turbines. They were silent. Switched off while they sandblasted the penstocks, white-bearded Jim Graham explained, showing me into a control room that looked like something out of a 1950s sci-fi movie and dazzling me with talk of valves, exciters and cusecs.

As I left, he handed me a photocopied leaflet entitled 'Jim's Holiday Suggestions: Going to Hobart'. With Jim's leaflet on the passenger seat the empty countryside took on a whole new dimension. 'Note the large pipes along the road. These are 102-inch steel and carry water from the Forebay to the Hill Top Valves near the Chalet. Make sure you see the view from the lookout. The two pipes become six penstocks . . .' By the time I came down to the lovely open country around Ouse, there wasn't much I didn't know about flumes and spillways and forebays and trash racks. And all so easily missed if you don't know what you're looking for.

Just outside Hamilton two hundred farmers were standing in a field being gently harangued by an auctioneer on a milk crate; I kept my eyes down for fear of accidentally buying a wood-splitter. At Macquarie Plains they were harvesting hops. The road along the broadening Derwent was almost French; poplars by the river on the left, ochre, Dordogne-style cliffs on the right. From the bridge at New Norfolk you could see boathouses and bronzed young people sculling. Then the river became a flat wild sweep of estuary, there were new mountains rearing up to left and right and I was on the main drag down into Hobart.

## Six Thousand Lady Bowlers

I had chosen the wrong week. The capital had been invaded by six thousand Lady Bowlers, competing in an Australia-wide annual championship. In the undulating backstreets of Battery Point and Sandy Bay the English-style B and Bs for which Tasmania is famous were all displaying NO VACANCIES. Even the motels and hostels were full. 'Your best bet, mate,' said the barman at a hotel on the waterfront, 'is to drive up Elizabeth Street and keep asking.'

Which is how I ended up (not) sleeping on a wobbly bunk above the noisiest pub in North Hobart. 'He's wearing a fucken shirt and a fucken jersey and a fucken jacket,' snarled a huge dough-faced woman at the bar before I'd even ordered a beer. Returning *much* later, I was harangued by a self-confessed jailbird on the subject of – well, well – immigration. He was particularly upset that the Australians had fought against the Vietnamese and now the place was lousy with the fucken slopes. 'This used to be the Free Country,' he told me. 'Not any more!' He did, however, offer a seriously thought-out solution. 'Send 'em back. That's how you'd solve all this fucken unemployment. Give 'em three months and flick 'em back.'

Next to him his mate Don was amusing the company by taking his false teeth out and waving them at the barlady. 'You wanna see my teeth,' he yelled, as his saliva puddled on the bar. They'd been drinking all day, my new friend told me, but he wasn't aggressive. 'I don't get aggressive,' he shouted, giving me another noseful of fumes. 'Do I seem aggressive to you? I mean, I haven't pulled your ears off yet, have I?'

## Channel Country Dreaming

After which the Tasmania inhabited by the writer Cassandra Pybus and her friends came as the most serendipitous of contrasts. We met the following morning outside Retro, a trendy coffee bar on the elegant curve of Georgian sandstone that is Salamanca Place. (I say a trendy coffee bar. It was the trendy coffee bar – in every sense: the only place to be seen and the *only* place to be seen, packed with funky people discussing scripts and fingering the rings through their noses and gearing up for the forthcoming Salamanca Writers Festival – guest of honour, Bill Bryson.)

Cassandra marched in and immediately marched out

again. 'Can we go somewhere else?' she said, leading me breathlessly up the pavement. 'There's someone I'm suing in there.' She laughed. 'That's the problem with living in a small place.'

She was in her mid-fifties, I reckoned: grey-haired, round-faced, plumper, perhaps, than she'd like to be. Though affable in manner, she didn't easily meet your eye, her lids flickering nervously like a blink caught on freeze-frame; but then, when she did, it was such a candid look that you had to turn away. She was a sixth-generation Tasmanian and proud of it, articulate in her love for her island, the landscape, most particularly her own bit, the 'Channel Country' just west of Hobart. 'You have to see it,' she said, and promptly invited me to stay. She had a cottage I could use. And an old car I could drive.

Snug was the delightful name of her village, and snug was what I decided I felt, looking down from my big table at my big window past the little jetty and over North-West Bay to the D'Entrecasteaux Channel beyond.

Walking up through thick woods behind Cassandra's house, the track led you out onto an open hill where you could see it all clearly: the cobalt blue channel and the long, low, tree-covered slug of Bruny Island beyond. 'That bit at the end,' Cassandra said proudly, 'belonged to my great-great-great grandfather.' (Arriving from Newcastle in 1829, Richard Pybus had been granted freehold title to 2560 acres, on which he'd been able to live like the 'gentleman' he hadn't been at home.)

There was something cluttering Cassandra's understandable love for this beautiful place; where she was the last Pybus; which had been the setting for 'the magical realm of my childhood . . . the overhung path which led to the rocky shore where we would play among the pools left by the receding tide . . . deeply shaded in parts and bordered with towering agapanthus'. Was 'guilt' the right word?

It is a perverse desire [she writes in her book *Community of*

*Thieves*] to make the past bear witness, to own up to its grievous acts. After all, what difference could it possibly make now? What was done is done, the newspaper letter-writers remind me. Those early settlers, my ancestors, were simply creatures of their time, which is to say they were men like other men; no better, no worse. The past is a foreign country: they do things differently there. Ah, but that is not how it seems to me on this morning, when a delicate shift of wind across the channel brings me the smell of broom on dancing white horses ... We have been very happy here in the territory of the Nuenone people. Has any of us paused to do a reckoning?

Cassandra's own reckoning takes the form of a history (from this tellingly personal angle) of the awful annihilation of the Tasmanian Aboriginals. In 1831, the infamous Black Line, her ancestor Richard Pybus among them, had marched across the island in an attempt to round up the surviving full-bloods. The project failed miserably – one adult male was captured, he afterwards escaped – but the intention was clear. By 1872 an old woman called Truganini was the only black left. In 1876, having ended her life being glamourised as 'Queen' Truganini, 'the last Tasmanian Aborigine', she died, and the race was extinct.

Or so the whites told themselves. And were things as simple as that, Cassandra's book, and the guilt-or-whatever it had grown out of, would have perhaps been most interesting as an example of how, when a problem is dead and gone, you can start to get sentimental about it, maybe even wallow a bit in your desire for 'reckonings' and such like. I might have thought: Yes, it's not surprising that she's the first white Australian I've met who is actively questioning their right to be on their own land; who comes up with thoughts like, 'I still don't know what I have to do to act responsibly as somebody who appreciates that they're the inheritor of stolen property' – nobody is actively threatening to take it away.

But things weren't that simple. The Tasmanian

Aboriginals weren't extinct. That there were no 'full-bloods' didn't matter. The generous logic of Aboriginality, which allows a child with any amount of Aboriginal blood to be Aboriginal, had meant that, as far as Aboriginals were concerned, there was a substantial community remaining in Tasmania; a community whose demands were now, paradoxically, more radical than anything that came from Mainland groups.

In her book, Cassandra continues her walk along the track above the D'Entrecasteaux until she finds herself coming down to Oyster Cove, (once Pybus land, now reclaimed as a sacred site) a welcome guest at a celebration of the survival of Aboriginality in Tasmania.

> It is a huge family gathering. On the stage two youngsters perform a wickedly suggestive mime of Dolly Parton and Kenny Rogers to wild applause. At a nearby table Aboriginal activist June Sculthorpe is selling T-shirts. Everyone is wearing them. In the land rights colours of yellow, red and black the message proclaims the reoccupation of Oyster Cove and Aboriginal sovereignty. I am wearing another message in the same colours. Mine says: 'Two hundred years of T-shirts'. We laugh at that and suggest a swap. Long ago we were close neighbours here, her family and mine. I feel absurdly pleased to be welcome at this celebration of their reoccupation. The mood is infectious, every face is beaming. People hug each other with spontaneous joy. Beside the bar-becue, Michael Mansell, recently returned from his meeting with Colonel Gaddafi, is coaxing the Federal Minister for Aboriginal Affairs to eat a wallaby patty . . .

Now, retracing her steps with me (there is no broom, the trees are blackened from a recent bush fire) we come down to the cove to find that the old VISITORS WELCOME sign has been replaced by one that reads:

> YOU HAVE ENTERED SOVEREIGN ABORIGINAL LAND AND YOU ARE THEREFORE BOUND BY ABORIGINAL LAW REGARDING THIS SITE. ASK THE SITE-KEEPER'S ADVICE:

1. **WHAT YOU CAN AND CANNOT PHOTOGRAPH**
2. **AREAS THAT YOU ARE NOT PERMITTED TO WALK ON**
3. **HISTORY OF THE SITE**

**WITH YOUR RESPECT OF OUR LAW, WE WELCOME YOU TO MENA LOONGANA, MANNINA, OUR OYSTER COVE.**

Behind, two couples are loading stuff from two cars into one of the huts on the site. It's not clear to the untutored outsider which is Aboriginal. Cassandra seems reluctant to go over and find out; nor do they come to us.

So we sit – a little uneasily – on the hillock by the entrance and, as we talk, it's clear that her feelings towards these descendants of the people her family displaced are now doubly complex.

It's five years since *Community of Thieves* came out and in that time 'its reception within the Aboriginal community has moved from being,' she pauses and thinks hard, 'um, well received and gratefully received, and a sense of, "Oh somebody's finally talking about what happened to us in a way that takes account of our being agents in our own story" to an attack on me for expropriating Aboriginal stories.'

The first chapter of her book is rather whimsically entitled 'Channel Country Dreaming'. Even this has got her into trouble. 'But what I meant was simply that when I was away from here I dreamt about it . . . I was aware of the multiple uses of that term and I did partly use it to mean, "This is a landscape that's got deep significances for me, over and above rational responses . . ." '

Poor Cassandra. She has had all the right reactions. She has condemned the neighbouring Crowther family who dug up the bones of the last Aboriginals and put them in the Tasmanian Museum; she has talked about the way the whites patronised 'Queen Truganini' in her final years, glamorising her and dressing her up in European clothes and taking her photograph and so forth as 'vile, it makes you sick'; she has understood, in a way that so many of her fellow Australians have not, that Aboriginals never considered their children to be less Aboriginal because they had a white father; she has taken her own complex feelings about all this and honestly addressed them within the covers of her book . . .

And yet, and yet . . . she is not one of them and things aren't the same as they were on that happy, inspiring day five years ago. She is quite adamant that she is not upset by any Aboriginal criticism of her work. 'Some people get hurt by rejection of their best intentions which are always paternalistic. But I'm not hurt by it, just a bit wary. I keep my distance from the Tasmanian Aboriginal community now because I think any interventions I make any more on the issue of Land Rights and stuff is probably not welcome.'

'D'you want to say "hi" to those people?' I ask.

'Yeah, you see they're pointedly ignoring us so what we'll do I think is – oh here's my mother now.'

## Not a Snowball's Chance in Hell

Still, this being Tasmania, where everyone knows each other, Cassandra is still on excellent terms with Michael Mansell, who is certainly, after his famous trip to meet Colonel Gaddafi, the best-known Aboriginal in Tasmania.

I've already heard, many times, that this celebrated black leader has blue eyes and fair skin (as it turns out, fairer than mine) but what I'm not prepared for is his affability. Knowing some of his views in advance, I'm all set for anger, aggression, impatience; instead, as he bounds into his office in blue jeans and sneakers (his grey T-shirt matching his bushy grey hair), shakes my hand and settles forward with a smile, he seems more like an enthusiastic youth leader than 'the most radical Aboriginal in Australia'.

His demands, none the less, were uncompromising. Not since I'd spoken to right-wing Afrikaners in South Africa had I heard such a vociferous call for a homeland, in this case an Aboriginal nation 'operating unto itself'. This didn't mean a wholesale return to the bush. They were twentieth-century Aboriginals, leading pretty much a contemporary lifestyle. What was important was that they had absolute control over themselves. They should be able to raise their own economy, run their own affairs. The legal system would be Aboriginal. 'I don't know,' Michael said, 'of any group of people who have found meaningful justice for themselves under the control of someone else.'

But wouldn't this, I said, be creating an Australian version of apartheid? He laughed. 'That's just a slogan used by Australians whenever they want to maintain their control over us. See, the dispute is, the question really is, Should white people in Australia have a continued right to dominate Aboriginals? If the answer is no – it's apartheid.'

And what did he say to people who said, 'Look, Aboriginals have got the same opportunities as everybody else.' He laughed again. It was what the Government said. 'And we say, "Agh, come off it, you know as well as I do that white people run this country, it's a white man's country, based on white man's needs."

'Our kids know, from the time they're born, that our role is right at the bottom of the chain and that the only way to get up there is to behave like white people. I'm one of the lucky ones, fair-skinned, so no problem with me going through university. Where's the dark-skinned Aboriginals in Tasmania going through university? There aren't. The only ones who've gone through is us fair-skinned ones. You've got to stop talking about the theory of "Everybody's got an equal opportunity in Australia" which is just nonsense and look at the reality. And that's what Aboriginal Government's about.'

So there we were. The same old story. For all the maps on the wall, for all the carefully worked-out detail of how the economics of this homeland would work ('under our own Government if we got these lands back we'd be three

times better off financially') – in the end it came thundering
back to the same old thing. An escape from the racism that
white Australians didn't know they had.

I listened for a while to the details of the homeland
politics and economics and then I put it to him that the
core problem was a lack of respect. 'Say you could wave a
wand over Australia and abolish racism everywhere
tomorrow,' I said, 'would you still want the homeland?'

He smiled. But he didn't think you could. That was
the problem. Racism was structural. For example: all the
property rights of the country were built on racism. The
rights of private white landowners and leaseholders were
greater than those of Aboriginals. 'Now how could you
possibly overturn that so there's some equality?' He continued in this vein, scoffing at Mabo and the subsequent
Native Title Act as 'such a weak piece of recognition'. The
whole country was torn upside down, for twelve months,
'and that was just on Native Title. How do you get across
to Australia that Aboriginals . . .' he broke off, then, 'I
suppose this is what I'm saying,' he continued, 'that the
recognition of Aboriginal sovereign rights is the way of
achieving what you're talking about. On these lands Aboriginal people would be in control, it's a way of having
political equality.'

Okay, I suggested. Say he got his homeland, this huge
green area here on the map of Australia, didn't he think it
would create such enmity in the white population that the
happy, equal world he suggested—

'But so what,' Michael interrupted. 'What I'm saying is,
let's get our rights. Then say to them, "You can complain
all you like now and there's nothing you can do about it."
I think the ultimate question about how do you foster good
relations between blacks and whites in this country should
not be based on the old notion that Aboriginals have to
wait until white people are ready, it should be based on
the notion that Aboriginals have got these rights so it'll
take you a decade, maybe a generation to get accustomed

to it. If you look at history around the world people do get accustomed to change. Who would have predicted five years ago that Nelson Mandela was going to be President of South Africa?'

Back in Snug, Cassandra was blunt. Michael was taking an extreme position to make the middle-ground attractive. 'It's important to give people a sense that they have their own culture and their own law. They don't. What constitutes Aboriginal culture in Tasmania is a very fragmentary thing indeed. I think it's a tragedy but there it is.' His political position, she thought, had 'not a snowball's chance in hell'.

## Sodomites and Mutineers

Snug was a handy enough base for Hobart. I became one of the Channel Country commuters, rattling through the pretty countryside past Margate and Kingston, past the signs saying HORSE POO $1.50, DONKEY POO $1.00 and the big circular FIRE RISK sign (which veered daily from HIGH to VERY HIGH to EXTREME) then onto the freeway that swept round the side of towering Mt Wellington and steeply down – the blue harbour gleaming beneath – into town.

Central Hobart reminded me strongly of an English county capital – Exeter say, or York. It had the same loud hordes of schoolchildren waiting for buses in the middle of the afternoon; the same shaven-templed yobbos irritating the shoppers on the pedestrianised central mall; the same mix of lovely old churches, houses, museums and not-so-lovely modern office blocks. It had an annoying one-way system and an excellent bookshop. It had a big central park. It had graffiti that amused rather than alarmed. (ALL WOMEN ARE BEAUTIFUL said one; some controversialist had crossed out WOMEN and scrawled PERSONS above.)

The difference was the mountain, which gave the little

city an altogether more epic feel. The ever-steeper back-streets petered out meekly on its lower slopes. Even Fern Tree, a suburb which felt positively alpine, was only halfway to its towering summit, four thousand feet above, which even now, in high summer, more often than not, was wreathed in cloud. On the first completely clear day I drove up the alarmingly vertiginous road and treble-checked the handbrake before venturing out. The view was the best yet; you could see what Cassandra meant when she talked about Tasmania just disintegrating into the sea; blue fjords and a scatter of deep-green islands spread out to the distant horizon.

The Bowls Ladies were still very much in evidence, parading the streets in their white hats and smart jacket-and-skirt uniforms. I shouldn't laugh, someone told me; Lawn Bowls was the biggest sport in Australia, out-stripping tennis and cricket.

On Saturday morning they were out *en masse* for Hobart's famous Salamanca Market. There were a couple of hundred stalls selling everything from runic astrological pendants to Tasmanian mustard, from polished wooden apples to fresh tacos with local strawberries and cream. 'I just want myself a boy,' mused the woman in the floral skirt at the Crystal Healing stall, fanning herself in the heat. 'Forget the electrics, I'll have a human.' Next door, an old hippy played a harp. No less than four women of a certain age were offering tarot. And at a glance you could pick up the key elements of Tasmanian politics. RESTORE LAKE PEDDER said the posters on the Greens stall; ABOLISH THE MON-ARCHY said the badges presided over by the long-haired Republican couple; further along the (technically illegal) Gay and Lesbian stall had two brave young men handing out leaflets saying WE'RE HERE, WE'RE QUEER, AND WE'RE NOT GOING TO THE MAINLAND.

It wasn't so much that the police charged into bedrooms, said Rodney Croome, leader of the Tasmanian Gay and

Lesbian Movement, when I spoke to him alone a couple of days later. The last time that had happened had been 1983. It was more that the very existence of the law was invasive. You could lose your flat or job because you were gay, the justification being: you're a criminal. The Tasmanian Premier and Attorney-General said they wanted to keep the law, 'as a signal, to educate people'. Well yes, said Rodney, it did educate people – to discriminate.

It didn't matter so much down South. In Hobart, people were fairly tolerant, over seventy per cent were in favour of reform. Even in Launceston, where the figures were 50–50, it wasn't too bad. But in the North-East, where he came from, there was a problem. In places like Burnie, Ulverstone and Devonport where the big, open, anti-gay rallies of the last few years had been held. 'Hysterical out-pourings of hatred towards us.' Which weren't, he didn't think, explained by traditional theories of homophobia. 'It's much more specific to these places and it's about social and economic change.' These places had been highly industrial-ised, now the factories were closing and people were trying to hide from the decline. The social indicators – alcoholism, child mortality, domestic violence – were the worst in Tasmania. There were a whole lot of problems that needed to be addressed; the civic leaders couldn't look at them. 'It's too hard, so they blame us.'

'Sometimes' – Rodney shrugged and gave me a thin smile – 'they even explicitly blame us for unemployment.' I laughed. 'How so?'

'Oh, they get to it through the route of us supposedly having higher disposable incomes and better jobs. The homosexuals are taking their jobs.'

The anti-gay rallies had started in 1989, following the election which had seen a majority of Labour and Green MPs returned. There'd been a resurgence of homophobia last year, after a United Nations decision which found that Tasmania's homosexuality laws violated an International Covenant to which Australia was a signatory.

So who went?

'Mostly men speak. People who go – it's a mix. A lot of the people would be churchgoers. On the North-West Coast there's quite a lot of late nineteenth-century Evangelical churches. Gospel Hall, Bible Chapel, Christian Brethren, Church of Christ. There's also the newer fundamentalists like the Assembly of God.

'An interesting thing is that a lot of their rhetoric isn't religious, it's secular. It's about health and morality and virility and things like that. There's never actually reference to the bible. And it's not old-style Conservative politics. It's very new, very right, very vehement. It comes from the US. A lot of the material they put out is direct from anti-gay groups in California.'

The wheel turns full circle, I thought. But what was the problem in Tasmania, where moustachioed clones were about as common a sight as Tasmanian tigers? Partly, Rodney thought, it was the economic-social thing we'd talked about; the rallies as a conduit for 'a whole lot of fear' about Tasmania's changing political destiny: the decline of industry, the rise of the Greens. But there was also, he was sure, an historical element to it. Going back to the first half of the last century when the big issue in Tasmania was homosexuality among the convicts.

In the earliest history of the colony – say 1803 to 1830 – things had been fairly anarchic. But then from 1830 onwards the people in charge began to discipline the convicts more; they developed incredibly sophisticated systems of surveillance and supervision. Tasmania was a totalitarian society at this stage, people controlled in every aspect of their lives. There were informers everywhere; people didn't know who to trust, so they couldn't combine and resist. 'However, in a same-sex prison the one thing that undermines that are same-sex bonds, when people overcome their mistrust of each other through sexual and emotional relationships. The authorities wrote piles and piles of material on unnatural vice among the convicts.

They collected love letters. And what comes through again and again is the connection between mutiny and unnatural vice. Sodomites were mutineers and mutineers were sodomites; they were the same thing.'

The association still lingered in the minds of the Tasmanian Establishment; in their rhetoric this came out sometimes. 'That we're going to transform Tasmania beyond recognition.'

So how had it been for him, I asked, growing up in the untransformed Tasmania, in an area where over eighty per cent wanted homosexuals to be considered as criminals?

'The character of homophobia wasn't the same then as it is now. It wasn't a militant and aggressive condemnation, it was a terrible silence. Utter silence. I didn't tell anyone until I came to uni in Hobart. It was only then that I felt free enough to actually begin to talk to anybody about it. Before, I didn't know of anyone else in my world, in Tasmania, who was gay, except one person, and that was Bob Brown.

'People talked about him, obviously, in a derogatory way. I went out and bought his biography, *Bob Brown of the Franklin*. It was two hundred pages long but I went out and bought it for about two or three paragraphs that talked about him being gay. And I stuffed it behind the bookshelf so that no one would find it. Just in case they thought I was a poofter, or worse, a Greenie. Otherwise there was utter silence; and that's what it had been like for 140 years in Tasmania.

'I knew what I was, there wasn't much confusion about that. I mean I'd try and forget about it, but I knew when I was a child. There was absolutely no one in my world who was influencing me in any way but to be heterosexual. Everything assumed that that's what I wanted. Puberty hits, you know exactly what's what. Or I did. You know it's boys and not girls.'

And how had that felt, in that community?

'Well the feelings were wonderful in themselves, but I

learnt very quickly not to express them to anyone, to keep them under wraps.'

'Did you pretend to have girlfriends?'

'Yeah, I did, to some extent. But I was also fairly academic so that was a bit of an escape. I could pretend: Well, I'm too busy with my work.'

'Was there a point at which you thought: What I am is illegal?'

'Not really, because people didn't talk about it. I just knew that people thought it was wrong. And I accepted that. And I didn't want people to dislike me. Because of it. So I just kept it under wraps until I came to Hobart. Then I had to find my own way. Reading books and very slowly beginning to talk to people. The gay scene was invisible, very quiet. Anyway, it took me ages to . . . I had to come to terms within myself. Talk to other people around me and then slowly move out from that.

'Of course there are lots of people who were in a much more difficult position than I was and who just killed themselves because it was too difficult. Thinking, how can I possibly live . . . Thinking that those feelings in here weren't acceptable to other people and how can I possibly be happy without incurring the wrath of the world and wanting to express your feelings but not being able to and not knowing anyone else you can talk to. Tasmania has the highest rate of male youth suicide in the country. The North-West Coast has the highest rate in Tasmania. You can't know for certain what the causes are, but anecdotally at any rate it seems that's a major contributor.'

'How did your parents take it?'

'Well, they were pretty traumatised. To start with. They were very unhappy. Because they had certain expectations of me. That I was going to get married, and this kind of thing. Which just wasn't going to happen. And they were also very unhappy with me for staying here. I remember my mother saying, "Why don't you just go off to – it'd be so much easier if you just went off and lived a quiet life in

Victoria." And that's precisely what I'm not going to do. We often get this. Give the homosexuals a one-way ticket to the Mainland, you know, get rid of them.

'Last year when I was at the Mardi Gras in Sydney, we had a float, it's the first time we've ever had one, we had a fantastic reception, people just loved it because everyone knew in Tasmania what was happening to us. And I remember we were marching along and there'd be people trying to grab the float and they'd put up their hands and there'd be tears streaming down their faces and they'd say, "Congratulations for being here, we're Tasmanians and we had to leave twenty years ago." And these people were so sad – overjoyed to see us, but there was an incredible sadness inside them, it was like they were sexual refugees and I thought then, Nobody is ever going to make me into a sexual refugee.'

## The Silent Prison

Half a day's drive out of Hobart, down at the far western end of the 'landscape breaking up into the sea', over two isthmuses once patrolled by guards and savage dogs, at the tip of the Tasman Peninsula, lies Port Arthur, where the very worst of the convicts were sent. Governor Arthur, who believed that a convict's 'whole fate should be the very last degree of misery consistent with humanity', divided his charges up into seven classes. Class 1 had tickets of leave and could, subject to his continuing approval, own property and work for wages; Class 7 – way down below the assigned servants, those who worked on Government projects or road gangs, those sentenced to hard labour in chains – were sent to Port Arthur, where they felled timber, quarried stone and were soundly flogged if they misbehaved.

Now, a pink-brick ruin surrounded by oak-lined walkways and restored Victorian gardens, it looked more like an old country house than a prison. On this sunny Sunday it was swarming with tourists, a good half of whom were Bowls Ladies and their consorts.

'Australia,' wrote Robert Hughes, in his history of the convicts, *The Fatal Shore*, 'has many parking lots but few ruins. When Australians see the ruins of an old building, our impulse is either to finish tearing it down or to bring in the architects and restore it as a cultural centre, if large, or a restaurant, if small. Port Arthur is the only major example of an Australian historical ruin appreciated and kept for its own sake. It is our Paestum and our Dachau, rolled into one.'\*

It had been a jail, our guide told us, for forty-five years, a tourist attraction for 125. The change from one to the other had happened almost overnight. Indeed, some of the ex-convicts had drifted back to act as guides. They would strip the shirts off their backs to show their stripes; and, artful to the last, manufacture leg-irons far heavier than the originals to elicit tips and sympathy.

Pacing thoughtfully amid the bright sea of leisurewear I came to the Penitentiary, where old photos of the inmates had been mounted by their original tiny cells. From *The Fatal Shore* I knew some of the crimes for which people had been banished to Botany Bay in the first place. Elizabeth Beckford, aged seventy, transported for seven years for stealing 12 lbs of Gloucester cheese; Thomas Hanwell, seven years for the theft of two hens, one dead and one alive, total value four pence; John Wisehammer, aged fifteen, sent down under for grabbing a packet of snuff from an apothecary's counter. But removed to this place? Here was James Foley, three months' hard labour for 'misconduct in smoking in the Colonial Hospital'; Arthur Smith, nine months' hard labour for 'misconduct in talking to an officer's son without authority'. They all had one thing in common, these sad Victorian mugshots – the eyes:

---

\* Robert Hughes, *The Fatal Shore* (Collins Harvill, London, 1987) – p. 399.

bright, sullen, unrepentant, even in the last resort; the eyes of the wounded cleanskin bulls at Coniston Plains.

'Brian's been wanting to get into the lunatic asylum all afternoon,' cooed a Bowls Lady. 'This is his big moment.' But it wasn't strictly an asylum, this grim little oblong with cells only three foot wide. It was the Silent Prison, the last stop on the long road from the original horse-theft or stolen packet of snuff. Where transportation to Australia, banishment to Tasmania, removal to Port Arthur, and sound floggings had failed, this place worked. The most serious recidivists were kept in silence in here, and for the few minutes they were allowed out each day had to wear a hood covering their heads. It had, like many evil things, been a philanthropic idea in conception. Contemplation of crimes in silence would bring men to reform, they'd thought in Philadelphia, America. Instead it broke men's spirits and drove them mad. By the time they came to building this one, the authorities knew this. Despite their talk of correction the Silent Prison was cynically devised and used as the final punishment place.

I decided not to stay for the hugely popular Lantern-Lit Ghost Tour, which offered a chance to walk through these cells in darkness. 'Since the 1870s unusual occurrences and sightings of apparitions have been documented at Port Arthur. Judges, Reverends, visitors and staff have all had experiences,' said the brochure chirpily. *'DO YOU BELIEVE?'*

The shudder I had felt in daylight was quite enough for me.


## Wilderness

Why, I thought, as I drove northwards, do they put TAS-MANIA – HOLIDAY ISLE on the numberplates? What a bland, almost offensive, reduction. If I lived and worked here I'd prefer TASMANIA – WILDERNESS ISLE or even TASMANIA – GOTHIC ISLE OF DARKNESS.

At Sorell I was all for heading back to Snug but my car had other ideas. It wanted to show me just how many trees there were in Tasmania. Rowlandson landscape after Rowlandson landscape unfolded before me along the empty Tasman Highway up the east coast. There were rocky rivers, there were moors, there were green fields, there were mountains. Every fifty kilometres or so a tiny seaside settlement: a cluster of houses, possibly a motel. At Swansea I stopped for the night at the Historic Motor Inn, so called for its lovingly realised 1970s feel. There were moth-eaten flowers on every table in the gloomy dining room, the red *vin de table* was priced as a luxury item, the 'roast beef' was swimming in Bisto-style gravy, and – winning touch – for pudding an enormous banana split, complete with thick swirls of whipped cream, fan wafers and a glacé cherry. All I needed was Gary Glitter in a silver catsuit at the next table.

The rest of the coast up to its largest settlement of St Helens (pop. 1000; coffee, tragic) was nothing but a string of unspoilt white-sand beaches. Inland, a man in a cabbage field was a scarecrow till he scratched his head; elsewhere the countless sheep grazed on.

To Rodney Croome, homosexuality was the issue; to Michael Mansell, Land Rights; but to Cassandra and her husband Michael Lynch it was the Green debate that dominated. The fight over the Franklin Dam had been a precursor. Now the island was divided between those who wanted to reduce the highest unemployment in Australia by encouraging industry, development, logging, hydro-electricity; and the Greens, who yearned with a passion to preserve the pristine emptiness of their wild and beautiful island; who spoke with contempt of policies that were turning tract upon tract of irreplaceable, 'old growth' forest into *toilet paper for Japan*.

'It's not made into *toilet* paper,' chuckled David Bills, General Manager of North Forest Products, Tasmania's biggest woodchipping operator. 'It's printing and writing paper. It's the sort of paper you would wrap your fiancée's engagement ring in. They're beautiful papers, works of art. I mean Sandra, if she leaves anything to this world, it'll be on paper.'

It turned out – this being Tasmania – that he'd been in kindergarten with Cassandra. And Helen Graham, one of the founding members of the Tasmanian Wilderness Society, was his first cousin. 'Her mother and my mother are like two peas in a pod. My mother is very pro-development and my Aunty Di, who only lives three hundred metres away, can't understand the need for any development. In fact, for many years, she gave Bob Brown free board and lodging in a little villa unit at the back of her house.' He laughed. That was the sort of place Tasmania was.

As for the forests, by the time I'd had an hour with David it was perfectly clear that not only was the woodchipping industry no threat whatsoever to Tasmania's trees, it was in fact the only sensible way forward. There were 42 million hectares of forest Australia-wide, only seven million were committed to forest industries; even those, on average, were only logged once in a hundred years. 'The real future of this world,' he enthused, '*must* lie in ecologically sustainable development.' Which meant using biological resources. Otherwise you were mining hydro-carbons or making nuclear power which was, clearly, unacceptable. And of forests, fisheries and agriculture, the three major resources, forests were not only the most sustainable, they didn't stress the soil too much, maintained genetic stocks, didn't affect the water, produced bio-degradable, recyclable non-toxic products . . . what on earth was I worrying about?

It was perhaps fortunate, for the balanced view, that Bob Brown was coming to dinner. I was lucky to be seeing him at all. He'd spent the last week in jail (and in the headlines of the *Tasmanian*) having been arrested over the Greens' latest battle, an attempt to stop the bulldozers carving a road through the Tarkine Wilderness, the empty section of the island north and east of Savage River.

He was as impressive in the flesh as I'd hoped. Cassandra had told me that he had a way of making instant converts, and yes (not that I needed converting) I was immediately a fan. When a nuclear ship had docked at Hobart he had sat up on top of Mt Wellington, in mid-winter, for a week on hunger strike in protest. In the darkest moments of the battle for the Franklin he hadn't given up. Even now that he was a famous campaigner he was still out there, still letting himself get arrested and jailed for his principles. And yet to meet he was entirely without side. There was no self-righteousness or sanctimoniousness; just a broad, inclusive smile and integrity in plain view.

Talking to him and Michael about the details of David Bills's arguments two things were clear; one, that I was way out of my depth among people who had spent years arguing about clearfells and old-growth forests and humus layers and understorey species; and two, that Wilderness was a concept that brought out a fight-to-the-death passion in its defenders.

You could define it, Bob told me (when Michael had gone off to cook the 'feral salmon' and we were sitting alone with the mozzies at the bottom of the garden), as 'a large tract of wild and quite natural country which is devoid of the impact of modern technology – roads, factories, fences, sounds and so on – where you can be with your senses entirely steeped in Nature.

'Over thousands of generations we've developed our bodies and our minds as wilderness creatures in an entirely wild planet. And it's only in the last few generations that agricultural and industrial revolutions have rolled back the wilderness as we've concreted and straightened and ordered everything and at the same time heightened our anxieties, increased our population, restricted ourselves, cut off the bond from Nature which is ineluctably there because of our origins. You run a great risk of severing altogether our anchor in that wilderness background. It's a very very special asset to humanity, and yet every day we wake up and there's less of it, there's more of us and we're facing a future where there will be none.

'My involvement and the public role I've taken, is grounded very much on a deep-seated conviction that this is something we have to make a stand on. In our time. We're privileged to be in a democratic, wealthy part of the globe. It's not just an opportunity, it is incumbent upon those of us who can see what is happening to do something about it.'

I put it to him that 'what is happening' was his perception; that David Bills had described the Greens as 'sentimental and middle class'; the reality was that people had to live, the state had to make money.

'Well, these were epithets aimed at the suffragettes, and the anti-abolitionists and the people who wanted to bring kids out of the mines. On every occasion the bulwark of the opposition was that they were going to wreck the economy, they were bad for business – exactly the same situation we find ourselves in.

'The second thing is what's wrong with sentiment, and what is wrong with caring and what is wrong with love and beauty and these other values which don't have a dollar tag on them?

'The other thing to ask is – well, what if they're wrong? We can't get back the forest ecosystems, we can't get back the extinct species. The precautionary principle would be that we should look after what little we have left of wild Nature until we know that we can dispense with it and it's for a better good.

'As a society we're there for the instant, the moment. We've lost the long-term view, what all people who came before us, be they Celtic, Aztec or Aboriginal, have had, which is that we must consider the people who come after us.

'We are out of control. We don't know how to bring

things back in control and, what's worse, the conventional economic rationalism is: technology will fix it – let's rip. We actually can see the cliff coming up and we're putting our foot on the accelerator. It's extraordinary.'

## Mardi Gras

On the little beach just round the headland from the cottage the blackberry bushes tumble to the sand, ripe, dark, untouched. The February sun is too hot and bright to sit in. Even looking at its reflection on the wavelets of the bay hurts my eyes. In Sydney this weekend it's the famous Mardi Gras, now the world's biggest gay festival. All the sophisticates have urged me to go. It's a one-off, it's incredible, it's where Australia is now. Sitting here, in the shade of this *eucalyptus beachsplendidus*, looking out over the bay at the red and white sails of the Snug Scouts Regatta plying back and forth against the blue channel, I wonder.

I drive round the bay and find a scene from a remaindered colour picture book on Australia. There are orange canoes and white dinghies and pink-cheeked teenagers and fierce, green-scarfed scout leaders. In the middle of the beach there's a temporary swimming pool and above it a Greasy Pole on which clean-cut boys bash each other with bags full of wet laundry. Further along is a Girls' Tug of War. 'Clear the beach please!' comes the voice from the public address system. 'Here come the runners! Get out of the runners' way, please.'

Darkness falls and down the centre of Oxford Street, Sydney, Rodney Croome and his colleagues march on foot, holding up a big sheet-banner saying TASMANIAN GAYS AND LESBIANS. Alongside the extravagant floats of the better-resourced same-sexers of the Mainland they look absurdly straight. There's a whole truck-full of Judy Garlands, a man dressed as a giant condom, a lot of people making lascivious tonguey-tongueys at the camera, and hosting it all from the studio everyone's favourite international gay, Julian Clary, fondling a pink eiderdown phallus and regurgitating the camp quips of yesteryear. ('Adelaide is the City of Churches, isn't it? I spent a few days there once. I was on my knees the *whole time*.')

Back down on Snug Beach the fun and games go on. Beneath floodlights and a huge banner saying YOU CAN NEVER DO BETTER THAN YOUR BEST a gaggle of prepubescents are trying to climb between two roped-together poles without touching either rope or pole. A lanky thirteeen-year-old called Catherine is stalling like a horse. 'I can't do that,' she moans to the bespectacled young scoutmaster in charge, and it almost looks as if she's going to get away with it when a terrifying-looking redhead with a scrunched-up face and swinging green skirt arrives on the scene.

'Come on, Catherine,' she bellows. 'It's not a question of being an individual, you're part of a troop.' She turns to Spectacles, who's shaking visibly. 'That's what I've been trying to instil in them all day. They're not individuals. It's about trust.'

'Excuse *me*,' shriek two little girls over by the 1st Tamar Sea Scouts tent, 'we're going to be *lesbians* together.' 'Anastasia!' screams a boy, circling wildly. 'Where are you? You little turd-jammer, you little poo-sniffer, you little *toad*-sniffer?'

## The Hobart–Launceston Rivalry

At a dinner party in Fern Tree, the woman on my left said, 'So where are you going next? Of course you've heard about the Hobart–Launceston rivalry?'

*HELP!*

I flew to Canberra.

# 20

# And Last, But By No Means Least . . . The Capital

There's always this smell, isn't there, when you arrive in a new place; this feel, that remains with you and defines the place for ever. Here, tonight, it's damp eucalyptus; pine needles; dew on freshly mown grass.

Everybody, but everybody, is rude about Canberra. 'The toytown capital of a toytown country,' said Vitali Vitaliev. 'A suburb without an urb,' said Alan Coren. 'The great Australian civic cock-up,' said Mark Lawson. And those were just the visitors. What the Aussies say doesn't bear repeating.

But I don't imagine it would be *so* bad to live in one of these houses with a veranda looking out on the tall trees of a mature garden. To stroll down to this quiet crossroads and into this roomy-looking pub on the corner. It's empty but has a good feel. Deep crimson walls and ceiling; deep crimson carpet on the varnished wood floor; little dark-wood drinking booths; up on the bar, three big copper vases of fresh roses, red, pink and white; a stage, with cabaret chairs and tables grouped before it. At one, a blonde in a business suit drinks alone.

No new beer, appropriately, just a choice of everywhere I've been. I return to South Australia with a Coopers. The tables fill up. The young lady I've studiously not been looking at is joined by a girlfriend and I, in my booth, by two young couples and Lindsay, who's not only a public servant but works in the Prime Minister's office. (The first person I speak to in Canberra!)

He tells me that this place, Tilley's, is a famous lesbian pub. Recently, it's started to allow men in. Up at the bar Belinda corrects me. She founded the joint and runs it still, and no, it was never exclusively gay, the rule was simply that you had to have one woman in the party. She wanted something gentler than that rough male atmosphere that you usually get in pubs. But if there's a noisy child and people are trying to have a business meeting she'd still throw it out.

'Would you rather have a song about Death – or Little People?' shouts the lead singer of Weddings, Parties, Funerals when the place is jammed to the eaves. Lindsay's surprised I've never heard of them; they're one of the most famous Australian bands. They only play a little venue like Tilley's because, well, Tilley's is Tilley's, bands play it on their way up and they'll play it again just for fun when they've made it. Two down a girl with a Glaswegian accent screams, 'Little People!'

In twelve hours I've exchanged the blue waters of Snug for a black-haired beauty who plays the violin in a tiny denim skirt with exaggerated silver buttons down the front and the slope of her shoulders and the swerves of her big, mascara-framed black eyes reveal that she is burning for the visiting Pommy singer, one Rory Macleod . . .

'This is about their most famous song,' shouts Lindsay in my ear. "Cause each and every Sat-ur-day is . . .' yells the band. '*Fath*-er's Day,' screams the crowd.

Rory Macleod sings of England, preoccupations I've long forgotten about. 'Farewell, welfare,' one is called. His voice smoulders with all the resigned frustration of the Exsanguinated Country. Whereas Our Other Island has such a different note, doesn't it? 'My grandmother died,' says the tall blonde singer on next, 'and I had this dream where she came back to say goodbye. It was kind of spooky, so I wrote this little song about it.' *Kind of spooky*. Oh give me Australia any day.

The violinist is going to have Rory if she can. She's limp when she gazes at him; and after the last song, when they all troop off and return for an encore – she doesn't, nor does Rory, and when she runs on late she's lost it, tousled and flustered, all that sensuality she's been giving off collapsed in her evening's triumph.

Heading back to the YHA I get hopelessly lost in this maze of identical grassy verges, identical green rubbish bins with identical yellow tops, tall, nonconformist trees lit by identical streetlamps. Boobialla Street, Clianthus Street, Grevillea Street, Swainsona Street. Oh for god's sake! Surely I've already been down Swainsona? Surely this bush was . . .? No . . . Wasn't that bungalow . . .? No. That garden fence . . .? No.

There's not a soul on these dark pavements. Occasionally a car slides by, a shark nosing through the suburban weed. Should I wave it down? I keep walking, knowing that sooner or later, sooner or . . . I'm just about to give up and knock, Hansel-like, on the door of one of the few houses with a light still burning when I come down a back alley and there, ahead of me, welcoming and reassuring through the darkness, is – Tilley's.

## Just a Little Country Town

Canberra was built, as every schoolchild in Australia knows, as a compromise. It is in fact the concrete embodiment of that festering Melbourne–Sydney rivalry: a treeless frost-hollow in the hills turned into a capital city whose essential merit was that it didn't belong to one or the other.

Its genesis was hardly spectacular. After Federation in 1901 numerous possible sites were toured, the most favoured location being on the coast at Eden; but the magnificent harbour at Twofold Bay posed a threat; the jealous cities didn't want to create *another* rival. So the Molonglo valley was finally selected and names that included Wheatwoolgold, Democratia and – incredibly – Marsupalia suggested, before a bastardisation of the Aboriginal 'Kamberra' (meeting place) was selected.

Ingloriousness followed ingloriousness. The prize money for the International Competition was so meagre that both the British and Australian Institutes of Architects blacklisted it. Then, in 1911, having chosen the American, Walter Burley Griffin, as winner of 137 entries, the Federal Government promptly appointed a board who decided his design was 'impractical' and prepared one of its own, incorporating features of several of the winning entries. This was only abandoned when the appalled architects of Australia ('it is the work of an amateur who has yet to learn the elementary principles') set up a 'Save Canberra' campaign. This, and a change of Government, brought Griffin back in 1913, but for the next seven years his attempts to put his ideas on the ground were continuously hampered by the bureaucrats whose plan had been foiled. His three ornamental 'water basins' were rejected; his road design was altered; in the end he quit. Only in 1958, with the establishment of the National Capital Development Commission, was something salvaged of his original.

Nobody seemed to care much for this chuntering compromise. Only six thousand people turned up for the grand opening of Parliament House in 1927, and twenty thousand meat pies had to be buried in a mass grave. People hardly flocked to live there. It became the city even Poms could be confidently rude about.

Now Canberra seemed to be trying to turn its back on its history and say, 'Look, I may be a late developer but now I'm splendid enough to be your capital after all. See, here by the lake is your National Library, your National Gallery, your (with a little help from the Japanese) National Science and Technology Centre. Don't keep accusing me of being merely artificial and ceremonial, I am real now. Look, here is your High Court, where all those Huons and myrtles along the Franklin River were saved and White Australia thrown into turmoil by the Mabo decision. And here, just up the gentle slopes of Capital Hill from the old Parliament House which has the Aboriginal protesters camping outside it (they want it for their Parliament; surely this kind of futile protest is a mark of my maturity?) is your splendid new Parliament House, set like a bunker into Capital Hill, with neatly mown lawns for a roof and and an eye-catching giant bent paperclip for a flagpole. From here I can offer a view to rival Paris, London, or Moscow (well, certainly Washington, Brasilia or Ottawa), over the lake and left up one arm of the Ceremonial Triangle to the City Centre, or right up the other to the largest War Memorial in the world.'

The only Australian I'd met who'd had a good word for Canberra was Julie, the 'art-secretary' at Murray Hills, who'd been born here. Now I phoned her home, only to discover that having returned briefly from Alice at Christmas she'd gone off North again to work as a camp cook in FNQ . . . but look, where was I staying? The YHA, ah, goodness, *in a dormitory*, no, I couldn't continue there . . .

So I was swept on a final wave of fair dinkum Aussie generosity into an altogether different Canberra. The grand and ceremonial 'city of pollies' was a glittering front, I discovered; underneath it was just a little country town, with more social clubs than you could shake a stick at.

Julie's Dad Michael was another public servant, a genial accountant with a more than passing resemblance – with his swept-back hair and dashing Victorian moustache – to Lord Lucan. His wife Helen was the very soul of unfussed hospitality. A huge tea appeared on the white lace tablecloth at six-thirty every evening (and this after a long day working). Did I have any washing she could just chuck in with Michael's stuff? Don't let the dogs annoy you. Just help yourself from the fridge while we're out . . .

So how *was* I going to get around? Look, Helen could

drop Michael into work and I could have the second car. Of course not (I demurred hopefully) I could use public transport. Public transport! Helen laughed. There was a bus into the centre only once an hour; then you'd have to take another bus out to wherever you were going – the car was mine.

So I got lost again. The bold epic triangle of the centre was easy enough, but once in the endlessly spreading suburbs, divided and surrounded as they were by countless identikit pine forests and Nature Parks, it was hard to know *where* you were. And once you were travelling the wrong way on the Tuggeranong Parkway or Yamba Drive you could be in Waramanga before you could get off ...

## Democracy at Work

A few weeks before, the circular drive around Parliament House had been blockaded by lorries belonging to Australia's loggers protesting against Keating's new pro-Green restrictions on the woodchipping industry. Their infuriating presence, in the cool, clean seat of Government, had eventually forced a policy rethink.

Now, there was just a small encampment of tents, one lorry and a temporary Portakabin. Some were farmers protesting about the drought; some were bankrupts protesting about banking practises; from the Portakabin flew a banner reading LONE FATHERS EMBASSY FOR THE AUSTRALIAN FAMILY. By its side a board read:

LIFE WASN'T MEANT TO BE – Bankruptcy, Suicide, Divorce, Starvation, Futureless, Childless, Leaderless, Aimless or a Joke. GET OFF YOUR BUTTS AND HELP US!

There was quite a gang of them inside the Embassy, mostly bald and wearing panama hats. They were, in a simmering fashion, extremely angry and upset.

'Are you married?' one asked. 'No, no,' I replied blithely

and they were off. 'Well, I tell you what, the day you get married you enter a new world of Government control, you'll give up everything you value most dearly, which is your ability to have a choice or to exercise your rights . . .'

I would in fact become nothing more than a sperm bank for women. Because what women saw in children was an economic commodity to be exploited. I thought that was a bit extreme? It wasn't. Australia was now spending *six to seven billion* dollars a year on single mothers. In Canberra *right now* they could get a brand-new, three-bedroomed house, hot and cold running everything, transport, electricity, concessions – no it was a lucrative business being a single mum.

The legislation had been drawn up by women. Not ordinary women, mind, but the people who had taken over the Women's Movement, who, one Lone Father told me, 'tend to be people who may be lesbians and male-haters. I coined the phrase "malephobiacs" ten years ago to describe them.'

The institutions of Government had been taken over by these 'femocrats'. In there, he gestured at the grass-roofed edifice above us, they had an Office for the Status of Women which set the agenda, which spent *billions*, which had now actually opened up their own office *within* the Australian Bureau of Statistics where they concocted their misleading, indeed downright fallacious, figures, such as, that one in three women in Australia had been battered, which had then turned out *not* to be true . . .

We were interrupted in this torrential account of injustice by – good god – a woman! Grandmother Diane, in fact, who had made not just the local *Canberra Times* but the national *Australian*. She was living proof that the Lone Fathers weren't – as they were so often portrayed – anti-women, they were pro-family. Her son was twenty-nine, married seventeen months, with a seven-week-old baby. His wife was twenty-one. She'd said, 'Hey, I don't love you, I'm out of here,' and what rights had he? None. What rights had she, as a grandmother? None.

As we walked across the broad piazza to the main public entrance of Parliament she took my arm and tears glazed her eyes, 'Mate,' she said, 'when you sit in that portakabin and listen to the heartache, like I have for two days, it's unreal. It's this Feminist Movement just crucifying the men. You should hear how much it costs them, and you should hear what they've lost. Because it's such a strong movement, has it overshadowed the men's rights? Are they paying the price for the mistakes of the past? Here I am, a woman, with all this woman's status stuff, and yet I'm being penalised . . .'

By the time we reached the grand glass doors to the front lobby I had tears in *my* eyes. 'I don't know,' Grandmother Diane was saying, 'I'm just an old grandma, a frustrated old grandma that had a *baby* and knew that wonderful feeling for seven weeks and then to have it taken away . . .

'Aw, politics, mate,' she concluded, tossing her head and laughing as she headed off to harangue her MP, 'I'm just a Greeny spelt Granny, protecting the family tree.'

Alexandra came down the grand, polished marble steps of the lobby to meet me. Raven-haired, dressed slinkily in purple, she was, if not yet a femocrat, one of an elite sisterhood of (dare I say 'attractive'?) young research assistants and journos to be seen swishing through the back corridors of power.

We took cappuccinos to the Members Lawn. Alexandra was full of the latest Parliamentary gossip, which was of course also – glamorous stuff this – the news. Hadn't I seen the papers this morning? I should have done. A huge row had blown up around the Minister for Aboriginal Affairs, Robert Tickner, over his handling of some sacred papers belonging to Aboriginal women. It was all to do with Hindmarsh Island in South Australia. There were plans to build a bridge from the mainland, the local Aboriginals didn't want it ... Yes, yes, luckily I knew all about Hindmarsh Island (even how Ngurunderi had created it).

Anyway, in a cock-up worthy of *Yes, Minister!* a box of sacred Aboriginal papers addressed to one of Tickner's juniors – by name McLaughlin – had got delivered, by accident, to Opposition Liberal frontbencher Ian *McLachlan*, whose constituency, in a remarkable coincidence, happened to include Hindmarsh Island. Pro-development, and anti-Federal intervention in what he regarded as a local matter, Mr McLachlan had photocopied the papers and handed them to solicitors acting for Hindmarsh Island's developer.

Riding, as he thought, high, McLachlan had then, during yesterday's Question Time, asked Tickner whether he'd ever read the secret and sacred material in his possession. Receiving a 'no' he'd asked for an assurance that there were secure arrangements for ensuring confidentiality of this material. 'Yes,' Tickner had replied. In a dramatic moment McLachlan had then thrown down on the central Parliamentary table an envelope containing copies of the papers.

But the move had backfired. The papers contained Women's Business so secret they couldn't even be seen by Aboriginal Men. They had only been given to Tickner's Department in strictest confidence to prove how important the site was. Now the Ngarrindjeri women of Hindmarsh Island were weeping and wailing and up in arms, and even better, Alexandra laughed, McLachlan had been made to look like a total fuckwit. Question Time should be lively, even if, sadly, His Majesty, as they called the Hon. Paul John Keating, was away on a European Tour.

It was an even worse bear-house than Westminster. Not only did the majority of the participating members clearly not give a toss about the issues before them, they didn't even pretend to give a toss. For well over half of the hour, the newly appointed Opposition leader John Howard (who'd been furiously trying to establish his credentials with the media as 'Honest John') sat in his swivel chair so that his back faced the Government and he could chat and joke with his mates on his own frontbench.

'The actions of the member for Barker,' droned poor, po-faced Mr Tickner, 'have caused great disquiet, hurt and sadness to Aboriginal people in South Australia, particularly Aboriginal women. The hurt suffered by these women is being felt in Aboriginal communities around the length and breadth of this country . . .'

But not around the length and breadth of Honest John. 'Ha ha ha!' he went, shoulders shaking at some frontbench witticism. Only when Tickner demanded the immediate resignation of the Shadow Minister for Aboriginal Affairs, did Honest John bother to turn round and engage in the argument.

As the usual ballyhoo and cries of 'Order! Order!' ensued the little pink-jerseyed (Australian) lady next to me in the public gallery asked if I was English. Yes, I said, and she shook her head sadly. 'It makes me ashamed,' she said, 'to see foreign visitors here, and it makes me ashamed to see children here. It really is the pits.'

God knows what the row upon row of grinning, nodding Japanese thought of it, but up in the special glassed-in teaching galleries the year-6 students of Beverley Hills in Sydney were leaning forward keenly. 'Now if we have a look at the man there,' said the teacher, 'with the dark hair who's standing talking now, I think you might know who that is, because we often see him on television, particularly lately . . .'

But none of them knew. 'That's Mr *Tickner*. And what's he the Minister for? Goodonyer, Daniel, he's the Minister for *Aboriginal Affairs*.'

Outside the Members Entrance the pollies and their attendant researchers and journos climbed into special free limousines to whisk them home. First stop for almost all of them was the airport. Canberra, Alexandra explained, was dead at the weekends.

Outside the Public Entrance the Lone Fathers paced in

the gloaming, looking down the long avenue of trees and over the lake to the War Memorial. An unfashionable minority for the time being, no heads were going to roll for them.

## Ridiculously Happy

One of the great Canberra things to do, Helen told me, was the Happy Hour at the Hyatt Hotel. Most particularly on Friday evenings, when it was generally quite an occasion.

At the grand front door there was a distinguished old buffer in a straw hat and bow-tie to greet us. Behind, two handsome young chaps in berets and baggy trousers to lead us through to the crowded lobby. Here were silver trolleys full of free titbits; tables laden with beer, wine, champagne. A smart and youthful crowd spilled out into the garden twilight, where there were strings of fairy lights in the trees and a band. How many were talking about Ian McLachlan's resignation, just announced on the 6 o'clock news? Not many. As the elegantly dressed young lady with the silver trolley came round and asked us whether we cared for any more champagne at this time.

Saturday night: Helen's and Michael's other daughter Amy is back from the Snowy Mountains; her friend Kate is having a housewarming. Not only is everyone at the party a public servant, they all work, like Kate, for the PM's office. Sprawled on the floor indoors or standing outside by the barbie there are experts on China, South Africa, Aboriginal Affairs, all drinking wine from paper cups and saying things like, 'I've walked past you fifty times but I've never met you.' Later, everyone dances to the new compilation CD put out by the Mardi Gras Committee. 'It's great if you like the *Priscilla* tape but are sick of all those songs,' says the Cambodian expert, grooving past me in torn blue jeans. In this group of forty young people there are no public couples; everyone dances together, alone.

On Sunday morning Michael and Helen and their close circle of friends have a regular tennis party followed by a regular brunch – today down by the lake. Though the sun is bright, it's blowing a gale ('Autumn is coming,' says Helen), so the rugs are spread in a spot protected by a thicket of evergreen shrubs. The men stand at one side drinking cold beer, the women sit on the ground by the picnic baskets and the eskis, drinking champagne, at intervals getting up on their knees to hand round the food. 'You see, Mark,' shouts Wendy, 'this is a typical Australian party. All the men on one side, all the women on the other.'

Besides Michael the accountant, there are present: Tom the air-conditioning millionaire, Robert the electrician, Derek the High Court judge, and two other fellows who could be dustmen or cabinet ministers for all I know. I'm doing my best to keep up with the chat about the Rugby Sevens in Hong Kong next weekend, to which Tom and Derek are headed. 'It's probably the biggest piss-up in the world,' Tom tells me.

Down on the rug, Wendy and the ladies are trying to come up with a title for my book. 'I've got it,' she calls out at last. I go over. '*Ridiculously Happy*. Because we're happy and we've got a sense of the ridiculous. Don't you like it?'

'Well . . .'

'What's he doing,' calls one of the men, 'chatting up a married woman!'


## That's Australia!

And then I found a third Canberra, neither the ersatz political capital nor the little country town, but the comfortable, unthreatening, superbly resourced nesting place for intellectuals.

Here, out in Fyshwick amongst the lewd-film makers and brothels (derestricted Canberra is, among other things, the porn capital of Oz), is Bob Hefner, Literary Editor of the

*Canberra Times*, who'd be willing to bet that there are more published writers in Canberra per square kilometre than anywhere else in the country. Why? It's an easy city to live in, there are wonderful libraries.

Here, just a stone's throw from Tilley's, is Mark O'Connor, a professional poet who makes a good enough living from his art to 'subsidise a couple of political habits', the major one of which is his group, Australians for an Ecologically Sustainable Population. (They're against uncontrolled immigration, pro-birth control and eager to get across 'the unfashionable, hard-to-comprehend reality that there is a significant link between population and environment'.)

And here, in a flat in a block on Captain Cook Crescent is Humphrey McQueen, the celebrated social historian and regular columnist for the *Australian*. He's tall, with round, horn-rimmed glasses over a benign expression. He's in his early fifties, I guess, walks with his hands crammed into the front pocket of his jeans, and knows everything I've discovered about Australia and much, much more. He has written a string of books and countless articles on Australian social issues: on the notion of racism as the pivotal point of Australian nationalism; on political apathy; on the piano as a symbol of embourgeoisification (oh dear, missed that).

Of *course* white racism is at the bottom of the Aboriginal desire for self-determination. One of the leading Aboriginal activists of the 1950s was an Indian who lived in the Kimberley. 'His point was, If the whites treat me like an Aboriginal I might as well be one.'

He also seems acquainted with virtually everyone I've met. 'Oh yes, *his* father was professor of Political Philosophy...' '*She* runs something called Freedom to Work in Front of Your TV Set or something...'

We step out of his book-lined, curtain-darkened flat and into the sunshine. 'Let's go and look at our local sacred

site,' he says, leading me across the busy road to the cappuccino curve of Franklin Street, Manuka.

'Now this place, Abels, is the record shop where the PM
buys his Mahler. And in a sense the owner of the record
shop is educating the PM's musical taste. Keating is, you
see, very dependent on people telling him things. Although
he hasn't taught him yet not to say things like, "belt a
Mahler Symphony into myself".' Humphrey chuckles
urbanely.

But this is one of the interesting changes that's come over
Australian society. In the old days if you wanted to be
cultured you voted Liberal, 'for Menzies, his lovely voice
and all that'; now, post-Whitlam, Dunstan, Labour subsidies for the Arts, all that has changed; and one of the
things the Liberals haven't been able to do is reconstruct
the historic bloc that you need to get elected. 'The Liberals
now sound like rednecks. Keating's culture is, partly, one
of the signs of the working class on the way up.'

(I nod sagely and agree; though, as it happens, just under
a year later, the Liberals are to be re-elected with a surprisingly large majority.)

On we stroll, slowly and observantly, with sociologically
rich dissertations on the suit shop, the parking-station over
the road, the 'greasy Joe's', until we come to the Back Alley,
where, Humphrey says, 'Bad Things Happen'. He has
already told me twice, once on the phone and once as we
left his flat, that Manuka has now become the street-crime
capital of Canberra, so I ask, 'But you've never had anything happen to you?'

'Never!' he says with tangible relief. 'Or *seen*
anything . . .'

At a gleaming steel table in the coffee shop on the corner
he is back in command, dazzling me with his grasp of my
subject. We joke and understand and contextualise our way
round my little seven-month journey. Humphrey has been
writing about Australia for two decades.

But it's interesting, when he returned from a spell in

Japan people would endlessly ask him about the Japanese. But *which* Japanese? For example, he got to know a group of communist professors, it being a little-known fact that nine per cent of the Japanese are communists. Humphrey smiled and raised his eyebrow a fraction. 'Which Australians?'

No, he laughed, in the end, as far as any country is concerned, there's a point at which explanation stops and you just have to say, as the Germans do, *'Das ist Deutsch'* – 'That's Australia!'

# Acknowledgements

This trip would not have happened without Christopher Sinclair-Stevenson, whose idea and commission it was. Nor would it have continued without the support of many organisations and individuals who went out of their way to help.

Air New Zealand generously provided me with a supremely comfortable return seat to Sydney. (Claire McKay organised this with great warmth and efficiency.) In Sydney, the charming Victoria Court Hotel in Potts Point gave me cut-price bed and breakfast while I found my feet. Ansett Airways flew me from Cairns to Alice Springs and then on to Darwin. The Plaza Hotel and Ivan's Backpackers' offered very different styles of free lodging there while the Northern Territory Tourist Board organised for me to go out bush with Australian Outback Expeditions. At Manyallaluk, near Katherine, I was treated to two nights and some stunning Rock Art. Pioneer Greyhound contributed a half-price ticket to Perth. In Kununurra, Kimberley Wilderness Adventures donated a trip to the Bungle-Bungles and Heliworks Helicopter Co. whisked me exhilaratingly over that spectacular escarpment. In Melbourne I drank VB courtesy of the funky Sambuca Bar in Brunswick Street. The splendid Spirit of Tasmania spared a low-price cabin across the choppy Bass Strait and the Tasmanian Tourist Authority came up trumps with a cheap car, passes to the National Parks and excellent advice. Finally Tilley's Bar in Canberra stood me a complimentary evening of Australian Rock. Thank you all, and may huge amounts of new business come your way.

Before I left, kind friends and acquaintances in England gave me advice and, more crucially, names and addresses. In particular, Virginia Allen, Charlotta Beeley, Katie Biggs, Jo Capell, Owen and Ruth Chadwick, Fran and James Cook, Carrie Donald, Laura Faber, Mark Gottlieb and Sara Hart, Rebecca Hossack, Tara Howard, Caroline Labb, Amanda Lay, Mark Lucas, Anne McBurney, Robert McCrum, Sarah Miller, Sue McCartney-Snape,

Sarah Milwidsky, Georgia Newbury, John Potter, Gabrielle Russell, Victoria Bathurst, Jeremy Walsh.

Once Down Under I met with immense hospitality and helpfulness almost everywhere I went. Advice, drinks, meals, beds, parties, laundry – here is the rollcall of Australian generosity: Prue Aitken, Charles and Angela Allen, Damian and Naomi Bender, Steve and Sue Biggs, Fiona and Rory Callinan, Tim Calnin, Peter and Julia Cannon, Susan Chenery, Judy Chisholm, Roy and Janet Chisholm, Tory Collison, Frank and Eleanore Cranston, Stephen Crooks, David and Joni Curr and family, Jamie Dods, Andy Durbach, Guy Faber, Eleanor Hall, Meg Gaffney, John Gallagher, Elisa and Domenico Gambaro, Michael Heyward, Don and Janet Holt, Peter Jansen, Edwina Johnson, Kim Kilvington, Megan King, Ron Manners, Cath McDonnell, Trish McEniery, William Mora, Gabe, Jacqui, David and Kelly Mullen, Laurie Muller, John Murphy, Margot Noone, Bridget and Casey O'Hare, Peter and Jane Phillips, Cassandra Pybus and Michael Lynch, Mark and Jenny Rixley, Bruce Robertson, Peg and Rick Rogers, Ed Sellar, Joc Smeichen, Serena and Craig Smith, Graham Tanner, Clive and Ros Tilsley, Lisa Towner, Joe Tuma, Claire Turner, Amanda Urquhart, Peter and Nancy Underhill, Philip Vivian, Lloyd Waddy, Murray and Mandy Walker, Michael and Judy White, Anna and Dean Williams, Gill and Leigh Woolley, and Kate Wyvill. Countless others offered help, gave advice or their time for interviews.

Oliver and Sophie Butcher provided a wonderful decompression chamber in Los Angeles; Leonie Edwards-Jones flew to Perth and decided I was worth it after all; my parents sustained me with news of family and garden. Several kind people read my first draft and offered advice and suggestions: Katrin Williams, my parents, Leonie Edwards-Jones, Patricia Alfonso, Benedict Flynn. My agent Mark Lucas always phoned back within the fortnight; Emily Kerr skilfully pruned my first draft; and Myrna Blumberg improved what remained with her fine but ever encouraging toothcomb.

I am also indebted to the Society of Authors who awarded me a grant from the Katherine Blundell Trust which bought me invaluable time away from freelance anxieties.

Finally, in 2000, thanks to Susan Lamb of Orion for resurrecting this title.